Living the Changes

Living the Changes

edited by Joan Turner

The University of Manitoba Press

© The University of Manitoba Press 1990
Winnipeg, Manitoba R3T 2N2
Printed in Canada

Design: Norman Schmidt

Unless otherwise noted, all illustrations are reproduced courtesy
of the artist or photographer.

Printed on Acid Free Paper ∞

Cataloguing in Publication Data

Main entry under title:

Living the changes

Includes bibliographical references.
ISBN 0-88755-624-8

1. Women – Social conditions. 2. Women's rights.
3. Feminism. I. Turner, Joan, 1936-.

HQ1154.L585 1990   305.4   C90-097151-7

The publication of this volume was assisted by a grant from the
Canada Council.

In Memoriam

This book is dedicated to the changing of the seasons, the changing of our lives, and to women who have died since this book was begun: Ethel Turner, Kathy Fleming, Margaret Francis, Ryn McDonald, Bev Christianson, Debee Paquin, Bette Robbins, Muriel McDowell, Daphne van der Put, and the 14 women murdered on 6 December 1989 at École Polytechnique: Geneviève Bergeron, Hélène Colgan, Nathalie Croteau, Barbara Daigneault, Anne-Marie Edward, Maude Haviernick, Barbara Maria Klueznick, Maryse Laganière, Maryse Leclair, Anne-Marie Lemay, Sonia Pelletier, Michèle Richard, Annie Saint-Arneault, Annie Turcotte.

Contents

Contents

Contents

Illustrations

Acknowledgements

I wish to acknowledge the assistance of a number of women who, from March 1987 to the fall of 1988, were the Living the Changes Committee. This group sprang out of a Sunday morning brunch attended by interested Winnipeg women and Helen Levine of Ottawa at my home in Winnipeg.

Together we defined the intention of this book, the style of writing, and the guide for writers reflected herein. They also suggested contacting writers they knew; for example, Joan Miller recommended Connie Kuhns of Vancouver. I wish to recognize the committee members individually: Lillian Esses, who thought of the title, *Living the Changes*, and assisted with a grant application, Therese Chatelain, April D'Aubin, Patricia Dowdall, Marni Kalef, Joan Miller, Nonqaba Msimang, Sari Tudiver and Diane Fitzmaurice.

When our momentum as a committee waned, Lois Emery agreed to assist with the first critical reading of incoming papers. Her involvement came at a crucial time, or this book might never have been. Thanks Lois, and Mary Sheldon, for reading the manuscript.

Kim Clare participated in the anxiety and fun of purchasing a computer, and Betty Henry learned not only how to use the new technology, but quickly became an expert. Thank you, Kim and Betty. Betty was responsible for the enormous task of inputting and printing the manuscript, correcting and revising draft after draft until we were satisfied. Thanks too to Lyle Henry and Joe Connor for all the times they couriered work between Betty's house and mine.

Funds that enabled the production of this book came from the estate of my aunt, Ethel Turner, of Cupar and Regina, Saskatchewan. Ethel Turner was a farmer, as was her mother, my paternal grandmother, before her. From Aunt Ethel I learned about diligent effort and perseverance even when times are uncertain. I learned from her the stories of the Red River carts and the early days of settlement in Saskatchewan, and an appreciation for the friendship and exchange of skills between some Native and white women of those times. Aunt Ethel served as a model on the importance of conservation of resources, and in her nieces' and nephews' judgement made the best rolls in all Saskatchewan. She died just before her hundredth birthday.

I thank the authors, poets, artists and photographers who shared their creativity with me. You stimulated my personal growth and my understanding, and have increased my deep appreciation of women. Thank you for your gifts, and for your willingness to share them publicly in this book. To those who considered writing but were unable to do so, and to those who wrote papers or poetry that do not appear here, thank you. Perhaps we will be able to work together another time.

To my friends and family, and my co-workers – Anne Kent, Heidi Eigenkind, Pat Rawson, Susan Peterman and Shellyse Szakacs, at Bold Print Inc., the Winnipeg Women's Bookstore – thank you for your patience and support and for taking on extra work during the times I was engrossed in the editing of this book.

Thank you to Patricia Dowdall, Carol Dahlstrom and Lena Klassen of the University of Manitoba Press for your questions, your criticisms and your support, and particularly for your expertise in the publishing of books.

Thanks also to the Winnipeg Arts Advisory Council for the Grant to Individuals (Spring 1990), which permitted completion of this manuscript.

Living the Changes

Setting the Stage

Joan Turner

Living the Changes is by North American women, primarily Canadian women. It is about Canadian women and our lives and situations and how the times are changing. One obvious indicator of change is that most of us now work on computers in our homes and offices, although we may still begin to write by jotting our ideas down with pencil and paper in the way we learned at school. *Living the Changes* began with pen and paper as Lillian Allen, Toronto-based Canadian-Caribbean dub poet rhythmically sang "Nellie Belly Swelly" and "Revolutionary Tea Party" at the Canadian Women's Music Festival in Winnipeg on Labour Day Weekend in 1985.[1]

"What are you doing?" an acquaintance asked me when the music and the swaying and the clapping stopped. She pointed to the notes I had busily, almost unconsciously, written.

I could hardly believe my own ears. "Working on another book," I said. "You're what?" a voice in me, the reasonable, wise and protective one, protested. "How do you think you are going to do that, too?" The determined part of me retorted, "It's important. I know how to edit a book, having already done one. I think I have the necessary connections. I will do it." At that time I had no idea how full my life would become or how much I would change over the next five years. Logically, I should never have begun this book, for anthologies require thousands of hours of focused attention and communication over months and years with many authors, some of whom never appear in the finished product. In 1985, I was still employed by a large bureaucratic institution, receiving the privileges of a tenured academic, which included access to free secretarial service and to a photocopier. A regular bi-monthly pay cheque automatically entered my bank account. I had begun a part-time private practice offering counselling and therapeutic massage, and teaching services, primarily for women and women's organizations. I was a single parent like many women these days. My two daughters were studying at university, financially dependent and living at home with me.

This stage of my mid-life journey was marked by new adventures. I had the advantages of being fair-skinned and educated, with excellent health and abundant energy, a job and some money, and the support of friends. I was becoming identified as an individual in my own right and by my birth name, my father's surname. (I wondered what it would be like if I had my maternal grandmother's name, but then she would have had her father's surname too.) I was getting used to being a divorcee, a label I had never expected myself to carry. Also, I was "letting go" of the need "to fix" the scarred lives and difficult relationships of my first marriage. The Polish family into which I had married and whose name I and my children bore had immigrated to Canada after the Second World War, bringing with them exceptional determination, distrust and fear, and emotional scars that may never heal. Only recently have I clearly and deeply recognized how scarred civilians were by the War, myself included. And the violence and destructiveness of war goes on today. The pain of childhood trauma and experience (war, abuse, violence and neglect) is carried with us into adulthood as Lucille Meisner and Heidi Eigenkind graphically describe in their contributions to this book.

My childhood was the life of the first-born daughter of a farmer and his young bride, and first grandchild of the matriarch whose name I was given. Widowed with four preschool children, my grandmother, Margaret Turner, struggled for years to acquire the right to hold title to the land she homesteaded. Eventually she was successful, the second woman in Saskatchewan to acquire legal title to property. Until that time women were considered to be the property of their husband or father, but in her case both were deceased. Thanks to women like my grandmother, I had the right as a person to acquire legal title to the home I purchased for my daughters and me in the 1980s. And since I had been employed for years, I was able to acquire a mortgage in my own name.

In my middle years, not only did I become a single home-owner with all its anxieties, responsibilities and advantages, but I also became stronger and more alive, bolstered by membership in a powerful international sisterhood. New opportunities frequently opened to me. *Perspectives on Women*, the anthology that Lois Emery and I co-edited in 1983, and the video documentary with the same title that Shirley Kitchen and I produced, thrust me into speaking engagements, workshop presentations and into teaching with a feminist focus.[2] I even sang publicly from the steps of the Legislative Building to open the Take Back the Night March, an annual event to publicize the right of women to walk outdoors without fear of violence. Musician Karen Howe and I developed workshops we called playshops to "lighten our natures and lift our spirits through movement and music, touch and anti-stress activities." And Karen and I had a wonderful time as we let the children within us out to dance and play and sing. We encouraged and supported each other too through the challenges of being adult women and single parents of the '80s. Our relationship grew and flourished over time and distance.

On the whole, I found I liked being an independent woman and a single parent living in an entirely female household. I thought that feminism was arming my daughters and me with an analysis of the world that would help us live relatively successfully in what we knew to be a male-defined and dangerous world. One of my daughters was at first flattered and then harassed, after her picture appeared on the sports page of a local newspaper, by a man we believe to be a pornographic photographer. My other daughter was threatened with violence and death by a male "friend" who was also her coach. I was angrily verbally threatened with death by a middle-aged man with whom I had been in a significant relationship. A male teenager we befriended stole from us probably to buy drugs until I finally had to involve the police. All of this and more happened within a period of three years. I would like to be able to name these men, but it is not yet safe to do so. None of us is immune to the threat of violence, not even the most privileged among us.

Simultaneously, listening more and more to our bodies, my daughters and I incorporated more vegetables and grains into our diet, gradually eliminating meat and becoming vegetarians.[3] More women's voices, women's literature and women's music filtered into our little home, and we scraped and painted and planted shrubs until our home acquired a feminine ambience we had never before achieved. And finally we had the opportunity to purchase the larger safe place we needed for ourselves and for my work, and we moved into the home I occupy today. While my daughters pursued their competitive sports and their studies, I planted more shrubs and flowers. We opened our home to those we chose to share it with us. Even our plants have grown and bloomed as if they, too, have found the sun and warmth and the opportunity to expand.

So, now it seemed that I could contribute concentrated time and energy to the women's movement, a movement that had enriched and empowered me. I had learned in childhood to value being busy, for it was said with pride in my rural Saskatchewan farm family that "man's work is done at set of sun; woman's work is never done." Naively, I suppose, I did not realize the scope of the projects I was beginning. I agreed to be a board and committee member of a local women's resource centre. I was hired by the YWCA to do an evaluation of the local shelter for abused women, then later to study the Manitoba Committee on Wife Abuse, an organization that no longer exists. Also, a friend and I opened Bold Print Inc., the Women's Bookstore, in Winnipeg. I was to be background person, participating in policy decisions and financing, and officially a legal partner of an incorporated business. After one year the partnership ended and I was left with decisions about whether to close or to continue with the store. Business partnerships and relationships with women as well as with men can be difficult, as many of us have painfully discovered.

The concept of power often helps me to make sense of difficult situations, for we live in a patriarchal world where all of us learn about power over others. We experience oppression and may become envious, resentful, angry and/or self-protective. We have learned how to dominate and how to submit in order to survive. Many of us grew up in families where the theme of domination by men and submission of women was played out daily. Women were expected to be silent, affirming male views of the world, worshipping a male god, and teaching their daughters to be handmaidens to men. All too often, male (and sometimes female) parental power was, and is, regardless of class, religion or culture, expressed destructively. The concept of power is referred to often, in different ways, by different authors in this book. The evidence of dysfunction, and of physical, emotional and sexual abuse, and of the violence that permeates North American society is threaded, too, throughout this book. Sometimes prescription drugs, or alcohol or other substance abuse is associated with dysfunction and illness, and this too is a recurring theme, specifically addressed by Sari Tudiver, "Candy" and Evelyn Lau. Books on these subjects and on healing the pain line the shelves of our women's bookstore. Women today hunger for ways to understand ourselves and to heal our pain. Women's words and art can help us to heal ourselves and to heal the earth.

Since I became a bookstore owner and therefore a "business woman" (a title I still wear like a hat that serves a purpose but fits uncomfortably) I have learned how males dominate the Canadian book industry. For evidence of this, just look at the shelves of almost any bookstore or at the book-review column of your local newspaper. I have thought a lot about feminist values and about alternate ways to structure and finance women-focused programs. In this anthology, Joan Pennell examines in detail two different battered-women's organizations, one in Saskatchewan, the other in Pennsylvania. The structuring of women's associations and businesses in a non-hierarchical way continues to challenge our imaginations and creativity. We know the questions, we have the critical analysis, and we are working on the alternatives. As more feminists gain experience in women's organizations, and in the business and legal worlds, we will develop our knowledge and our confidence and find the answers. On the darker side, funding of feminist organizations, publications and businesses continues to be a very critical issue. In this book Both Helen Levine and I briefly address the issue of funding.

Some of the authors in this book – Joan Pennell, Emma LaRocque, Uma Parameswaran, Margrit Eichler, Kathryn McCannell and Barbara Herringer – are professors currently teaching at Canadian universities. Rosemary Brown, best-known as a politician and now as director of MATCH International, describes what she learned about women and academia when she was chair of Women's Studies at Simon Fraser University. She challenges us to make university-based work known and accessible to women in the community. By including academic women and writers, musicians, homemakers, women in the media, immigrants to Canada and women with street experience – women whose voices are different – and by intentionally writing for women of the broader community, we anticipate that this book will help to bridge the gap between academia and the public, and that it may be used in a host of ways. We anticipate that it will be adopted as a text and resource book in women's studies programs and in women-focused courses in faculties of social work. Authors Brown, Herringer, Levine, MacKenzie, McCannell, Meisner, Pennell and I have been educated as social workers. Native Studies, sociology and English departments may find particular parts of this book of interest since professors and students of those specialties are included. Emma La-Rocque tells us about her journey from a small Metis community in Northern Alberta to a teaching position in a university department of Native studies. Uma Parameswaran, author of "Mangoes to Maples," is a professor in the Department of English at the University of Winnipeg.

I no longer identify myself as a professor. Lying under a mosquito net in the home of my friends the Nags in Calcutta, India, in 1987, it became clear to me that I had more work than one person needed. I was profoundly moved by some of the women I met in India, women like the matriarch whose picture is on page 210. She and I could not communicate with words, but we did so through body language and translation. Recognizing in India that there are many different possible lifestyles and that my life could be simplified, I made the decision to resign from the security of almost 20 years of teaching social work at the University of Manitoba. As a feminist in academia, I felt, too, like I was bashing my head against a wall. It was clearly time for me to move on.

Now only occasionally do I identify myself as a social worker. I am no longer a motherworker, my daughters having graduated to independent adulthood as physicians. I am able to talk more openly about having been abused, and I have experienced feminist counselling for my own healing journey. I can sing and yell and cry more easily. My eyesight is changing; I am less short-sighted. My body is bigger, my hair is shorter and greyer. I feel personally stronger and wiser. I am more and more writing in my own voice rather than the voice of a restrained academic. I struggle with the rules of language and punctuation, and of referencing sources, in order to say what I mean, simply and clearly. My home is no longer an entirely female home. I am in an intimate committed relationship and, therefore, I no longer declare myself "single."

In spite of all the changes in my personal and professional life, and the challenges to putting the manuscript for this anthology together, the kernel of the idea for *Living the Changes* was never lost. For a while, a small group of women were involved in defining the over-all intention and guide for authors for the book: "It is our intention to be as inclusive as possible of the experience of Canadian women across cultures, religion, class, sexual orientation and geography. Writing will reflect awareness of women's position in patriarchal society. The book is intended for a wide audience." When federal funders we approached to underwrite some of the costs were not helpful, the Committee's momentum waned. For a time the project "sat on a back burner," sheets of white paper in my filing cabinet. And yet, I found myself from time to time describing the anthology and asking women I met to write for it: Kathleen Shannon, after she gave an address at the Winnipeg Art Gallery; Di Brandt and Carol Rose, after we had worked together in therapy[4]; Ellen Goodman, after she wrote an article about my daughter's experience as the only Manitoban ever to cycle in the gruelling Tour de France; Heidi Eigenkind, while we worked together at the store; Mary Meigs, after a Canada Council sponsored reading at Bold Print Inc.; Rosemary Brown, when we met at the Third International Feminist Book Fair in Montreal. Entering the bookstore with her mother one day, Emily Warne gave me her passionate handwritten piece, never anticipating that it might become part of a book. Gradually as papers arrived and were edited, a book began to take shape.

We wanted to include women from all regions of Canada and are disappointed that this was not completely achieved. I had no success contacting women of the Northwest Territories, Yukon, Labrador and Newfoundland. But we discovered that women of the Northwest Territories have published a book called *Gossip: A Spoken History of Women in the North*, which reflects their voices in a fuller way than would have been possible in this anthology.[5] *Living the Changes* is, therefore, about Canadian women from the southern part of Canada, from the west coast to the east coast.

Essentially, the authors of *Living the Changes* are women whose paths crossed mine in some way as we moved through the late 1980s and entered the 1990s. We represent a mosaic of North American women, across race, culture, sexual orientation and religion. Diversity is evident. Most of us are involved in the women's movement in some way, and most, but not all, of us call ourselves feminists. We write about our lives, our sisters' and our mothers' lives; sometimes, like Evelyn Lau, about the men in our lives; and about the problems and the obstacles that confront us. We are reflective, sad and angry, hopeful and concerned, energetic and exhausted. It seems to take so much effort, so much time, to inch towards sexual equality and to chisel away at the barriers of sexism, racism, ageism, ableism, urbanism, homophobia and lesbophobia.[6] Sometimes it seems that so little has changed. Sometimes, like Dorothy O'Connell, we can write with humour. Although we may not agree on priorities, each of us, in our own way, is trying to write from a place of consciousness about our personal and familial lives and often too about local and global issues. Our ideas about how to work towards sexual equality, justice and peace, assuming and sharing responsibility for what happens on this planet may differ. In "Something to Think About," Emily Warne, a young woman in elementary school, reminds us of the connections between the issues, and confronts us with the urgency of the tasks.

Most of the authors, poets and artists, including Emily, are residents of Manitoba. This was not intended originally, but it makes sense that it would be so, and it pleases me. I have resided more than 50 years on the Canadian prairies, as did my homesteader grandparents before me. Prairie women's voices are important yet under-represented in books, even recent books about Canadian women.[7] Poetry is included in this book, for as Adrienne Rich says: "The necessity of poetry has to be stated over and over, but only to those who have reason to fear its power, or those who still believe that language is 'only words' and that an old language is good enough for our descriptions of the world we are trying to transform."[8]

Having decided that we wanted to be comprehensive and representative of diversity, we reached across the country to include women of different races, cultures, religions, abilities, sexual orientation and ages. We have succeeded, as you can see from the description of who we are in the list of contributors at the back of this book and from reading the content. The ages of the artists and authors range from Emily, aged 9 when she wrote her piece, to Mary Meigs, who in her seventies writes about the process of aging. Most of us are between 35 and 55. Our writing and our images reflect our experiences, our knowledge and our wisdom, and our culture. We have struggled with the accurate expression of women authors' voices. Traditional ways of expressing ourselves, which reflect the assumptions of white, educated, urban North American men, may be obvious, but more often are subtle. I began to understand how it might be to be Black or Native, a farmer or a fisherwoman, poor or differently abled and to have your words misunderstood to fit mainstream ideas about how one should express herself more like an American or a British man. This anthology is reflective, therefore, of contemporary arguments about style, of our history and the times, and sometimes of our differences. We are diverse women, with diverse experiences. We write in different ways with different voices: "The last fifteen years have seen an explosion of women's writing – both in Canada and around the world. Women are using poetry, research, fiction, theory, prose, and popular theatre to understand themselves, initiate change, communicate with others, hammer out theoretical perspectives, document women's day-to-day lives, explore commonalities and work through differences. "[9]

We expect that this book will help us to understand ourselves and other women in the Canadian context, provide access to some of the research that is being done by women like Margrit Eichler, Sari Tudiver and Joan Pennell, document women's realities and clarify some of our commonalities and differences. We believe our lives, our experiences and our thoughts are important and ought to be recorded now. Too little about women has been documented in the annals of history. We hope to stimulate and to encourage you. We are optimistic that our words and images may give you courage to find your own voice and your own forms of expression, whether you share your thoughts and feelings publicly, or for now keep them to yourself in a journal or a sketchbooks, or write letters to a friend. Perhaps, like Katherine Martens, you might conduct an oral history project or, like Heidi Eigenkind, express yourself in art as well as poetry. Or perhaps, like Carol Rose and Lu-Ann Lynde, you might create other forms like the Motherpath cards, one of which is reproduced on page 106. Or, like Joss Maclennan, perhaps you will create political posters to document shattering events. Or like Connie Kuhns, Faith Nolan and Ferron, you might write songs and sing. We invite you to take a critical look at your local theatres, the presence or absence (absence is more likely) of women playwrights and directors, and to look critically at the themes presented, and how women are depicted. You might talk to women in the theatre to learn from them the hard realities of finding work. For an overview of feminism and Canadian theatre, read the *Canadian Theatre Review* (the summer 1985 edition), which I was lucky to find in our women's bookstore lending library.

You will notice that the authors in this book write in the first person about ourselves, our sisters, and the context of our lives. We often refer to each other by our given names – a practice that is frowned upon in prisons and in academia, for it has been decreed that we should be known by our father's or our husband's names. We live in a patriarchal world where men's names and words are given prominence whether it is in churches, universities or homes; in the media, on film, in the theatre or bookstores. This is a fact we too often take for granted.

Until the manuscript was finally accepted for publication, *Living the Changes* was financed entirely by women. It will likely be sold and bought and read for the most part by women. We hope men will buy and read this book too, but know from experience few will do so. And that disappoints and saddens us, for we have read and learned so much in our education about men, their history and their wars. In fact, history, as it is commonly taught, is men's his-story. Nevertheless, we write to record our history (her-story) and to empower ourselves, our daughters and our sisters – and that is important enough. Perhaps one day society will recognize women's work and creativity equally with men's. Until that day we must support women-focused endeavours. Some of us go as far as stocking only women's literature in our bookstores, sponsoring readings by women authors only, and purchasing only women-authored books, music and art.

Owning a women's bookstore and becoming more aware of the book industry, I am sometimes amazed at how much literature, music, art, film and theatre Canadian women, and in particular feminists, manage to create in spite of the sexist patriarchal context in which we live. The Third International Feminist Book Fair in Montreal in June 1988 was an incredibly enriching experience, bringing women together from all over the world. Linda Nelson and Lise Weil wrote about that experience in *Trivia*, and since it was an excellent critique we bent our rule that authors must be Canadian to include them, the two U.S. Americans represented in this book. The Book Fair deeply affected our consciousness about the struggle of women of colour to be taken seriously and to publish and market their writing. We learned how easy it is for white, English-speaking Americans to dominate and influence the discussion. I remember how Jamaican-born Canadian Rosemary Brown strongly differed with Sonia Johnson, an outspoken white American. And I understand that Native Canadian Lee Maracle's first book, *I am woman*, was the Fair's best-seller.[10]

In an interview in *Kinesis* (also the June 1988 edition), Trinidadian-born Canadian author and poet Dionne Brand said that as we hear from Black women and women in other parts of the globe, feminism is changing. A white, middle-class movement is no longer possible. As a consequence, feminism "is changing for the better, becoming broader and deeper."[11] And there are stretching and growing pains for white women as we hear the anger and frustration of Black and Native women, and women of colour, who define white women as part of the problem. The majority of authors in this book are white women, the editor is white and so are the staff of the publisher. Even the women invited to read the manuscript to judge its suitability for publishing were white women. We cannot escape who we are.

Some days I feel optimistic about our expanding consciousness and about the changes women are making. Then within one week I listen to an Aboriginal author express her frustration, I attend a conference on violence against women and a symposium about sexual abuse of children, one of my clients learns through accessing body memories and dreams that she is an incest survivor, and I suspect it of another who is in terrible emotional pain. I estimate that at least 70 percent of the women I see in counselling have been sexually abused as children. I wonder if women's pain will ever end. Mother Earth too is struggling for survival and our ecological efforts seem so late, so minuscule. Wars still begin and continue on and on.

When I re-read "Conquer this Earth and Subdue It" by Shirley Kitchen, "Working for Access" by April D'Aubin, "Women's Music and the Mothers of Invention" by Connie Kuhns, "In Search of the Right Prescription" by Sari Tudiver, "Tides, Towns and Trains" by Emma LaRocque, or "Removing our Blinders" by Rosella Melanson, I realize we have come a long way. Uma Parameswaran and Jacqueline Barral tell about their experiences of immigration through poetry. I am proud to have Di Brandt, Heidi Harms and Katherine Martens included in this book, for it is only in recent years that Mennonite women have begun to develop a body of literature. Di says: "I came to writing as a profoundly transgressive act: there was so much silence in me, so much that had been silenced over the years by my strict religious Mennonite farm upbringing."[12] Every step counts – Di Brandt's and ours – as women find our voices and our power. We are changing our lives, our laws and social conditions. The process is certainly slower than we would like it to be, trying our energies, our patience and our limited resources. And the resistance we meet along the way is often disheartening, especially when it comes from family members or from "comfortably situated" women. In "Family Portrait," Heidi Harms describes family pride and politics, and in "Giving Birth," Katherine Martens documents Mennonite women's birthing experiences. Debra Krahn illustrates "Healing Hands."

This book may be viewed as a piece of tapestry, a weaving of bright and sombre colours of different tensions. It is tapestry unique in design and form, each of the threads carefully spun by different women, one not knowing what the other has done. Some of the threads are strong, others more fragile. Some of the pieces are by experienced authors, while others are by weavers new at this craft. As editor I have been entrusted with decisions about what "rules" will or will not be followed, how the book will begin, how the middle will unfold, and when and how the book will end. It is time for this tapestry, this interweaving of women's art and writing, to be seen and shared, to go out into the world for viewing. We feel anxious and excited. How will you receive us, in your hearts and minds, homes and classrooms? We are ready for your feedback and your criticisms, although since we write about ourselves we feel personally exposed and vulnerable. One woman, "Candy," chose to use a pseudonym for this reason.

There will be more tapestries, more weavings, more books. And hopefully this one will stand the test of time, be read and used by our daughters and granddaughters, by students and teachers, politicians, women in the media, the arts and music, physicians and scholars, and by lovers of prose and poetry. We hope *Living the Changes* will not be relegated to the "out of print" category that Kathleen Shannon refers to, a phenomenon that women booksellers know all too well.

A decade from now, will families be like those described by Kathryn McCannell and Barbara Herringer? Will lesbian women be able to write openly as does Mary Meigs, or continue to have to be concerned about losing jobs, friends or family, or credibility? Will disabled women have the rights of access, the understanding and acceptance, and the opportunities they strive for? Recently April D'Aubin reported on a conference of disabled women and how they communicated through simultaneous translation, sign language interpretation and bliss board symbols. In contrast, I think of how limited we are when we depend only on written words that reflect the dominant male-defined culture.

I wonder if prostitutes will be appreciated as children and women and the violence directed toward them be eradicated, or will even feminists continue to have a good deal of trouble relating to them? And will the number of runaway kids on the streets continue to grow? Will Canadian women have the basic right to choose whether they will abort or carry an unplanned pregnancy (and I think most pregnancies are unplanned) through to term? Or will the matter still be heatedly debated primarily by men and considered a matter for the courts where usually male judges preside? And will women, including women on university campuses, in their homes, and on the job continue to be harassed, abused and killed, necessitating more sexual harassment officers and policies, more police and more organizations focused on services for abused women and children. Another woman was murdered in Winnipeg this week. Another vigil quickly organized by women. Now women politicians attend, and a colour picture of the circle of mourning women hits the front page of a local newspaper. Yes, times are changing.

Will "slimmer is better" continue to be the rule for women, keeping us in our small place, anxious about our seemingly imperfect, too-fat bodies? Will we become comfortable with our sexuality and with the word *sex*? This word, and the word *gender*, not surprisingly, I suppose, caused us to re-think and research definitions. Will farm women and poor women fight for survival on a planet that is being polluted and becoming less able to support the world's population? And how will we cope with the new reproductive technologies and with the stockpiles of technology intended for warfare?

Although Canada is one of the richest nations in the world, will we continue to be small cousins to our American sisters who seldom see books by Canadians? And what will my sisters in India think of this book and of our privileged lifestyles? Will Canadian women who live abroad, often sacrificing their careers for their husbands', find anything of relevance here? Originally I hoped to include a piece about Canadian women living in Europe, and my Canadian friend Joy Berthelsen, who lives in Denmark, sent me ideas. But it seemed that I could not go beyond the relative comfort of their lives to touch their pain and frustration or even their questions. My inability to cross language boundaries is as real a limitation and a barrier as is distance and geography. And yet we are a global village. And this is why images are important and are included in this book in the form of drawings and photographs and a poster. Literacy was identified as a priority women's issue in India, and now we recognize that many Canadians are illiterate, many women among them. While words may allow communication, they may also be problematic, understood and misunderstood. Images allow for individual response, "make visible the lives and experiences of women . . . as social subjects,"[13] and for interpretation do not usually require education in either of Canada's official languages. Women's art and women's images stimulate and please and provoke.

Some of the authors challenged traditional rules of style and propelled us into examining contemporary Canadian women's use of the English language. The key word in my decisions about style was *diversity*. You will see that we opened the door to a variety of styles and forms of writing. Sometimes the form is a well-documented academic paper, sometimes it is a summation of interviews, or a personal story based on experience, or reflections expressed in a letter to the editor, or in poetry. Sometimes the author used capitalization or punctuation in a special way, changing traditional usage, and setting us thinking about how we might use language in new ways to say what we really mean in the personal/political way that reflects our particular politics. "Feminists have moved from a universal conception of women that denied difference to focus on multiplicity. . . . [We are] claiming our right to speak and name the world according to how it looks and feels from our particular social and political locations."[14] Catherine Mc-Kinnon says: "The first step is to claim women's concrete reality."[15] In this book we are claiming Canadian women's *realities.*

My thoughts and questions could fill a book, but that is not my intention. Author Kathleen Shannon, best-known for her work with Studio D, National Film Board, not only poses questions, but also tries to answer the question "Why Worry about 'Culture' at a Time like This?" and introduces films by Canadian women into the discussion. So, please read on.

Worry about "Culture"
at a Time like This?

Kathleen Shannon

I had been talking about women's culture for some time before I started musing about how I would define the term. "Culture" is a slippery word. It slithers.

Peculiarly, one could say, "In North American culture, Culture is often considered a luxury." Our governments tend to reflect the deep suspicion that many Canadians, and U.S. Americans, seem to harbour towards "higher culture." I think this results from our history as a colony. The colonizer looks down its collective nose at the "uncultured" practicality of a largely rural population; and, the formerly colonized react with reciprocal defiant pride. Out of this attitude comes the concept that money spent on culture is being "wasted" on frills.

"North American culture" is often used loosely to mean simply "the way things are these days." It is almost a synonym for the content of the mass media, which reflects our knowledge that the mass media are the major means by which the culture is continually recreated. The media do not merely reflect reality. They play a major role in creating it, and they create it very selectively.

We speak of "Canadian culture" as distinct from North American culture, and here we tend to mean our books, movies, opera, ballet, painting: the Arts – the Culture (with a capital C) that happens north of that long undefended border. If it is a member of our current government speaking, he (and it is likely to be a he) may talk about "cultural industries," a particularly baffling term.

Anthropologists use the term "culture" to encompass the beliefs, values, traditions, laws, economic system, etiquette, food, clothing, health-care system, ways of rearing children, ways people relate to each other – the entire context in which a people live their lives – *which includes the ways in which they transmit and reinforce all these things*. This process may be oral or visual, through paintings, songs, stories and formal teaching such as history. In other words, culture is transmitted through language and images; through the information and communications media, and through the arts (the Culture of the culture).

We have this more inclusive concept in mind when we refer to Native culture, northern culture, Acadian culture, pop culture, teen culture, Black culture, Quebec culture, urban culture or prairie culture. It is implied that Canadian culture is a mosaic of all these things and more. But, "Multiculturalism" does not mean such a wonderful amalgamation. "Multicultural" means anything that is not "us," the "mainstream."

Who is this "mainstream"? The example of the word "man" comes to mind here. The most bewildering words we have in English are "men" and "man." It is possible to utter (it is even demanded by official grammar that we *do* utter) such nonsense as: "Nearly half of all men . . . are men." Women are assured that the term "man" means everybody. Of course "man" includes women. But try carrying this argument to its logical conclusion: try saying, "more than half of all men menstruate." Someone will point out that as only *women* menstruate "men" don't menstruate.

Pondering this, I came to realize that, yes, women are considered to be included in the term "man" – *except where we are different*. The use of that supposedly collective term *erases our differences, renders invisible our uniqueness.* We are included only in so far as we are two-legged, upright, talking mammals. We are not included when we do not conform to the ways men are, and, to be more specific, to the way white, middle class, heterosexual, ablebodied men are. In so far as any of us does not conform, in so far as we are different, *we do not exist in the official culture.*

What passes as our collective culture is Euro-American men's culture. If the culture that claims to be our collective culture is men's culture, then what is women's culture? the part of culture that is left out?

If the scholarship of the last 20 years had been available to women of my generation, we would have felt saner! There is evidence that women use language differently from men, listen differently, and even hear a wider range of frequencies. We interrupt less frequently.[1] There are distinct differences in the process of moral development, between women and men.[2] Studies have shown that we read nonverbal languages better than men do[3] (and I believe this shows up in the few dramatic films women have had an opportunity to make). Margaret Atwood asked people she knew what they most feared. She concluded that women fear for their lives; men fear being laughed at.[4] Men's novels tend to be more hopeless, more cynically despairing than women's, and to rely on the intervention of cataclysmic change. Women's novels tend to reflect more subtle interaction with surrounding forces, more complex characters, and a more enduring optimism and faith in human potential.[5] Women's recent academic and literary work gives authority to the gut knowledge we have had. Women's culture *is* different from men's.

"Women's culture" embodies many meanings. It means the culture specific to women: what we talk about in our kitchens; our experiences as we interact with the dominant culture; our knowledge of our collective past, of our foremothers; and *our means of communicating these things*, and *communicating about them*: a song about childbirth, a film about menopause; Margaret Atwood's novel in which all the terrible things that have been done, or are being done, to women, somewhere, *because they are women*, are legislated in an all-too-possible future society.[6]

"Women's culture" also means the missing half of what would be a truly human culture, the perspective and skills that women bring to all public issues, based in the experience of women that is unique.

We ourselves often fall into a narrow use of the concept "culture" and we discuss "women's culture" as though it were just something to entertain us at a conference dinner: a song written here, a tapestry woven there, some poetry in one of our now defunct Canadian women's magazines. In our organizations, at our conferences, some of us dismiss culture as not one of the "real" issues – like employment, housing, the economy, child care, peace, the environment. But "women's culture" is as urgent as our other issues. It encompasses and symbolizes our other issues, providing a shorthand for shared experience, a common language. It is in our culture that we find our means of communication, and confirmation that other women feel as we do, that our experience is shared.

Adrienne Rich says:

The power of art is to create connections denied by the intellect alone, to transform the unnameable into something palpable, sensuous, visible, audible, to take our unexpressed thoughts and fling them with clarity and coherence on a wall, a screen, a sheet of paper, or against the long silence of history – this power has instinctively been recognized by women as key to our deepest political problem: our deprivation of the power to name. In beginning to create art which claims this right, we begin to create a politics which is a critique of all existing culture and all existing politics."[7]

Put that way, it is easier to understand the reaction of the malestream cultural gatekeepers. Their reaction shows up in criticism and negativity, in the underemployment of women in the arts and media, in the underfunding of individual women in the arts, and in the politics within society's cultural institutions.

When women are considered for cultural funding, our work is often perceived as less important, or less "interesting" than men's. We are funded disproportionately, whether measured against the proportion of women in the population, the proportion of women applying for funding, or the skills and experience of the women applying. When it comes to public spending, in times of government restraint – in plainer words, budget cuts – we're first to be cut, and the heaviest brunt of cuts falls on us.

Government cutbacks in other areas, like social services, have already affected women disproportionately, as social services provide a banded for the deepest inequities of income and opportunity, which are already exacerbated by the lack of necessities such as child care, affordable housing, adequate public transportation.

And then our ability to communicate about these realities is stifled by cuts to our means of communication – cuts that strangle our organizations, our films, cuts that terminate our magazines. Where are *Branching Out, Makara, Herizons, Broadside*? They were our means of speaking for ourselves, among ourselves.[8]

Cuts to the public agencies that fund communications activities affect women first. We had begun to get a share of the resources from the Secretary of State and the National Film Board of Canada, at least partly because these agencies do not accord primacy to commercial interests. Nevertheless, they cut back on women's activities before they touch the "mainstream." The late 1980s has illustrated these points quite well.

There is no publicly funded press, and the publicly funded television network is remarkably like the other networks, due both to the commercial and ideological interests of sponsors, and to the overwhelmingly male bias from which it is operated. The CBC regularly has refused Studio D films (films made from the perspective of women) on the grounds that they are "biased."[9] Piously quoting the Broadcasting Act guidelines, they interpret the term "balanced programming" to mean that if women make a film from our point of view, we ourselves should refute it in the self-same film. I interpret "balanced programming" to mean that if hours and hours of coverage are given to a visit by a pope reiterating his expertise on subjects known by direct experience only to women, for example, balanced programming would be achieved by the broadcast of such women's films as *Abortion: Stories from North and South*, or *Behind the Veil – Nuns*.[10]

What the charge of "bias" really means is that our films reflect a bias that is different from the bias of the watchdogs of the airwaves. That bias is so pervasive that it is invisible, and is declared not to exist. That bias assumes the alias of "objectivity," and produces two kinds of "objective" documents. The first kind of "objective" report will give time to a particular position then hunt for someone to express the opposite view (even if it borders on the lunatic), endowing each "side" with equal value and calling this "even-handed." The second kind will simply uphold the status quo, and dismiss other views as naive or mistaken.

Upholding the status quo is a political position. We have not arrived at the status quo through some kind of natural balancing process where all views have shaken down into consensus. We have arrived at the status quo through a process that includes a great deal of censorship and vested interest. Deriding all those who object to the status quo deprives the public of access to new information and new ways of seeing and understanding the world, therefore interfering with our ability, as the public, to decide for ourselves.

"Objectivity" is another word I have much pondered. By my standards, Studio D was the ideal group to make a film that would be perceived to be objective about pornography: none of us poses for it, none of us produces it, and none of us uses it. Interestingly, the arbiters of taste and judgement did not once apply the word "objective" to *Not a Love Story*.[11]

Here are some examples of situations "objectivity" is reserved for: A man is put in charge of women's affairs in a certain province. He will be "good for the job" because he is "objective"; he is not "too sympathetic." That makes him good for the job? Indifference, almost distaste, seems to be a better qualification than an open mind. A journalist calls me for an interview for a magazine. I ask what his interest is. He says that he does not have any. The magazine thinks that makes him a good choice to write about Studio D. Because he is a generalist, he can be "objective." It seems to me that expertise is considered desirable if someone is writing about new kinds of hybrid corn, or affairs in the Middle East. Travel columns are written by someone who has been there. I can think of few subject areas where ignorance is held to be a qualification for reporting other than about women . . . and UFOs.

The same kind of people who bring you this kind of objectivity will write headlines for two meetings at which exactly the same thing happened. One headline reads, "Serious Differences Shadow Outcome of Talks." The other reads, "Tiffs Break up Women's Pow-wow."

Objectivity is what some people claim they, and those who agree with them, have. Reviews of our films could lead one to suspect that "objectivity" is a simple grammatical contraction, with an apostrophe. Spelled out in full, it would read "I *object* to your *activity*."

Critical response to Studio D films is representative of male reaction to women's culture generally. Critics are often hostile to the point of actual incoherence, though they try to maintain their accustomed lofty pose of cynical detachment or patronizing derision. These critics routinely label our films "controversial." We never set out to make a controversial film, though our point of view is unusual for the reasons I have outlined. In fact, we do not in our films polarize issues into the either/or, win/lose, debate model. The Debate is the paradigm of masculine culture. Identify two opposite points of view, then take a side (no matter whether you believe in it or not) and argue and defend "your side" until you win or lose. A simple example of this is the patriotism to the team proclaimed by professional athletes until they are sold to an opposing team, for which they will then equally and "loyally" fight – whoops, play. We women ponder something, talk together, review and revise, and then our considered belief may, sometimes, include contradictions. Life is often contradictory. We have learned to live with ambiguity.

Most women's films present issues in their inherent interconnectedness, their lifelike ambiguity, and most let people think for themselves. Few of us end our films by telling people how they must think, but instead by inviting them to *think*. We try to show our films in situations where an audience of real live people can communicate with each other, the film having been a catalyst, so that the stage is set for the wonderful creative synergy that can happen when people put their minds together, and new creative and innovative solutions are sparked.

Some of my well-meaning male colleagues at the National Film Board have assumed that we make our films differently from theirs out of ignorance rather than choice. They have often tried to "help" us "clarify" the issues to make a film "less confusing" by distorting multi-level truths into two neat opposites. And though we do not take their advice, many of the critics still see only two opposites, and will insist (though we never referred to it) that if we are anti-pornography we must be pro-censorship!

Reviews of *Not a Love Story* provided a wide enough sampling of reaction for a pattern to emerge. One reviewer initially reacted with sober respect, but after seeing the fulminations of his brothers, he switched to affronted indignation. Michelle Landsberg devoted one of her columns in the *Globe and Mail* to a review of the reviews. They were remarkable enough to merit it. But I did not really detect The Pattern in the critics' response until I saw it manifested in a *New York Times* review of a new book by a woman theologian. Not being directly involved, I could see with more clarity. Here is how it manifested in a review of *Not a Love Story* by a critic I had previously admired. The reviewer pronounced what he perceived as the thesis of the film. He had it wrong, but it went something like this: *Not a Love Story*, "a shrill diatribe," claims that men are evil and women are victims. He cites the woman photographer who appears in the film as *evidence that this thesis is faulty*. Then he finds something that a woman has said, somewhere, that seems to disagree with his thesis of our thesis, and triumphantly quotes her, thereby providing his clinching argument: women cannot even agree among themselves! He is, therefore, under no obligation to waste any more of his precious time, or column-inches, on any of us. It did not seem to occur to this person that we knew that Suze, the photographer who appears in the film, was a woman.[12] In fact, the director, Bonnie Klein, went to considerable trouble to find a woman photographer (since female pornography photographers are rare). She did this quite deliberately in order to build into the film the evidence that would enable audiences to go beyond the temptation to "just blame men." He dismissed the evidence that our thesis was *not* what he claimed it to be, and upturned that same evidence in support of his diametrically opposed interpretation.

Do I need to comment on the demand that all women have to agree before any of us merits being taken seriously? The disagreements between white men have created more churches than is good for anyone, a political party system that makes consensus impossible, and two world wars.

Why does this matter? Many hold the belief that debate and disagreement make things more interesting. "Wouldn't it be boring if we all agreed?" Well, not much danger of that! The problem is that we are not able to disagree with equal exposure. The majority of film critics are men. Most of those who select programming for television, theatres and home video are men. Most of those who dole out cultural funds are men. Most of those who administer those funds are men. Most of those chosen by political parties to stand for election as our representatives are men. And, not least, for every dollar earned by these and other men, women earn only 60 cents. Having less money, we are less able to create our own alternatives.

CRTC reports have shown how rarely women – more than half the public – appear at all over the airwaves, which are ostensibly public.[13] We appear as experts even more rarely. The result is that fully half of human ability, skill and resourcefulness does not appear as part of the official culture.

Tillie Olsen and Dale Spender have documented how the exclusion process works.[14] It is poignant reading. The very women who, in centuries past, addressed the exclusion of women, and its results, have themselves been victims of that exclusion process. Their books are out of print, not available to women of our generation to let us know that our perceptions, our pain and confusion, have been shared by others. Authors Marilyn French, Elizabeth Dowdson Gray and Riane Eisler have addressed what this exclusion has cost us as a society and a civilization.[15]

The way women solve problems, using tongues instead of fists (or technological equivalents of fists), is not known as a behavioural option at negotiating tables. We do not encourage children to fight it out so that the strongest, or nastiest, or palest bully gets the biggest piece of cake. We invent deals like the one in which the person who cuts the cake gets last choice of pieces. I use the example of children not to suggest that we all have, should have, or will have our "own" children. I speak of children as an example of how we tend to relate to other people. They are a convenient example of one group of people that many women deal with, personally and/or professionally, and an example of the kind of influence we bring to bear in a situation where we have the opportunity. A race interested in survival should want to draw on all its resources of wisdom and choice of behaviours.

While few men feel very personally powerful (though every one of them shares some privilege denied to women, even if from his standing point he may not be aware of it) we do, of course, have a great deal in common.

The most urgent issue we face in common is our very survival as a species. And even if we achieve the overwhelming task of avoiding nuclear annihilation, our job will not be finished. The mentality, the culture, that invented the possibility of nuclear annihilation has set other lethal plans and processes in motion. Physicist Fritjof Capra documents that fully half of all scientists and engineers in the world are engaged in the technology of making weapons, while 35 percent of humanity lacks safe drinking water. In the United States alone, it is currently estimated that 1,000 new synthetic food additives, pesticides, plastics and other chemicals are marketed every year. There are numerous signs of social disintegration: a rise in violent crimes, accidents and suicides; increasing alcoholism and drug abuse; a growing number of learning disabilities and behavioural disorders in children.[16] More children with cancers. Dr. Rosalie Bertell, an expert on the effects of low-level radiation, says the casualties from World War III are already among us, and already – conservatively – number 16 to 17 million. These are the deaths and terminal illnesses related to the production and testing of weapons, the mining and transporting of weapons materials, and disposal of their wastes.[17] The crisis is unprecedented, though not entirely unanticipated.

In 1913 a Canadian woman, Sonia Leathes, spoke to the National Council of Women about how women's social concerns forced them to be politically active:

It is on this account that women today say to the governments of the world: "You have usurped what used to be our authority, what used to be our responsibility. It is you who determine today the nature of the air which we breathe, of the food which we eat, of the clothing which we wear. It is you who determine when, and how long, and what our children are to be taught, and what their prospects as future wage earners are to be. It is you who condone or stamp out the white slave traffic and the starvation wage. It is you who by granting or refusing pensions to the mothers of young children can preserve or destroy the fatherless home. It is you who consider what action shall be considered a crime and how the offender, man, woman or child, shall be dealt with. It is you who decide whether cannons or torpedoes are to blow to pieces the bodies of the sons which we bore. And since all of these matters strike at the very heart strings of the mothers of all nations, we shall not rest until we have secured the power vested in the ballot: to give or to withhold our consent, to encourage or to forbid any policy or course of action, which concerns the people – our children every one."[18]

I wish I had been able to read this when I was a teenager or a young mother. I contemplate what I might have been able to say and do if I had had my thoughts and feelings validated. We have the ballot now, but the whole process of men's political culture still excludes us. The media colludes, charging that feminist candidates are "single-issue" candidates – their "single issue" being women. But women tend to have a far wider perspective than do white men, whose single issue is the maintenance of a patriarchal system, a system based on power and control, and the idea that some people matter less than others.

A United Nations statistic tells us that, worldwide, fully 70 percent of the membership of peace and social justice organizations is female. Most, if not all, of these organizations were initiated by women. But peace conferences these days are overwhelmingly male. I have observed a peace-conference head table with 13 men and two women. The women who pointed this out were belittled as though they were merely hurt at feeling left out, or petulantly demanding equal visibility. Brilliant and experienced women get lumped together in workshops called "Women's Perspective on Peace and Security," instead of being included in every panel and workshop. Because the culture around us so consistently denies our perceptions, making our culture invisible, many of us lack confidence in our perceptions. We will hang back until someone else takes the risk of pointing out that the emperor has no clothes. In a world being run by naked emperors, we need to trust our inner knowledge and wisdom and dare to act on it. We need to remember that, in reality, no one else has the same vantage point that we each, individually, have. If no one gives voice to what I see, I no longer assume that that must mean it is too trivial, or naive, or uninformed, or idealistic, to count. It means that no one else is seeing things precisely as I am. What do we have to lose by speaking out?

Our planet and all life upon it is at stake if we remain silent. We need the determination not to be diverted, not to be co-opted. We must not be so anxious for male approval that we compromise the strength and vision of our organizations in order to maintain male endorsement and participation.

We must all speak our truths. Let us put our minds together to find the way to return our planet to a healthy place for all that lives: to reclaim our home as a place where all can flourish. We know now that, if we do not all flourish, none of us will. As women, we need to celebrate and trust aspects of our culture that we take for granted, to honour the skills that we sometimes fail to recognize as skills, and to support other women.

It is through our culture, as women, that we can find our voices. We must demand the funding to support women artists who enunciate for us, putting into language and images, music and motion, the perceptions we cannot use until they are given form. We must demand our own media, and our share – which means more than half – of the public media. We have a right to our share of all the resources earmarked for culture. This will enable us to present our knowledge and information and to find new ways to express that which has not yet been named in our invisible experience. That is not all, though: it is also to heal ourselves and affirm that we exist. Confirmation that our experience is real will empower us to act and to speak. To see people like ourselves, to hear perceptions like our own expressed and endorsed will reassure us that we inhabit a world in which *we* are not crazy. We need to know we are producing ideas and creating traditions that we can build on so the next generation of women will no longer have to discover and name the same things all over again.

Then will our knowledge and wisdom, our culture, have substantial form. Then, and only then, will we have the continuity necessary to contribute our full share to the creation of a fully dimensional human vision. That vision will accord at least as much value to nurturance as to competition, to co-operation as to aggression, to the traditional skills of women as to those of men, to diversity as to conformity, to the power of autonomous ability (power from within) as to power over others. And then, maybe, we will still have the chance to create a newly, and truly, collective human culture, before it is too late.

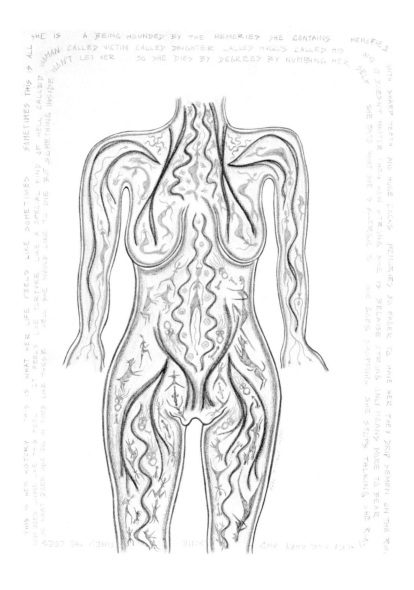

Hounded, Heidi Eigenkind

Women's Music and the Mothers of Invention

Connie Kuhns

In the summer of 1974 I performed an original song at the local bar where I worked. Up until that night my repertoire had included "Four Strong Winds," "Take It Easy" and "The Night They Drove Ol' Dixie Down." On this night I wanted to give my audience something more personal. In my naivete, I thought a tongue-in-cheek talking blues about my recent abortion would be appropriate. I called it "Abortion Baby Blues." I will never forget the silence that followed my last chord. Likewise, I will never forget the applause that erupted once everyone caught their breath. Those cheering the loudest would later go out and hold up half the sky. My life changed that night, too; it was only a matter of time before I was writing and singing to the all-women audiences that thrived during the seventies.

What I had written was "women's music," inspired by the euphoria of the women's movement. It was in reaction to that nameless emptiness many of us felt while listening to the radio, to our records, or to the music in clubs. Although there were notable exceptions, most of the music in the 1970s did not encourage independence in women. It was rare to hear music that accurately described our lives.

In 1974 a woman did not have to belong to the women's movement to feel its power. Women's liberation was the coffee-break topic of the year, whether that coffee was being poured in the kitchens of Saskatchewan and Nebraska, or in the office lunch rooms in Toronto and Denver. No woman was left untouched. It was an incredible feeling to stand poised, ready to make history.

Women's music was born during these urgent times. It was music that valued honesty. It encouraged women to take control of their lives. Its subject matter was rich and varied. Some women wrote hard-edged, overtly political lyrics. Others chose to celebrate the accomplishments of women they knew: mothers, grandmothers, sisters, friends. Still others documented the intricate subtleties of relationships between women, including between lesbians, and some composers dared to demonstrate female sensibilities in purely instrumental music. Bravely, songwriters revealed the painful secret of abuse. Women's music was easily recognizable. It was to the women's movement what civil rights music was to the '60s, and it paved the way for the freedom of expression that newer female artists now enjoy. Historically, it was an unforgettable force.

With the growing acceptance of socially conscious songwriting in popular music today, and with the acknowledgement by women of the hard-fought gains made by our musical foremothers, the term "women's music" is not easily defined. In fact, many Canadian performers with feminist sensibilities now find the term vague, or inappropriate and limiting. But it was not so in the early years.

Although women's music could certainly be considered a spontaneous outburst, one of the first written definitions of women's music is traceable to California and the all-woman recording company, Olivia Records. In 1974 it described women's music as music that "speaks honestly and realistically to women about our lives – our needs, our strengths, our relationships with each other, our anger, our love."[1] And the creators of this new music committed themselves to confronting oppressive behaviour and bigotry.

As time passed, however, and a sophisticated women's music network developed in the United States, the term "women's music" was often used to mean "lesbian music." Lively debate still continues in the United States amongst concert and festival producers, musicians and supporters, as to whether this is true. Also, confronting discrimination and prejudice in the world at large is often a difficult process until we have confronted it in the world within.

But in the mid-1970s, many Canadian feminists involved in the growing women's independent music scene acknowledged and accepted the definition of women's music as envisioned by the American pioneers; this was particularly so in Vancouver, where there were more cultural exchanges with Washington, Oregon and California than with the Western provinces, and in Toronto and Montreal, where the Michigan Womyn's Music Festival provided an annual cultural fix.

Through the work of Anne Michaud, the organizers of the Michigan Festival became aware of the existence and needs of the French-speaking women of Quebec, and made it possible for there to be French translations of all relevant material as well as space for Francophones to meet. Later, those services grew into a multi-cultural and international support service, with Anne as the co-ordinator. Anne explained:

At the same time, it was important for me that the road be open for Francophone performers and musicians. It took a couple of years of lobbying to get them to have Lucie Blue Tremblay. I really wanted Lucie to be the first one because she was speaking and performing in both languages. I was sure it was a great way to have a Francophone woman start in the States. It's still a part of my work that is close to my heart.

Having access to Michigan has been very important in terms of having a strong sense of community. Because there are so many lesbians in the States and money to have, there are more possibilities in terms of what you can do. For me, it was a place to get the nourishment that I needed to come back to my own community and go on with the work I had to do. Michigan is the only place in the world where for two weeks your choices as a lesbian are validated.

[At the Michigan festival] there is also the part of listening to all that music that is part of your day today. That music is very connected to what we live when we are among each other. But there are few places out there where we can be with each other. So to be outdoors, to be with so many women and to see live on stage those women you listen to when you do your dishes, or when you are with your lover is another reason women go.

Michigan was also the place where Canadian women learning sound engineering got a chance to work. Engineer Nancy Poole and Womanly Way Productions producer Ruth Dworin are still an important part of the women's festival scene in the United States, and Edmonton sound engineer Cathy Welch made her debut at Michigan in 1988. As for performers, what started as a trickle about 16 years ago with classical musicians Carol Rowe and April Kassirer (known in Toronto as C.T. and April) taking the stage at the National Women's Music Festival in Illinois has turned into a stream. Most feminist performers in Canada have found their way to the major festivals in the United States. Quebec's Lucie Blue Tremblay has signed with Olivia Records; Connie Kaldor, Sherry Shute, Ferron, Lillian Allen, Faith Nolan, Lorraine Segato and Heather Bishop have all made names for themselves south of the border.

Heather Bishop's manager and business partner, Joan Miller, and Ruth Dworin sit on the board of directors of the Association of Women's Music and Culture, which meets yearly in the United States. For two years I wrote a regular column called "Live! from Canada" in *Hot Wire,* the Chicago-based journal of women's music and culture. But, however connected many of us were, and still are, to this American movement, here at home a transformation was taking place that was uniquely our own.

In Canada, in the mid-1970s, there were coffee houses and clubs that offered women-only space on a full or part-time basis. These places became centres for the development of women's communities. Among them were the Full Circle Coffee House in Vancouver, Clementines (later renamed the Three of Cups) and the Fly by Night in Toronto, the Powerhouse Gallery and Co-op Femme, also known as Co-op Lesbienne, in Montreal. Almost every Canadian city had one women's coffee house during this period, whether it was in temporary quarters in the YWCA in Halifax, "down an alleyway in some guy's dance studio" in Dalhousie, at Women's Night at the Guild in Regina, or an evening of live music at the Women's Building in Winnipeg. Some coffee houses offered an evening for women and their men friends, and on occasion some concert producers designated lesbian-only space. But this usually occurred only when American performers Linda Shear or Alix Dobkin came to town.

Most cities had an all-woman production group, although for the most part the women were novices, with only their energy and desire to guide them. Often these women were associated with a women's group or political organization that produced concerts for a particular benefit. However, there were some exceptional companies that produced the first women's music concerts in this country, for example, Womankind Productions in Vancouver, and Sappho Sound in Toronto (which later gave birth to Womanly Way Productions).

These women took on an incredible task as they imported talent, often at their own expense, and introduced us to our own kind. They also weathered a lot of criticism as they tried to respond to the needs of a growing political community trying to define itself.

In conjunction, there emerged a small garden of women's music festivals, beginning on the West Coast and eventually spreading to Nova Soctia. The talent was often local and the trappings were few but, for those women and in some cases, men, who openly celebrated the contributions of women, while being videotaped by local police (as was the case in the Kootenays of British Columbia) and who hiked into the backwoods to sit on the ground and get eaten by bugs, there were great rewards: the a cappella and acoustic music of women on the edge of time, including Ferron and Rita MacNeil.

It is appropriate that the first Canadian women's festivals took place in the Kootenays. The area has a mixture of Doukhobor people, the rural working class, urban exiles, American expatriates and an active women's community. Even a provincial tourism brochure states that the area has a reputation for seclusion, and several generations of settlers have found a safe haven here from the anxieties of religious persecution or social unrest.

The first festival, held in 1974 in Castlegar, B.C., was organized by Marcia Braundy for the Kootenay Women's Council, an ad hoc group of Status of Women organizations in several small towns. The two-day festival featured local and regional musicians, workshops on witchery and crafts, a film festival, square dancing and an arts-and-crafts fair. It was open to both women and men.

The second year, the festival was held in nearby Kaslo and lasted for four days. The first two days were for women and their invited guests, and the final days were for women only. These were historic events. It was revolutionary for women to put themselves first and to celebrate and promote each other. To designate women-only space, especially in a public place, was entirely new. Equally ground breaking was a workshop on lesbianism led by the Lesbian Caucas of the B.C. Federation of Women. But as one woman told me, "lesbianism was not an issue" for rural women at these festivals. The primary purpose was to bring all rural women together for the first time. As Rita MacNeil sang "Angry People in the Streets," so did the Doukhobor Women's Choir sing the music of their culture.

Although the idea of women-only space was controversial in the '70s, and is often misunderstood in the '80s and '90s, within that environment something wonderful happened. Women spoke honestly to each other. We sang together. We loved one another. We rejoiced in the telling of our stories and our secrets. With music as the salve, women were healed. For a brief time, the slumber party had come of age.

However, Canada has yet to support a national women's music festival on an on-going basis. The West Kootenay Women's Festival in British Columbia, now in its fourteenth year, is the oldest. For the 150 women who attend, this festival is primarily a community celebration complete with potluck supper, talent show, auction and dance. The Kingston, Ontario, Womyns Music Festival has been in business since 1985 but operates on private land that accommodates only about 300 women. Both festivals are for women only, with some restrictions placed on boy children.

In 1988 avant-garde musicians Diane Labrosse, Danielle Roger and Joane Hétu produced the ambitious five-day Festival International de Musiciennes Innovatrices in Montreal. Nadine Davenport, Carol Street and a dozen other dedicated women produced Vancouver's First Annual Women's Music Festival. In 1989 and 1990, Vancouver offered Women in View: A Festival of Performing Arts, which featured mostly theatre. Ruth Dworin of Womanly Way Productions remains one of our most prolific producers, as she continues to organize two and three-day events in the Toronto area, including Spectrum: A Festival of Music, Theatre, Dance, Skillbuilding and Strategizing (1985), Joining Hands: A Deaf and Hearing Theatre and Music Festival (1987), and Colourburst: Multicultural Women in the Arts Festival (1987). She has also worked on several co-productions including Spirit of Turtle Island: Native Women's Festival, co-produced with Dakota-Ojibway Productions (1985), and the Rainbow Women's Festival, co-produced with Multicultural Womyn in Concert (1984). But, overall, women's music festivals in Canada are sporadic. And, the

Kootenay and Kingston festivals being the exceptions, women-only festivals are rare.

When Ruth Dworin founded Womanly Way Productions in 1980, she decided on an open-door policy for her concerts and festivals. She says:

At the time, I wanted to do something politically that would nurture and support women, feminists, who were out doing front-line organizing work. I also wanted a situation that would educate people who were just coming for the entertainment value, and I figured a concert was the ideal way to do both. Art is a really strong tool for consciousness-raising because it goes for people's emotions and in a lot of senses bypasses their intellect.

It may be a little bit annoying for some women to sit at a concert and be singing along and hear male voices singing along, but the trade-off is the fact that those women aren't having to make themselves personally vulnerable and the men are learning more about our issues. As far as I'm concerned, it's probably the most painless way to educate people.

It is on this point of exclusivity that the Canadian experience differs radically from that of the American. It became obvious in 1984 when Our Time is Now!: Canadian Women's Music and Cultural Festival, was held in Winnipeg. Although it was intended to be a once-in-a-lifetime experience, the festival continued for three years. And it came to symbolize what Canadian women's music had become. Quite accidentally, it was the first national festival that defined women's music in a Canadian context – but not without controversy.

Produced in 1984 by Joan Miller and a core group of five women, at the request of a Winnipeg organization called the Same Damn Bunch, Our Time is Now! was the largest gathering of Canadian women musicians ever assembled in this country. The first festival introduced dub poet Lillian Allen, Inuit throat singers Lucy Kownak and Emily Alerk, native singers Suzanne Bird and Alanis Obomsawin, as well as Connie Kaldor, Arlene Mantle, Nancy White, Ferron, Marie-Lynn Hammond, Four the Moment, Heather Bishop and Suzanne Campagne in a program composed of almost 50 women performers. The second festival, produced by the newly formed Canadian Women's Music and Cultural Festival, Inc., presented 70 individual women including comedian Sheila Gostic, jazz musicians Wondeur Brass and The Swing Sisters, gospel and blues performer Louise Rose, and the punk band Ruggedy Annes. Canadian women's music was not limited to one musical genre. Nor was it the sole expression of one race or sexual orientation. Breaking from an early tradition, women's music was not for women only.

The organizers knew what many of us did not: that the established women's community could not support a women-only festival of this magnitude. Musicians born out of this movement would not make a living if they sang only to women. This was devastating news to women who were accustomed to the American women's festivals (which, with the exception of Sisterfire, are closed to men and to boy children) and to women who needed the lesbian-positive atmosphere that women-only festivals provide.

The issue was further complicated when the festival organizers did not designate a lesbian stage. It was their belief that the musicians had the right to choose how they would identify themselves. It was an acknowledgement, as well, that many performers in Canada who are lesbian choose not to declare their sexual preference publicly or to make it the focal point of their careers regardless of their public stands on issues. And this right to privacy had to be respected.

Despite this painful controversy, the majority of the feminist press applauded the festival, as did the *Winnipeg Free Press*. Ironically, a few letters to the editor appeared in that paper complaining of "women hugging and kissing each other in this family-based park," and that "taxpayers' money is being spent on hate propaganda," but the responses from other readers were swift and encouraging. Heather Bishop told me: "What it did for all of us women musicians was just short of a miracle. It put us all together in the same place. It changed people's lives. That's a victory."

Although the attendance at the second festival in 1985 was over 2,000 people, the organizers were left with a deficit. They chose to hold a much smaller festival in 1986, and then to discontinue producing the festival for the time being. But they had already made a bold statement about women's music in Canada. Women's music could benefit everyone. This was not news to the performers.

For over a decade the Vancouver and Winnipeg folk festivals have been promoting music by women at their annual gatherings. For at least three years Winnipeg had a women's theme tent and Vancouver has consistently brought new songwriters and regional legends from around the world, including the first wave of feminist and lesbian performers. It was on these stages that women's music met the music of the world. In an atmosphere of tolerance, the ideals and issues so sacred to women's music received an international hearing as politically aware performers – women and men, gay and straight, white and of colour – stood together, worked together, and learned each other's songs. Likewise, the audience was integrated, giving women an opportunity to gather and yet be part of the whole. To stress this point, Rosalie Goldstein, artistic director of the Winnipeg Folk Festival since 1986, told me: "I think there are some important principles around which the festival operates. I mean, in addition to its concern about women. Its concern in general is about people who live in a society that's alienating. And the concern is to bring them together, the artists, the audience, the volunteers, and give them a quality-of-life experience which is something hopefully they take away with them and use as a model for their lives on a daily basis. Because I really think that is how the world changes."

Certainly the Vancouver Folk Music Festival is an example of this as well. At its peak, 20,000 people gather for two days and three nights at an oceanside park in a beautiful area of the city. The counter culture attends, as well as seniors, politicians, teenagers, students, children, professionals, and a large contingent from the feminist and lesbian community.

When women's music began to rise to prominence in the United States, the Canadian artistic directors took note, and, urged on by women working in the ranks (in particular in Vancouver by Susan Knutson and Wendy Solloway), began to book the first wave of feminist and lesbian performers. In his first year as artistic director for the Vancouver Festival, Gary Cristall sent talent scouts to Michigan. He called "someone who knew someone," who eventually got him in touch with Holly Near. And in 1980 the flood gates opened. On stage in Vancouver, in front of 10,000 people were Sweet Honey in the Rock, Cathy Winter and Betsy Rose, Ferron, Robin Flower, Nancy Vogl, Laurie Lewis, Barb Higbie, Holly Near and Adrienne Torf.

"Feminist" appeared as a music category at the Vancouver festival, alongside "gospel" and "Celtic" in the festival publicity. The festival program printed articles about women's music and songs by Rosalie Sorrels, Ferron, Holly Near and Betsy Rose. There was a workshop with women performers called A Good Woman's Love. All of this happened in an environment that included traditional folk and blues music, and performers from other parts of the world. In varied proportions, it has remained this way ever since.

The big breakthrough at the Winnipeg Folk Festival came in 1982 when Heather Bishop, Holly Near, Betsy Rose and Cathy Winter, Meg Christian and Diane Lindsay, Ginni Clemmens, Frankie Armstrong and Mimi Farina were invited to appear in The Big Tent. Winnipeg also introduced a women's theme tent, which operated between 1984 and 1986. In 1984 nearly 30 women appeared on this stage, including Toshi Reagon, Judy Small, Anne Lederman, Teresa Trull and Barb Higbie, Heather Bishop, Holly Near, Ronnie Gilbert, Patsy Montana and the Reel World Stringband. In 1985 newcomers included k.d. lang, Margaret Roadknight, Four the Moment and Rory Block. The final year was a blowout, with Ellen McIlwaine, Christine Lavin, Tracy Riley,

Heather Bishop, Connie Kaldor and Sweet Honey in the Rock, among others.

Despite its popularity, when Rosalie Goldstein became artistic director after the festival in 1986, she disbanded the women's stage. "I did so with the most loving care," she told me, "because I believe it's important for women to be dispersed throughout the entire body of the festival. I would not put up a tent at the festival and say here are all the blacks, or here are all the Jews. And that's exactly what was happening with women. I don't think that's fair. I don't think it shows women to their best advantage. I don't think that it invites people who might, under other circumstances, come and see that programming. It doesn't make it easy for women, whatever their sexual orientation, to put their music across. And I want that to happen in a serious way. It's what I believe in."

The feminization of the Winnipeg and Vancouver folk festivals came about in part because of the large number of women who volunteer each year to work on the event. Currently half of the 800 volunteers at the Winnipeg festival are women, and in Vancouver women are in the majority. The inclusion of women was also aided by musicians such as Connie Kaldor and Heather Bishop, who carried around lists of Canadian women performers to show any and all who would blame the lack of participation by women performers on the fact that there were not any, and by Marie-Lynn Hammond, one of the first Canadian feminists to grace the main stages of festivals. Connie Kaldor called Hammond "the shining light in that scene."

Although the Vancouver and Winnipeg festivals are now the biggest producers of women's music in the country (with Womanly Way Productions an impressive contender), it should be noted that not every folk festival has been open to the idea. The Regina Women's Production Group operated a women's stage for three years at the Regina Folk Festival against all odds.

But the feminization of the Canadian music business in general has been aided by our feminist musicians who, while supporting our independence movement with music, did not separate themselves from the rest of Canada. They fought for equal access, for their right to perform in the best venues in the country, for their right to control their own careers and their creativity, for their right to speak out on behalf of women. Now a collective consciousness is at work spreading the word.

Our job is not over yet. There are wounds to heal and bridges to mend from those early years. There is living history that must be analyzed and documented. And there are issues to be addressed that are as urgent today as they were in the beginning.

The advent of women's music brought new standards to concert production; it brought sign-language interpretation, wheel chair accessibility, provision of child care, and the lowering of the barrier between performer and audience. The network that supported women's music gave women the opportunity to develop skills that had previously eluded them: concert production, photography, sound engineering, music journalism, management, graphic arts, record production and distribution. It also ushered in a wave of unprecedented criticism.

Because the performers of women's music became the voices for a newly forming and still largely silent women's community, their accountability was demanded by the women they represented. In the early years a performer could just as easily be chastised for wearing makeup or shaving her legs as she could for making a racist remark. There was no qualitative difference. The length of a performer's hair and the style of her clothing could be used as indicators of the depth of her political commitment. Appearance was a serious business as women attempted to reject images that were perceived to be contrived, traditionally "feminine," or "man-made."

Although women's audiences were notably enthusiastic, a musician was often judged more by the content of her material than for her skill. It was the message, not the means, that won over an audience. And since the primary battle at that time was designated to be between women and men, performers who chose to sing about being mothers, or the wives and lovers of men, were not always welcome. Children were not always welcome either, as women asserted their right to be with women only.

There is no gentle way to say that these times were not always the best of times. Often as one group of women claimed its territory, it did so at the expense of another. Any history of oppressed people includes the difficulties encountered as those people define their issues and themselves.

Many of our musicians were victims of our desire to design a perfect woman's world. Heterosexual performers were made to feel like traitors, lesbian performers who made their sexual preference public were taken for granted, and women whose careers began before or outside the women's movement were seen as having no validity. (This was particularly the case if they played anything other than acoustic music.)

We also failed to recognize cultural, racial and class differences between women. Assimilation was required by all, with one language spoken here.

The Alliance for the Production of Women's Performing Arts/-l'Alliance Femmes et Arts de la Scene, now in its third year, is attempting to address these problems, as well as to unite women in communities across the country. Although hundreds of women have worked tirelessly to create and support women's music in Canada, they have often done so in isolation. Their stories are just beginning to be told. There are also other voices to be reckoned with: the black women of Nova Scotia, the immigrant women from the Caribbean, the native women from across the country, and the women of Quebec.

Today the mothers of invention are hard at work. Many of the early performers are now keeping pace in the music business. Other women are at home, choosing instead to nourish their communities with their very personal music. Women's music is still changing lives. It is also changing the way Canadian society feels about women. And each time a woman decides to tell her story, a revolution takes place.

We must always remember how these changes happened. We must honour our predecessors and the women who work daily to enrich our cultural lives. History is a precious gift. It is how we learn. Only with hindsight will we shape our vision. Only with vision can we carry on.

I Black Woman

Faith Nolan

I Black woman can barely dance
I'd rather read a book than jive and prance
I hate wild parties and cheap romance
I'm a woman on my own, taking my own stance.

I Black woman will not be used

Don't call me brown sugar or sweet-time gal
talk like that don't give my heart a whirl
I'm not hot in bed, it ain't my scene
I am not part of your make-believe schemes.

I've seen mama beaten up by strange men
sister's on the street turning tricks for them
brother's out pimping and talking jive
I saw daddy drunk – couldn't make this life.

Don't call me your mama, your sister, your girl,
Don't call me anything in your fantasy world.
I ain't voodoo queen, an african dream
I'm my own woman with my own damn scene.

I wrote this song to say I will fight against the racist/sexist ways we as Black
Women are forced to live.

Testimony

Ferron

There's godlike
And warlike
And strong
Like only some show
And there's sadlike
And madlike
And had
Like we know
But by my
life be I
spirit
And
by
my
heart
be I
woman
And by
my eyes
be I open
And by my
hands be I whole

They say slowly
Brings the least shock
But no matter how slow I walk
There are traces
Empty spaces
And doors and doors of locks
But by my life be I spirit
And by my heart be I woman
And by my eyes be I open
And by my hands be I whole

You young ones
You're the next ones
And I hope you choose it well
Though you try hard
You may fall prey
To the jaded jewel
But by your lives be you spirit
And by your hearts be you women
And by your eyes be you open
And by your hands be you whole

Listen, there are waters
Hidden from us
In the maze we find them still
We'll take you to them
You take your young ones
May they take their own in turn
And by our lives be we spirit
And by our hearts be we women
And by our eyes be we open
And by our hands be we whole

Beyond the Barrier:
Women in the Media

Ellen Goodman

My early impressions of the life of a journalist were charged with idealism and romanticism. Like many others unfamiliar with the field, I believed journalism would offer a woman an unconventionally exciting, attractive life of meeting interesting people, travel and freedom. I thought it would provide a wonderful creative outlet for personal expression. I later found that the profession can offer all of these things at different times. Initially, I never thought that a woman would need to attend to a personal life, or take time away from this stimulating and gratifying work. Why would anything else really matter when she could have such an intoxicating and rewarding career? After all, the job would provide a thrilling life unto itself. Or so I thought.

Once employed as a reporter, I realized that the work can, indeed, be all-encompassing. I also discovered that reality does not always match fantasy. Like any other job, it has peaks and valleys that have an impact on one both professionally and personally.

In the early 1970s, when I first considered a career in journalism, I never understood that getting ahead could mean taking some tedious steps, and would present one with the stresses and strains of any other tough job. A journalist can work excessively long hours and, especially at a smaller publication or broadcast station, earn a meagre wage. What I quickly learned is that you can feel like you are bashing your head against a wall. If you do not accept the drawbacks, there apparently are hundreds of others who are eager to snatch up your job. The work can be extremely demanding, yet also have a mysterious appeal. A journalist can find it difficult to abandon media life entirely.

Along her career path, a journalist can enjoy the satisfaction of producing a good piece of work (though perhaps not for long before having to get on with the next assignment). When there is a shortage of congratulatory pats on the back or lucrative cheques as visible rewards, one needs to be able to draw up that recognition from within herself to maintain a sense of job satisfaction. Like other traditionally male-dominated professions, where women forge a wider career path for themselves and perhaps establish a new tradition for other women, the journey can be both gratifying and difficult.

So what is it really like for contemporary women who work in print or broadcast news media? In January 1989, I selected five women in Manitoba to interview. I wanted to find out how they felt about their media work and how it has affected their lives. Their experiences, of course, reflect only a fraction of women who work for media companies predominantly controlled by men. Although their backgrounds varied, and their ages ranged from the late twenties to the late forties, they shared some common views as women who want to succeed in their professions and to balance their personal lives.

The women interviewed generally are ambitious, dedicated to their work – and, in some cases, are more idealistic than the management for which they churn out their money-making product. I recognized that these women and others like them – as in other professions where women need to expend additional energy to chisel away the walls of male tradition – have special talents and determination beyond the average person's to maintain the pace required to attain their goals.

In the 1970s and 1980s, women emerged from behind the social, or "women's" news sections to stretch their talents. They often hopscotched through career obstacles and career-related stresses, many unique to women, to arrive in their current positions.

As an ever-increasing number of women graduate from journalism schools, their sheer presence is apt to open the tightly shut doors of the almost exclusively male newspaper publishing and broadcast executive offices, particularly in the private sector, which has blatantly resisted the inclusion of women in upper management.[1] Canadian journalist Marjorie Nichols nicely sums up this attitude when she points out that the Catholic Church would allow a woman pope before there would be a woman newspaper publisher.[2]

Some Canadian media, such as the government-owned Canadian Broadcasting Corporation (CBC), have been slowly opening more doors to women. Prior to the late 1960s female news announcers were never seen on television. Women started appearing as local television reporters during that time, but men still held on to their bastion of network news where ambitious reporters often strived for positions. Only since the early 1980s has women's participation in television journalism increased significantly.[3]

Jane Chalmers, now senior producer of current affairs at CBC-TV in Winnipeg, started in the early 1980s, ambitiously carving out a television news-reporting career for herself. Working her way through private television stations and the CBC in western Canada, often undertaking unpleasant tasks and dealing with non-supportive employers, she finally broke into a position as a national, or network, reporter. That break came when, at CBC-TV in Calgary, she covered the trial of Charles Ng, who was wanted in connection with a horrific series of murders in California. Soon after that, she reported on the fall of the Northlands Bank. Jane was asked to do both stories for "The National," which led them to hire her as a full-time reporter. She recounts her experience as a national reporter:

To be a good network journalist – and I would say all the women on "The National" are very good – it's talent, looks, ability, knowledge and education. I think you have to work ten times harder, be ten times more persistent than any other reporter doing a local show. I did some great stories and exciting stories. At times I'd pour out every ounce of love, passion, sex and hate – every ounce of myself. Mind you, I'd come home a zombie at night. Everything would go into that story. My average [work] week was 70 hours. It was really hard on my personal life. I was burned out and stressed out . . . because every story had to be great.

Jane says she made a careful and deliberate choice "to put the brakes on," to accept her production job. She considered an option to work for the CBC in Toronto preparing for a possible future opening as a foreign correspondent, which had been a major professional goal: "It was a choice between going to Toronto and being groomed down the road for something like that, or choosing to have a more balanced life and a personal life and to develop myself differently professionally." Though the work was intense, Jane stresses that she loved working as a television reporter, especially at the national level. "I don't know how much I'm going to miss the reporting field," she says. "That worries me." In the end, she decided to leave "The National": "It was an agonizing decision. I'm still feeling the pull of the field. I loved doing my job. I love reporting. I'm a good reporter, I think. You know, I worked very hard to get where I was. I gave up everything for the job."

Jane says she began to realize she could not "be everything and do everything." Acknowledging the high price that must be paid to stay on top as a national reporter, she says: "There's burn-out, bitterness, anger, feelings of being used, and just losing total control of your life. It's that severe."

She notes that being a single woman permitted her the opportunity for total immersion in her work, but left little or no outside time to herself or for others:

Other reporters, especially women who have kids, are limited as far as where they can be sent. They can't send you gallivanting all over the world away from the children. The husbands, the fathers can. The mother's can't. It's too hard on them and the kids. Because of the competition and nature of the work, it's doubly hard, because I'm a woman. Women have to make choices, and it's not their fault. It's the reality. For me, it was a choice between being alone with the job. And the job isn't home at night. And the job doesn't care if you die.

I asked if workaholism was a requisite to reach the top echelons of television reporting. "It is," Jane admits, "but you get into the whole thing that it's not fun anymore. It's competitive. Every story has to be good. It's a standard thing. There's also the fact you always work way beyond 35 hours a week. You can't make any other plans."

Jennifer Dundas, legislative reporter for CBC Radio in Winnipeg for two years in the late 1980s (and for a fill-in year previously), describes her introduction to the long hours required early in her career when she was at "Broadcast News" in Toronto:

I was doing a current affairs program syndicated to a bunch of stations. That was a lot of fun. I think that's what helped me get the job at CBC. But there were lots of other things I did at "Broadcast News" that were really high pressure. During that time, there were assassination attempts on the Pope, Anwar Sadat and Ronald Reagan. I was in charge of the audio service when each of those things blew. I learned what it was like to work under intense pressure. I found it quite exhilarating. But after three and a half years, the shift work was too hard.

I asked Jennifer whether she, too, felt the effects of job-related burnout. "I wasn't exactly burned out," Jennifer recalls. "But I was getting sick a lot. I never felt well-rested. It was fun being at work, but the rest of my life was in shambles."

I asked if a hectic work pace was common in news media. "It's really expected, especially when you're first starting out," she replied. "If you're young and don't have much experience, if you're not willing to put in 12 or 14 hour days, you're not taken that seriously."

Jennifer later reported for CBC Radio in Prince Rupert, B.C., for one and a half years, then went to the Winnipeg station to work as a general reporter. Soon she replaced the legislative reporter, a position that is considered one of the most important reporting jobs at the station. Then Jennifer took time off to have a child. She returned to the position of legislative reporter on a permanent basis. Jennifer says, "I think it's one of the best jobs you can have in CBC Radio. It's always changing. I do like it. I'm self-assigning. I don't have to deal with the news room too much. I let them know what I'm doing and send my material in."

Jennifer says the job serves her life-long interest in politics and allows her to be close to active political decision-making: "Actually, I've come a long way toward meeting my professional goals. I got into CBC hoping to get into legislative reporting."

According to Susan Crean, author of *Newsworthy: The Lives of*

Media Women, public radio has provided a "shining oasis of opportunity for women."[4]

I asked Jennifer how she manages to balance her busy work schedule with her responsibilities as a single mother. She replied that "it can be extremely stressful. Last year was really tough. It started out at a fast pace. Intense." She explains that provincial and federal election campaigns made 1988 an incredibly busy year for political reporters in Manitoba: "During the long, hard hours, I had to depend on friends for child care. I had to do some travelling with campaign buses and would have to leave Alex, my two-year-old son, with somebody for a couple of days. That was really stressful for me and for him. It was quite upsetting, actually. It took a lot of fun out of covering an election."

Provincial-election coverage took a toll on her health. She says: "I'd drive out of the legislative grounds and not know which way to turn. I forgot where I lived, I was so tired. That was serious exhaustion. So I took six weeks off. The first two weeks I just slept while Alex was in day care. I couldn't read or do anything. I was in pretty bad shape."

Jennifer's experience is similar to that of Jane, who agrees the burnout factor can be so high for some reporters that much holiday time is spent sleeping and recovering before going back to the stresses of work again.

"I always knew it was important to find a balance," says Jennifer. "But I also knew I wouldn't be able to have that balance. In the early years, I didn't really mind that much. I wanted to work as much as I did. Now I don't want to – but sometimes have to."

Despite the pressures, she says she enjoys the fast pace of the job, and overall loves the work: "When I started, I was in it to have an exciting job. I'm not in it for those reasons any more. I'm in it because I see it as an important job to do and to be done well. I feel I'm there to help people understand this society." In May 1989, the YM/YWCA of Winnipeg named Jennifer Woman of the Year, in the communications category.

Nelle Oosterom, bureau chief for Canadian Press in Winnipeg, worked as a daily newspaper reporter in Thunder Bay and eventually, in 1981, was hired as a Canadian Press reporter. She also took time out to study, freelance and travel. Prior to her current job, she was the sole and first woman Canadian Press correspondent in St. John's, Newfoundland, where she apparently was treated with some curiosity before establishing her professional credibility. She says that being single has been advantageous as far as changing job locations and working long hours are concerned. Recently, she discovered the demands of a managerial job.

The position of bureau chief is a relatively new one for women in Canadian Press offices. I asked her how she experiences her supervisory role:

Largely because I'm a supervisor, I think there's some feeling – and that would be in any office where people haven't worked under a female before – "what's that going to be like?" I sometimes feel, not just by people in this office but also by others in the company, that I'm being looked at under a microscope to see how I'll do. It's partly because I'm a woman and partly because I did not have any managerial experience before I got the job.

Nelle's new job has required some adjustments, though familiarity with the Winnipeg office as a former reporter has helped. Her role is not only to give the news wire service editorial direction, but also to act as a liaison with the Canadian Press clients and members: "I'm aware of being watched and I'm aware of my image. So that certainly does add stress. I do feel I have to be careful I don't screw up."

I asked her how she views her input at the bureau. "I have a much different sense of the media role," she says. "I'm always a fairly idealistic person. But I've become a little more realistic over the years. I like to think what I do now makes a difference – what I value will somehow be reflected in what comes out of the bureau. I like to be active in giving it direction.... I'd like to leave the bureau a better place than when I got there."

I asked Nelle whether her job, too, is time-consuming. "I really fight to make room for personal time," she answered, noting that her current position imposes greater demands than her last reporting job. "I really have to plan ahead. You have to accept [the fact] that a lot of your intellectual and emotional energy does go into your job. And it does take up a lot of space in your life."

I asked Nelle if she thought a woman needs any particular qualities to work as a supervisor rather than as a reporter:

If you want to move into managerial work, to be a producer, in the planning aspect, more than in reporting, you have to deal with people and communicate with your staff. You have to be tough – that's pretty important. Not tough in a macho way, where you look and talk tough, but tough inside – so that you don't get upset by criticism or by things going wrong. You need not feel bad about getting knocked down and being persistent. You need almost to take a philosophical view when things go wrong.

I asked if she thought that workaholism is a factor in getting ahead in media. She thought that "being a workaholic is an advantage; the tendency, though, is not a healthy one. When I look around, the people who get ahead are the ones who put in the extra. If you're a nine-to-five kind of person and don't like phone calls in the middle of the night, you probably won't get very far. Another quality is the ability to respond to a crisis. When some big story happens, you've got to drop everything and devote your time, your energy, your mind, to doing that job."

Laura Rance, married and without children, works as Winnipeg-based correspondent for the western Canadian farming newspaper, *Western Producer*. She began working as a regional reporter for a rural Manitoba newspaper, moved on to the daily *Brandon Sun* as a general reporter, then reported for the *Calgary Herald* before coming to Winnipeg to get married and take a job at the *Winnipeg Free Press*. She worked at the *Free Press* for two years prior to her current job. Laura says being raised on a farm in southern Manitoba fueled her eventual interest in agricultural/rural news reporting.

I asked her to offer some observations about her career. How did she arrive where she is today? "The Brandon Sun was a training ground for me. We never were paid overtime. We worked late hours and weekends on a rotating basis and got a Friday off as compensation. When I went to the *Calgary Herald*, where they did compensate [pay] for overtime, I realized my time is valuable to me." She explained that the *Free Press* "wasn't as pleasant a working environment" as the other two papers. Reporters "had to fight tooth-and-nail" for overtime pay. "There was a real, concerted effort to discourage people from overtime. But if you're going to do your job, you have to work extra hours. That's all there is to it."

Although Laura puts in some long hours working as a *Western Producer* correspondent, she has found plenty of support from the Saskatoon-based management. Although the newspaper is managed by men, its western Canadian offices are run mainly by women. "By and large, I'm happy doing what I'm doing now. This job has benefits in terms of freedom and control over what I do. Staff have been provided opportunities such as training courses. I did not expect to go into agriculture reporting. It's been a progression for me. But I'm glad I'm here."

I asked Laura, whose husband is a newspaper photographer, how she has balanced her personal and professional life. "We're both used to putting in extra time in this business. It's always hard finding the balance. He works night shift and I work the day, so we see each other on weekends. The balance is, if you're happy in your career, I think you'll be happier in your home life. It's never been perfect. If we both were at home in front of the TV every night, I don't think we would enjoy that either." But she is not as eager to work long hours any more:

"Maybe I'm burning out. I don't know. I'm trying to find a better balance between my home and work life."

I asked whether she had noticed any differences in the way women and men approach their journalism careers: "Women need to change jobs more frequently than men to get ahead rapidly if there are family considerations," Laura observed, "because we are the ones who will make the sacrifices to our careers." She also thinks a positive work environment is more crucial to a woman than to a man: "When I think of women who left the *Free Press*, they left because they thought the environment was better for them elsewhere or they were going to be with their families. I've run into men who talk about spending 10 years of their career in one location. Women can't afford to do that."

Laura says that after two years she gets "itchy feet" and wants to move on to another job. The other women interviewed agree that it is common to take a new job every couple of years to move up the career ladder. Jane, for instance, says moving into a new job every two years was a deliberate part of her career plan. "I don't think you can ever be happy in this business," Laura says, adding that the characteristics making a successful journalist are those also causing difficulties. "I think we're so used to being critical of everything, we're critical of our own lives, and nothing is perfect." I asked why, then, she stayed in the business: "What keeps me here is that I'm doing something positive and productive."

Catherine Evenson has a rural-based perspective of her work as a broadcast and print journalist and editor. Married to a farmer, and the mother of two grown children, she has reported for southern Manitoba newspapers and radio stations for over 20 years. She has also done other media work, including some programming for community television, writing rural stories for the *Winnipeg Free Press*, and interviewing for a Winnipeg radio station. She says she "came full circle" when she recently took on a position as editor of one of Manitoba's largest regional newspapers, *The Pembina Times*. She started writing for the paper in 1969 at the invitation of the woman editor, who admired Catherine's note-taking as secretary of the local Manitoba Centennial Committee in Morden. Catherine says the newspaper was so small then she "ended up doing all jobs except running the press." Soon after, she was asked to join the *Dufferin Leader* (now the *Valley Leader*) for better pay (low pay is a common problem for rural newspaper reporters). She was editor of the *Leader* for four years during a time when the idea of regional newspapers was developing. Eventually, she quit to spend time with her young children, and took a job as a school librarian. But the writing bug again bit her and she began reporting school-board meetings while continuing her work as a school librarian.

A local radio station approached Catherine to report full time, but she compromised by freelancing for a few years for them and for three local newspapers. "You could do the same story four different ways. I also started at Valley Cablevision, where we went around with television cameras. My family went with me," Catherine laughs. "That's how you organize as a mother."

By 1980, when freelance budgets tightened, Catherine reported full time for local radio for several years and then became *Pembina Times* editor. She also reports for the paper. She prefers print to broadcast media, "for a story can be told more thoroughly in print."

I asked her about her work schedule. "It's quite amazing," she replied. "I know that city people may think that rural Manitoba is pretty ho-hum and not much happens. But where I used to cover four stories in a week, now I cover four in a day. We encompass a lot – a large area – three towns and a municipality. There are some real feisty folk out here who'll think nothing of calling me in the middle of the night. That's one of the hazards of being a rural reporter. I tried to quit reporting once," she says. "But I guess I want to be part of the community – that, and just being bloody nosy."

Catherine says that the erratic hours can make for a very tough job: "It's hard for a married woman – you need an understanding husband and kids." She wrote about her family's adjustment to a reporter's life in an article about making dinner in the morning for *Canadian Living* magazine. "It was a thing I actually had to do. Talk about adjustments you make."

I asked whether she had had to make many personal sacrifices for her work. "I don't think I've made any personal sacrifices," she retorts. "It's been worthwhile. The only time it was most difficult was when I thought my work wasn't appreciated by my employers. But then, I just never hung around for long."

I asked how she thinks she is viewed as a woman editor/reporter. Catherine says she is treated the same as a male editor, except she is not paid as well as male editors, though comparatively better than at an earlier radio station where less experienced male reporters were paid more than she. "I'm sure if a man had my job, he'd be paid more money. I'm unsure whether it's because of the type of community, because I'm a woman, or because I don't have a piece of paper [journalism degree] to say I'm qualified. But I'd like to be paid for my ability."

Aside from feeling short-changed in terms of pay, she says that rural reporting has offered her boundless opportunity to learn about media: "I don't know of anyone in an urban setting who could go from not having any education in journalism to working for every media outlet. I like to think I've made changes – and been accurate and fair. I've gone for the jugular on occasions when I thought someone was playing smart, and I've felt like sitting and crying with someone. At other times, people have gone up one side of me and down the other, ready to get me fired."

I wondered if she thinks there exist any obvious career barriers to women in rural news media. Catherine says she knows of a woman working at a local radio station whom she expects will "never be a news director" because of her gender. She feels bitter about such obstacles to women. However, she is optimistic that attitudes are changing, saying she felt patronized when some thought a woman could not write about agriculture. But the growing number of female agriculture specialists has helped alter those attitudes.

Laura says one adjustment (though not necessarily an obstacle) is that she must approach some interview situations with men differently from the way a male reporter would. "In this industry [agriculture], which is dominated by men, I can't have a drink with my sources like a male reporter can. My interviews are very structured and businesslike, so my intentions aren't misinterpreted. That's a limitation. You also have to work extra hard and make sure your sources view you as credible."

Laura cites a situation she found ridiculous: a banker tried explaining agricultural economics in terms of her buying dresses and shoes. "It was just hilarious. I couldn't believe what this man was doing. It was very patronizing because I understood the point he was making very well. I talked about it with another reporter and thought about quoting him on this, but decided it would not have been productive."

Laura also has encountered, but attempted to ignore, the "pat-you-on-the-back patronizing sort of thing" by men. "As long as I'm getting the information I want from them, if they feel they have to patronize me, fine."

"In some cases," says Nelle, "a female reporter may not be treated as seriously as a man in an interview, but it may work out positively for the woman. Maybe they're not taking a female reporter as seriously. So they relax more, then say more. It may work out positively, but it comes from a negative attitude in a way."

Jane says at the start of her career, because of her gender, she was frequently pushed into television news anchoring, which she detested. The first occurrence was at a station in Lloydminster, Alberta. "I got in there because I was a woman and the first woman there to anchor. They put me on with a man who looked like my dad. 'There's a cute young thing,' said the manager. 'We can promote the station.' I was handing out trophies to hockey players and front-lining their commercials. It was a big deal to have a female there." That was one unsettling instance, and it was followed by others, where her appearance – her sex appeal – was used to sell a station. She says that youthful attractiveness is still an important factor in hiring women to report television news.

I wanted to know how Jane felt. "I feel sad about that," she replied. "Because I think only after a number of years in the business do we really have something to say beyond the surface. I think it's become a very plastic industry." Jane agrees with the CBC's efforts to hire more women, at least partly as a response to government pressure to employ women and members of visible minorities. "In any broadcasting news room, sure, we look better. But there's still very few women managers and very few reporters over age 40 or even 35."

I asked her whether she ever has complained about this attitude. "No, you don't. It's a game," she says. "You don't come out and say something. You wait until one day you can change things. You work your way up. This is a very competitive business. Any job you have, there's a thousand who want it." Jane refers to numerous situations where she felt treated unfairly in the business because of her gender. "I learned quickly that you don't sit around and bitch about it. You go out and prove you can do something." For example, at a private station in Edmonton, she was given "fluff shit" to cover. For three months she worked on her days off to do an award-winning piece about the elderly on skid row. Although she turned her credibility in the news room "upside down," she nearly had to beg for a raise to match the salary paid to other reporters. She left the station for another job.

Jane says one reason she decided to work as a producer instead is to establish herself in a more secure a position, knowing the fragility of women's longevity as television reporters. "It is easy for your boss to push you down for some sweet young thing." She was particularly disturbed about the demotion of her former assignment editor, a single woman in her forties, who was "terrific" at her job at "The National," but was replaced by a younger, married woman reporter who wanted the position. "I think it's immoral. She's seen as a single woman, so what's she going to do? Quit? No, she won't. How's she going to quit and make the money she's getting here?"

Jennifer says she encountered problems when she issued a sexual harassment complaint against a male co-worker. "I complained to the president of the company. The man was spoken to and told to apologize to me. That was really hard because I ended up suffering more and it made people mad at me. It was common knowledge and treated more as a joke. "

She also has found some on-the-job obstacles as a legislative reporter. She finds, for instance, that Premier Gary Filmon is more curt in his replies to her questions than he is to those asked by male reporters. "I know there's another woman there who has experienced the same thing. So, that's a problem. You ask a serious, thoughtful question and expect to get an answer with some substance. "Sometimes I think it's their [politicians'] loss if they don't want to answer a question seriously. It's their point of view that won't be expressed to the public."

Jennifer says she has experienced some difficulty at the management level as well. She explains that CBC Radio journalists have their high and low cycles of excellent and mediocre work. "I had a three-year cycle where I was climbing. If a man were doing what I was, he would have done all sorts of things I wasn't encouraged to do. I was doing so well, I thought things were going to be coming. I realized after three years it wasn't happening. They saw me as having a lot of potential, but not being able to perform jobs that would have been promotions for me. So I am a little resentful. If I were a man, I probably would have been in Ottawa [doing political reporting]."

Jennifer says that, now she has a child, she does not aspire to the same goals as she did before. She remembers another time being treated with undue aggression by an all-male hiring board for a CBC editor's position. She regrets telling them she was pregnant – a factor she is certain accounted for negative treatment and not getting the job. "I was devastated. I was just destroyed by the interview. I wanted to quit my job. No job is worth losing your dignity over."

All of the journalists interviewed emphasized the importance of a gentle, as opposed to aggressive, approach in their work. But they stressed the necessity for a tough stance in some situations. "It helps, in some instances, not to have a hard-nosed, aggressive approach," says Nelle. "Although lots of women have that approach in media, I don't generally. It depends on the context you're reporting in. With politicians you have to be more that way – especially in news conferences or a scrum. . . . There's more aggressiveness needed there." She adds that people not used to dealing with media and those "who don't have a middle-class way of communicating" need to be treated with additional consideration.

Reporters not only should be fair, accurate and accountable, but also need to be aware of the human factor, according to Jane. Sensitive situations should sometimes involve a follow-up. Once, for example, she visited a hospital patient who broke down crying during an on-camera interview. "I wanted to see she was okay. I told her I felt badly – 'you really bared it all for us,' I said. 'That shows strength, and you spoke from the heart.' She really felt good about that. The difference between good reporters and the great reporters is that the great reporters can capture parts of the human spirit, put it in a story and not cause those people to lose dignity, not use them, but allow them to speak for themselves. Those little stories that capture a piece of the human experience – those are the best stories. And the great reporters are the people who can do it."

family portrait

Heidi Harms

in my fathers family sports and politics weren't one and two, the male
preoccupations   i think it was, first, family pride with all the attendant
jostling for position within the ranks and second, wit, both strongly
encouraged and influenced by my grandparents, partly by their
disconcerting habit of rarely expressing approval directly to any one
child, instead extolling his/her virtues & accomplishments to a sibling
thus ensuring continued competition   so the sport obsession came not
in the form of speculations about NHL playoffs or american college
football but rather in outdoing each other in remembering old quotes,
the stories behind them the historians were particularly good at this
part and in delivering them in a fresh way with just the right timing so
you couldn't help but laugh   politics was often a subject for discussion
too of course here everyone including grandfather deferred as they did
with any religious moral ethical questions to uncle anton, the eldest
son the odd one might disagree on the politics but it was always
perfectly clear & even a little embarrassing that he was wrong   there
were two who followed their own muddled theorizing   uncle ike who
by accident or necessity in this strong-featured family had come to
embody all its negative characteristics   he lacked ambition had the vilest
temper of them all and inexcusably couldn't tell when the others were
making fun of him   and aunt tina's husband, uncle erwin, with the
unnatural soft girth around his middle burgundy shoes and a bobbypin
subtly keeping his few strands of hair, rene levesque-style, around his
head   (there were three sisters amongst all these men oh yes
and i haven't forgotten them three strong women forced gracelessly into
the only molds available to women then   wives & mothers, two of them,
& one a missionary with vision allowed to join in the men's games yes
but only until it was time to prepare serve & clean up dinner, tasks all
three hated)

we cousins easily negotiated the different territories   the best times
were when aunt rita was sent out to keep us quiet until it was our turn
to eat aunt rita was magic she was the most wonderful storyteller we
were mesmerized by her soft voice and expressive eyes always she left us
clamoring for more   in summer the youngest uncles put up the rope swing
in the cavernous now empty hay loft it made you dizzy just

looking way high up to the beams where the ropes were tied   one
uncle stood at each end of the board seat four of us straddling it in
cabooselike formation, hanging on to each other or the ropes for dear
life   then with powerful legs and wicked grins they started pumping
gaining speed & distance until paralyzed with delicious terror we were
swooping heart-in-mouth the entire infinite width and height of the hayloft
afterward we walked away on jello legs agreeing it hadn't been scary at
all   we were privileged children wanted & valued precious inheritors
of the family legacies breathing this love this prideful attention

enormously articulate my uncles (& aunts always a resentfully deferential
halfstep behind)   even boldly   about bodily functions except for
sex sex **sex**   no words for that   so that when i was a teenager wishing
my body away with its clumsy new curves walking down the street with
my very favourite uncle of all and he put his arm around my waist i
thrilled to his strong protective arm and when his long probing fingers
started inching their way up to my RIGHT BREAST thoughtsfeelings stopped
dead there was only this a filthy sidewalk strangers feet shop windows
sliding by my right eye   until years later in broken words new
horrible language elizabeth told me what he'd done to her   to us
because at first my bewildered rage included her elizabeth my
fragile sister

oh he was a snake he knew his place knew just how far the silence
thicker than pride more profound than humiliation would
go keeping him safe paid his dues in advance always his mothers
favourite son the first one every year to remember about putting
up storm windows & etc he became a solid family man a minister in
the home congregation the fuckingnerve

God like sex was everywhere hidden & powerful for despite all
the words about him the awe & reverence they created deep inside he
was trapped in them pushed down with the guilt the guilt about
sex the unmentionable i couldnt find him in my grandmothers
living room noisy with laughter & sharp wit   the teachers
preachers missionaries visionaries   there was no thinking it into
place the lies denials betrayals the sex in me the hole inside
where god used to be

eyes and ears open lips sewn shut i grow a second skin stretch it tight over
my forbidden knowledge   caught   i live my fractured truth in flawed
allegiance to the family code *saving whom from what*   the clear fresh

loveliness of my young cousins, my daughters, haunting me the slow
acid burn of shame the great heavy weariness of my slowmotion lie
settling in my bones my grand gift of silence turned to dust

but if

finally in a small cracked shout terrified drymouthed my untellable
story breaks through the dense twisted layers of time & exquisite
circumlotion what then

Changing Terms of Endearment: Women and Families

Kathryn F. McCannell and Barbara M. Herringer

An 81-year old woman and her 97-year old husband live in an apartment in a rural prairie town. Their adult children and grandchildren visit often and offer assistance.

A couple in their late thirties and their teenage children from earlier marriages share a home and all family responsibilities. Both women are professionals.

A married couple in their early forties have recently had a baby. The woman's adult children from a previous teenage marriage live nearby and occasionally assist with child care.

A divorced professional in her mid-thirties has two young daughters. They live in a suburban neighbourhood. The daughters also have a residence at their father's, who has joint custody.

A 61-year old woman, suddenly widowed, lives in her own home in an urban area. Her adult children all live in different cities.

A couple in their early fifties, both artists, live on an island within commuting distance of an urban centre. They are child free, having made this decision prior to their marriage.

A 19-year-old woman and her three-year-old son live on income assistance. She is completing grade 12 on a part-time basis. They share a home with her mother and older brother.

Three women have shared a home for five years. One of the women has become pregnant through artificial insemination and plans to share parenting with her two friends.

All of these people define themselves as living in a family. The scenarios come from our own social circles, and vividly illustrate the point that there is no such thing as "the family." Indeed, the traditional family of one working parent (the father), one parent at home full time (the mother), and their children living at home is now the case in less than one in five homes in Canada.[1] In spite of this reality, the "other" family forms are often denigrated and unsupported by social policies.

Both of us are interested in families because we grew up in them, have worked with so-called dysfunctional families, and are creating new family forms ourselves. Kathryn grew up as part of a large extended family in a rural area. She was married for 10 years, and for part of this time her husband remained home caring for children while she pursued doctoral studies. After divorce, she and her daughters lived together, then shared a home with sisters. She shares responsibility for child rearing with her former husband. Currently she lives with a partner in a blended family, and he too participates in child rearing. Barbara has been in long-term relationships but has never married. She entered a convent and lived in a religious family for two years. Over the years she has lived in communal families of friends, lived on her own, and now shares a home with a friend she considers chosen family.

We believe that understanding the experiences of women in family life is at the heart of understanding the personal and political changes we are seeking. Interpersonal ties, with their themes of conflict and peace, nurturance and responsibility, present a microcosm of larger societal issues.

In this chapter we outline the shifting pattern of family life in Canada and explore the "labours of love" women engage in. Before doing this, we want to comment briefly on the impact of language in shaping our expectations and experiences in families.

LANGUAGE: THE TERMS OF ENDEARMENT

Language plays a crucial role in human existence. Its symbolic function allows us to structure our world and to form bridges of meaning. However, just as language can connect and unite, so too can it isolate and exclude. The fact that we live in a patriarchy means that we inhabit a world that has been named from a male perspective. Understanding the world from a female perspective can lead to a different understanding of many phenomena. For example, the term "maternal deprivation" has been used in social-science literature to describe the negative consequences experienced by a child deprived of mother's love. As Helen Levine notes, it implies an active "doing to" the child, quite unlike the image generated by its corollary term, "father absence."[2] From a feminist perspective, maternal deprivation can be used to describe the feelings of loss and grief a new mother may experience as she gives up some old roles to assume this demanding new one, or it may reflect her own hunger for nurturance.

There is tremendous power in naming. Several years ago, certain events that happened to women were "just normal life"; now these events have names such as sexual harassment and battering.[3] The act of naming gives validity to experience, and, as we begin to incorporate female reality and experience into our concepts, new directions emerge. For example, during the 1970s there were many journal articles studying the "effect of a working mother on the family," while research studies exploring the "effect of an uncooperative, demanding husband on the energies of a working mother," or "the effects of sex discrimination on a working mother and her family," were virtually nonexistent.[4] As the scientific community begins to incorporate female realities into the study of families, policy and practice will be more informed.

The language used to describe family life also reveals assumptions. For example, after a marriage ceremony, the couple is pronounced "man and wife"; he is a person, she is a role.[5] The issue of togetherness in marriage is reflected in the dictum, "and the two shall become one." Many traditional churches, particularly in the 1970s, refused to sanction a reading on marriage from poet Kahlil Gibran's *The Prophet*,[6] which advocates "spaces in your togetherness," because it is seen as opposing the ideology of male supremacy. Ownership of women and children is reflected throughout our language, from the nursery rhyme "Peter, Peter, Pumpkin Eater," to the notion of child custody, which implies possession. Custody is something that people "win" or "lose." Linda Cantelon has suggested that the term "joint responsibility" replace "joint custody," since the former more accurately reflects the intent of shared parenting.[7]

There is a subtle tendency within our language to view one type of family as ideal. Scrutiny of adjectives used to describe men and women in families reveals an implicit assumption of what is normal: consider, for example, the terms "working mother" and "family man." The adjectives modify the nouns in a value-laden way. The terms "working father" and "family woman" are not part of our vocabulary.[8] In the same way that the North American white male is considered the norm (and a male is considered white unless there is another adjective attached), the traditional nuclear family is held up as a norm against which other family forms are judged.[9] Family types are described, for example, as "blended," "two-earner," "matriarchal," or "single-parent" families, the latter term disguising the reality that there are many single-parent families in two-parent households.[10] A search continues for the "head of the household," and special derogatory words – old maid, spinster, dyke, hag, man-hater – are reserved for the never-married, lesbians and others who are not attached to members of the dominant class.

The area of sexuality is replete with examples of the power of perspective. When we read magazine articles on couple sexuality, do they speak of the man penetrating the woman, or of her enveloping him? Our knowledge of sexuality is from a male perspective; thus the emphasis in treatment programs for sexual dysfunction is on performance and skills, and "emotional orgasms"[11] are rarely discussed. The paucity of literature on gay or lesbian relationships reflects the heterosexual bias of "family science." Indeed, sexuality is an area where language encapsulates society's emphasis on male dominance. Julie Brickman suggests that a more precise definition of the term "emasculating" would be tantamount to refusing to acknowledge male authority.[12] The words "epersonating" or "epowerating" do not exist, because it is the value on masculinity that is central. This value on male genitalia is evident in popular expressions of admiration such as, "He (or she) has balls." As Sheila Gostick observes, "You've got ovaries" is not seen as such a compliment.[13]

The pervasive patriarchal biases in our language must be acknowledged if we are to move to a more complete understanding of families. Developing a sensitivity to such perceptual barriers and the power of symbols to oppress will alert us to what has been invisible. With this caveat in mind, we turn now to a summary of the demographic information available on changes in Canadian families.

FAMILY PATTERNS

Most of us grew up within a structure called family, or were, at least, attached to one. Some of us are adopted, grew up with relatives or friends, some of us were foster children, some of us only children or the "little mothers or fathers" of large families. Some were raised lovingly by our mothers, our mothers and fathers, or by several adults, or in blended families. Others of us grew up with the television role model of "Father Knows Best" or "Leave it to Beaver" and wondered why our families were so chaotic and destructive; why our parents were divorced; or why our fathers or mothers were alcoholics or addicts; why we were sexually abused by our fathers, stepfathers or uncles, or the man down the street; why we couldn't work things out as easily as the "Waltons."

Families are as diverse as the people who live in them. Historically women have been at their core, although not necessarily as the stay-at-home parent. That family picture has changed dramatically. Far more Canadians than ever are living outside traditional two-parent families.[14] Other significant trends include the fact that people are marrying later and are divorcing and remarrying in large numbers; couples are having fewer children; the number of lone-parent families headed by women is increasing (from 590,000 in 1981 to more than 700,000 in 1986); more than 1.9 million Canadians live alone, the majority of whom are women. The divorce rate nearly doubled between 1971 and 1983. There has also been a tendency to delay or forego childbearing.[15] In husband-wife families, the fertility rate was 1.3 children in 1986, compared with 1.7 in 1971. Women are having more children outside of marriage, and there is an increase in the number of children born to women in their late thirties or early forties.

Sociologists offer demographic, social and economic indicators as explanations for the shifting family structures. As statistics show, we live longer, marry later and have smaller families; in addition, family life is affected by the increased participation of women in the labour force. Increasingly high divorce rates and more liberal sexual attitudes also account for the transformation.[16]

Interestingly, while the structure of the typical Canadian family has changed, Canadian beliefs about gender roles conform to rather traditional expectations for women.[17] The diversity among Canadian families continues to be seen as "less than" the traditional model. The romantic notion of Mom humming in the kitchen as Dad strides in from work to be greeted by his children is still held as the ideal. Our intent in discussing other kinds of families is not to dismiss or mock this family structure; rather, it is to illustrate that there is more than one family form to be explored. There are alternatives to marriage; alternatives such as the choice never to marry, or to remain single after a relationship ends; to live in a gay or lesbian relationship, to have several relationships, to be celibate or non-monogamous, to have children without marriage, to have children through artificial insemination within or outside of marriage, to live in a common-law union, to co-parent, to maintain joint custody and joint responsibility of children after divorce. In the 1990s, the possibilities of family configurations are extensive.

Thus, defining the term "family" is not easy. In Canada, the popular model of the family usually encompasses a husband, a wife and children who are living under the same roof.[18] There are 5.8 million husband-wife families; of those, 3.6 million live with children.[19] Statistics Canada defines families as including husband-wife couples with or without children living at home, and lone parents with children living at home. Husband-wife couples include persons living common-law.[20] As Margrit Eichler notes, what is of interest is not only what (or who) is defined as part of a family, but also what (or who) is defined as not part of a family.[21] She describes the boundaries of family as being fluid, and believes that when asked, members of families are able to define the meaning for themselves.

Broader definitions are being explored, since not all Canadian families come under the umbrella definition of the nuclear or conjugal family. Sociologists also make a distinction between family and household.[22] Family members are related by blood, marriage or adoption, while a household could include unrelated room-mates, a family, a single person, for example. Many unrelated household dwellers do refer to themselves as family, particularly if they have lived together for any length of time. Some of us live in our "chosen" families; these may include gay and lesbian relationships or communities of friends. Families may include several generations living together, or a grandmother living with her child and taking care of the grandchildren.

The group of women having the most profound effect on family are those married women in the work force. It is this changing role that particularly upsets proponents of the new right and pro-family movements. While the anti-feminism of the new right (a coalition of political, religious and anti-feminist groups) is dismissed by some as being the ravings of religious fundamentalists, we see it as a continual threat to the gains made by women. As the new right continues to gain ascendancy and influence, it is an ideology and practice that cannot be ignored.

Proponents of the new right, both male and female, believe that nothing less than the re-establishment of the dominance of the traditional white, patriarchal family will revitalize the economy and create moral order. To accomplish this, married, wage-earning women must be encouraged to return to the home, for when they are situated in the work force, they become increasingly more aware of the sexual bias of the marketplace and their double load of paid work and "housework" and child care.[23] With this recognition comes the demand for equal rights. "Feminist demands are not just demands for civil rights, control over their bodies, and equal opportunity. They are simultaneously demands for a new conception of the family – namely that women be viewed as individuals – and a rethinking of the basis of law, philosophy and society."[24]

It became more and more difficult to ignore women's paid work, when, by 1985, 68 percent of all Canadian married women of child-bearing age (20 to 44) participated in the paid work force.[25] What about the woman who chooses to work at home raising her children? How is her housework and motherwork counted in the scheme of things? At the United Nations Decade of Women Conference in Nairobi in 1986, delegates voted to include all women's work in the gross national product (GNP) of every country. The resolution stated:

The remunerated and, in particular, the unremunerated contribution of women to all aspects and sectors of development should be made to measure and reflect these contributions in national accounts and economic statistics, and in the gross national product. Concrete steps should be taken to quantify the unremunerated contribution of women to agricultural food production, reproduction and household activities.[26]

According to the Canadian Advisory Council on the Status of Women, if women's unwaged work in the home were included in the GNP of Canada, it would account for 35 to 40 percent of it.[27]

A discussion of family patterns would not be complete without reference to the violence that is part of life in many families. The ideology that fosters an image of the individual family as a bulwark against the cruel world often keeps a battered woman and her children from being able to seek help, for it sees what goes on within the family as "private." It is difficult for any of us to comprehend statistics that coldly illustrate the fear, hatred and loathing directed at women and children in a society that purports to hold these members sacred. However, when one out of four girls and one in six boys in Canada will experience sexual abuse before they reach 18, when a Canadian woman is raped every 17 minutes, and when one in 10 women who live with a man in an intimate relationship can expect to be beaten at some time in their lives, the idea of home and family takes on macabre connotations.[28] These painful realities of family life have only recently been spoken of by women. Breaking the bonds of silence and secrets, and courageously telling the truth about family experiences, we bring about change.

LABOURS OF LOVE

The statistics cited above do not illustrate the work, the extensive labours of love, that women in families engage in. The effect of family work on women's lives has largely gone unscrutinized because of its invisibility and the low value assigned to it. Feminists, however, have asserted that the unpaid work women do in their homes is a fundamental factor in the creation of mental illness among women, and have used a labour analysis to understand stress in women's lives. Harriet Rosenberg suggests that postpartum depression, for example, would be more aptly labelled "on the job stress."[29] She notes that symptoms such as chronic anxiety, depression, fatigue and substance abuse are often seen as signals of strain produced on the job. Burnout is an extreme form of strain frequently experienced by front-line workers at the beck and call of needy individuals. Rosenberg outlines the stressors inherent in motherwork, both alone and in combination with housework: shift work with no shifts off; no time off for illness; a work site often not safe for children because of demands associated with cooking and cleaning; isolation in the workplace; no wage; little control over working conditions because of infant-defined schedules; and little feedback about performance. In addition, motherwork has a vague yet all-encompassing job description, reflecting what Pogrebin calls "scientific motherhood";[30] men are in charge of the concept of childrearing and write books on how it should be done, while women are in charge of the reality. Rosenberg argues that it is the job design itself that creates difficulties, rather than some flaw in the worker's personality.

The perplexing and paradoxical working conditions experienced by women who marry and assume the reputedly high status but in fact low-paying jobs of wife and mother are well summarized in a verse from Peggy Seeger's song, "I'm Going to Be an Engineer":

... what rights for a woman,
you can buy her a ring of gold,
to love and obey without any pay,
a cook and a nurse, for better or worse,
no you don't need a purse when a lady is sold. . . .[31]

Sociologist Meg Luxton has vividly described the labour processes performed by housewives in her book, *More than a Labour of Love: Three Generations of Women's Work in the Home*.[32] She analyzes the relationship between wage labour and domestic labour, noting that the low wages paid to women in our society help to keep the nuclear family together because they ensure few alternatives for women. The economic dependence of women has profound effects on male-female relationships. The male in a capitalist economy sells his labour power in exchange for wages, and his work is part of the production sphere in society. When he returns from work, hungry, tired, tense and frustrated, his labour power must be reproduced; he must re-energize.

The housewife's work is to ensure that lunches are made, shirts are ironed, mending is done, people are awakened on time and that breakfast is prepared. But just as important is her work in the management of emotional tension, defusing the feelings that arise from the frustrations of her husband's workplace. Luxton emphasizes that it is this emotional-tension management that is the most hidden part of reproducing her husband's labour power. For the housewife, there is no separation between workplace and home; thus work time and leisure time are indistinguishable, and it is difficult to tell when she is not on duty. Who then will reproduce the woman's labour power? She herself must. Luxton found the women she interviewed often ate less and slept less than their husbands; and they worked when sick, used "breaks" to mend or sew, and found it hard to relax because they were on call. Another component of women's labour in families has been called "kin keeping." It refers to the work involved in maintaining connections within the extended family, for example, writing letters, remembering birthdays and planning holiday celebrations. Luxton found the tensions created for home workers were managed in part by relationships with women friends and female relatives. The issue of who nurtures the nurturer is critical in any family, and depression, anxiety and guilt can be seen as ways of going on strike, or signalling that a woman is starving for nurturance.

Helpers working with families need to assess abnormal working conditions as well as abnormal interactional sequences. The toll that unpaid labour is exerting on the mental health of Canadian women must be examined. Family counsellors need to explore divisions of labour, for to do otherwise is to implicitly endorse the existing arrangement, which is in many situations oppressive. Intake questions such as "Who cleans the toilet?" quickly get to the heart of politics within a family, and are equally as important as explorations of how the couple met, or their communication styles.[33]

But what maintains the attitudes and expectations that feed into the situations we have described? While economic and religious factors play a major role, we believe the political ideology of romantic love also bears close scrutiny.

ROMANTIC LOVE: THE IDEOLOGY

Mainstream culture models the traditional family in its music, television, advertisements, religion and magazines. In its trendy up-beat situation comedies, for example, network television rarely presents realistic portrayals of alternate families or forms of intimacy. Poverty does not exist on television. In general, beautiful, middle-class families (sometimes black but primarily white), live very carefree lives, lived according to the status quo.

Perhaps the most insidious and inescapable socialization occurs through advertising, which the industry terms "art" and which some viewers experience as pornography. Even though we may criticize, ignore, or minimize advertising, the publication and broadcasting of subtle (and blatant) images shapes our values and the way we perceive ourselves. Advertisements are full of messages about love and romance and sexuality. The pursuit of sex and/or romantic love, wearing the correct designer jeans, furs and perfume, drinking the most delightful white wine or aged scotch in front of a fire, listening to music on high-tech compact disks and later driving off in a red BMW or Porsche, is presented as the American (and Canadian) dream. A powerful film, *Killing Us Softly*, vividly depicts how North American advertisers use romance and sexuality, and violence, to influence the public to purchase and consume.[34]

The ideology of romance portrayed in all pop culture is one of possession.[35] The romance novels read by thousands of girls and women present a picture of being swept away, where sex is associated with love and fidelity. In contrast, the pornography read and viewed largely by boys and men reinforces the union of sex with violence, and objectifies relationships. What gets lost is the broader meaning of sexuality. For example, Sonia Johnson defines sexuality as "everything that inspires touching and caressing and holding and kissing and petting and smoothing the hair of and saying sweet things to, lonesomeness upon absence and joy upon return. It includes our physical and emotional and spiritual responses to all that is beautiful – in nature, in art, in one another, in ideas."[36] Our mainstream culture's emphasis on romance and on sexuality plays a part in what is now termed "addiction to love," and feeds into competition between women for a man.

The notion of an independent woman, not attached in some way to a male, still seems difficult for people to comprehend. She does not fit because she is not meeting a man's needs. Thus, nuns are still referred to as "brides of Christ" and married to the church, while witches are seen as married to the devil. Today, women without men are often called lesbians, regardless of whether they are or not. Never-married and single women, whether heterosexual or lesbian, are labelled old maids or spinsters. Mary Daly and Jane Caputi gleefully infuse "spinster" with new meaning: "A woman whose occupation is to Spin, to participate in the whirling movement of creation; one who has chosen her Self, who defines her Self by choice, neither in relation to children nor men; one who is Self-defined."[37]

NEW DIRECTIONS:
CHANGING TERMS OF ENDEARMENT

As we make slow steps toward equality between women and men, new forms of family relationships become both possible and necessary. Margrit Eichler sees one factor of fundamental importance emerging: families are slowly moving toward becoming voluntary rather than non-voluntary units for their adult members.[38] As "choice not circumstance" gradually becomes a reality as well as a slogan, diversity in family structure will increase.[39] To understand experiences in families, we must turn our assumptions into questions. Thus, rather than assuming that a family unit means the people within share a residence, procreate, share responsibility for socialization of children, and meet emotional and sexual needs, we need to ask questions about the extent to which these dimensions are present in different arrangements.[40] This helps us to acknowledge, for example, that for some family members there may be two residences (current conceptions of family in Canada's census make it impossible to determine the number of children who have joint residences or to count as families couples who maintain residences in different cities), that for some families procreation is not a dimension, and that there are varying ways of providing for the socialization of children. Various authors have suggested that it may be useful to conceptualize families as networks of relationships; relationships between some members may end but may continue between others. As social scientists develop more apt ways of investigating family life, Canadian women will continue to search for ways to achieve the rich intimacy, comfort, caring and closeness that family life free of abuse and oppression can offer. It is our hope that, in Adrienne Rich's words, "women and men may one day experience forms of love and parenthood, identity and community, that will not be drenched in lies, secrets and silence."[41]

Claiming Kin

Heidi Eigenkind

It's late winter now
and the river's dark with dreams
of break-up.
Bad. Ugly.
Or so they told me as a child.
Ugly as dreams
that don't bear telling.
Dreams of violence.
Of breaking out.
Dreams slaves have.
Full of blood and knives.

It's almost midnight.
Almost the time the women come.
The seven in their robes
smelling of the earth.
Of the leaves pinned beneath
the remaining snow.
Of the grasses uncombed by any wind,
flattened by the weight of winter.

They told me of these women too
When I was small.
Women in black.
Hags of the night.
Witches with brooms and broken teeth
Foul bitches that couple with goats
and large dogs.
They trained me into fear.
Into believing their lies.
Me and the others.
All of us prod-wary milch cows
bred to respect fences.
To choose the barn and pasture
over any other life.

Once a year we still mock
what we are taught to loathe.
Dressed in pointed hats.
Blacken our teeth
and cackle like fools.
It shames me now
how we make them ugly,
these sisters.
How we shun our own natures
to appease our keepers.
The fathers, the brothers and uncles.
The teachers.
The priests and doctors.
Each with their horde
of convenient facts.

The one who keeps this house
I still call father.
Though the word is a lie
my throat gags on.
Father.
The one who grabs my breasts
in the hallway.
Who finds me doing laundry
and dirties my mouth with his come.
Father.
The one who mounts me like a bear in rut.
Who groans and shudders above me
whenever my mother isn't home.

The names he calls me vary.
Gold Piece, Goldfish. Sweetmeat.
Princess. Cunt. Slut. Whore.
It doesn't matter.
It's not me he rails at.
Not me he thrusts into.
I'm just the one at hand.
The daughter of the house.

He tells me he saves me this way
from the touch of filthy-minded boys.
Spares me the backseat rapes other
unprotected daughters suffer.
He says he needs this.
That without it he would die.
He swears I drive him to it.
That I want it just like him.
He outlines death plans for him,
for me
should anyone discover what we do.
I no longer listen.
I dream almost nightly of him dying,
or of how to kill him.
I'm afraid of knives.
Of what my hands might do with knives
should I unclench them.

Tonite his absence
is an omen.
In the master bedroom
my mother dreams of fire.
Of all her children burning.
Calls out their names.
Cries out for help.
In their beds
my brothers dream of being heroes.
Comic book orphans.
Caped crusaders vulnerable to nothing
but betrayal. Rare metals.
A temptress' kiss.
I lie here listening for the women.
Each time the curtains billow,
each time a sleeper shifts
in rhythm to a dream
I think it's them.

Eight times
they've come and freed me
from the tangle of my dreams.
Eight times they've held and soothed me.
with tales of other places.

Tales of mirrors of the moon,
blackwater lakes
concealed by granite cliffs
that offer footholds only to the chosen.
Tales of nameless rivers snaking paths
to old, forgotten caverns.
Caverns strewn with fire opals,
rage red rubies, diamond glitter.
Jewels they call the Mother's tears.
Tales of mermaids riding waves
as wild as stallions.
Of cliffwomen. Falcon tamers.
Lithe as cougars.
Fleet as deer.
Tales they claim are true.

As always
a new moon heralds their arrival.
Heralds too
my time of choosing.
This is the ninth new moon.
The last one to announce them.
They've counselled me to heed my dreams.
But I've had nightmares only.
Dreams in which my hands sprout knives
I thrust into my father as he rams me
with his blade.

Outside
the river rouses slowly
from a sleep as dark as any dream.
I'm weary of this house.
Of being father-haunted.
I crave a life unfettered
by the claims of any keeper.
It doesn't matter who these women are
or where they'll take me
or if what they've told me is untrue.

Their voices work a charm
that dispels madness.
Their deft hands are a balm
I can't refuse.
All I have is what these seven offer.
My need claims them as kin.

Where Did She Go?

Emma LaRocque

That orange-red glow
from an old black woodstove
in Sapp's "Making Rabbit Soup"
Teased out a pain,
a memory so deep
of a life,
a way of life,
of a face,
many faces,
of smells,
of sweetgrass smells
of stories told in a language
I will never know again.

Where do they go
The voices that sang
and cried
and cooed swinging babies
wrapped in canvas
suspended by rope
nailed to the browned poplar beams
holding up the tar-papered roof?

Where do they go
The faces
In many shades of brown
aging
in concentric circles
like old cultured trees?

My grandmothers, my grandfathers,
My aunts, my uncles,
My mother
Where did she go
Her voice chanting Cree
in the morning,
Her voice cooing Cree
to her babies
In mid-afternoon
Her voice crying.
In the evening
grieving the dusk of her ancient culture.
Her voice raging
in the night
of her sorrow of Woman,
her sorrow of Native.

Where did she go?
Her face triumphant
at chasing away Pehehsoo the Thunderbird
from scaring her children.
Her face in determination
Swatting mosquitoes
away from her blueberries
that will nourish her children.
Her face in lilting laughter
and animation
Telling on Wisakehcha
playing games on ducks and foxes
Wisakehcha playing games on humanself.

Where did she go
Her face at rest –
in zero absolute stillness
posed for morticians
it was almost more than I could bear.

Her face, her voice
fading
in concentric circles.
Damn crazy cells
felled her
like a mad axeman
fells
a regal northern tree.

Where did she go?
Her voices, her faces
that wake me in the night
Where did she go
Her voices, her faces
that turn my coffee
into a cup of tears
with the first wisp of day?

Where did she go
My great,
ancient
cultured Tree,
My mother, My Cree?

Tides, Towns and Trains

Emma LaRocque

Where and how do I tell the story of the many worlds my mother and I have travelled? How does one tell a post-modern society that one has traversed centuries in half a lifetime?

While I have undergone some "predictable" stages in the four decades of my life, my journey has been more than the "passages" of life described by Gail Sheehy.[1] Because I was born into a world quite different in race, culture, political and socio-economic status from the "ordinary" Canadian, there has always been an "un-ordinary" and multi-dimensional aspect to my life and, therefore, to my thinking. For me, there have been no road maps; there have been few role models. There have been days when I have felt that I was in some space and time warp. And, indeed, in some ways I have been. At the age of 20, I could identify with Chief Dan George who, in his seventies, poeticized:

Was it only yesterday that men sailed around the moon . . . ?
You and I marvel that man should travel so far and so fast . . .
Yet, if they have travelled far then I have travelled farther . . .
and if they have travelled fast, then I faster . . . for I was born a
thousand years ago. . . . But within the span of half a lifetime I
was flung across the ages to the culture of the atom bomb. . . .[2]

If Chief Dan George travelled far and fast – as indeed he and my parents did – then perhaps I have travelled farther and faster. It did not take half a lifetime, but barely a decade, for me to be flung across the ages, and across yawning chasms of experience between my world and the world of Town.[3]

I was born in the morning in the dawn of 1949 in a one-roomed, kerosene-lit log cabin, into a small family in the small Metis community of Big Bay, Alberta, near the town of Lac La Biche. I was born into a world of people whose roots of pride, independence, industriousness and skills go back to the Red River Metis, back to the Cree. I was born into a world of magic, where seeing and hearing ghosts was a routine occurrence, where the angry Pehehsoo (thunderbird) could be appeased by a four-directional pipe chant, where the spirits danced in the sky on clear nights, and where tents shook for people to heal. When my mother brought home from town a comic book of Henry Wadsworth Longfellow's *Hiawatha*, which I later learned was a "classic," I could identify with its world. The magic and natural world of *Hiawatha* was my world too!

Yet I was not born into a garden of Hiawathian paradise. Our own humanness and the effects of European colonization were very much with us. Even as we lived off the land, we also lived off the railroad, and by fighting forest fires, and picking rocks and sugar beets in the "deep south" of Alberta. Even as we ate moose, trout and berries, we also ate canned Spork, sardines and white sugar. Even as my grandmother's lover shook tents in the ancient ceremony of the Cree, we were kissing the Stations of the Cross in the annual pilgrimages of the Roman Catholic Church. And even as my mother chased away Pehehsoo, soon after I entered school I was lecturing her about the physics of thunder and lightning. And even as my father spoke of smelling the swooping night-spirit dancers, I lectured him about the gaseous flickers of aurora borealis. Even as we chanted to drums, jigged to fiddles and laughed, we were also crying, hurting and burying grandparents, aunts, uncles, brothers and sisters who were felled by tuberculosis (T.B.) and other diseases. And even as we generously shared foods and other kindnesses with each other, there were those amongst us whom we feared. And there were those from Town whom we feared. Violence stalked among us.

I was born into a complex community that was open to natural change but that simultaneously experienced forced change. Change was not and is not new to Indian and Metis culture. The issue is to differentiate between change that is imposed and change that comes from free choice. And change that is forced is oppression. Oppression over time, such as that of the colonizing of Native[4] peoples in Canada, has had various and varying effects on different generations. I believe changes came slower for my parents than for me, but my parents experienced changes that were more directly forced upon them by Canadian society, especially in regard to their children and schooling. It may be harder to unravel the effects of changes that were at once forced and at once sought after. Schooling was forced on me too, yet I actually fought my parents in order to go to school. At the time, I did not know that school was an institution of colonization invading and disturbing the way of life of my family, my community, my ancestors. Nor could I have anticipated the school's denigration of Native peoples, which was to affect my self-image profoundly. And what could I make of the violence by white and Native alike in the playground as well as in the classroom?

Even though I soon hated school, I idealized learning, and unknown to me I internalized much of what Metis author Howard Adams calls the "white ideal."[5] Early in my childhood I quite consciously rejected the roles expected of me by my family and community, namely, to attend to household chores and eventually to become someone's wife. So, I kept on going to school. I kept on going. And I kept on going.

My going to school presented numerous complications for my family. Living off the land was a family affair. Parents and children were engaged in the various activities associated with trapping, hunting, working on the railroad, fire fighting, gardening, processing food and animal hides, sewing clothing, making tools, cooking, healing, fishing, berry picking, creating and recreating, the sum of which formed a well-integrated, functioning culture. Our culture cut across all seasons and some geography. However, in the early 1950s, forced schooling and governmental confiscation of Metis trap lines in the northeastern area intercepted the seasons, geography and rhythm of our culture and, hence, our family life. My parents had to juggle between a land-based lifestyle, which was available to us only at Chard (a little whistle-stop on the Northern Alberta Railroad[6] [NAR]), and a lifestyle that could accommodate school, which was available only in the Lac La Biche area. The distance between Chard and Lac La Biche was only 100 miles numerically speaking, but it seemed much greater, because we were crossing more than the muskeg. But we managed. My mother stayed at our home near town so we children could go to school, and my father shared a trap line with my favourite uncle and worked seasonally for the NAR at Chard. My father came home regularly every two to six weeks, and we joined him in Chard whenever school was out.

Chard was our haven. At Chard we had our second cabin (the first one being at Big Bay) just a few yards from the railroad. On the rail line between Lac La Biche and Fort McMurray there were Metis hamlets about every 20 to 25 miles. Metis men worked as section hands for the NAR and the women worked tirelessly at home.[7] I have many fond memories of our numerous family trips on the train, going back and forth between town and Chard. I learned to play poker from the best on those train trips!

Just prior to my reaching grade seven, we learned about a dormitory that was opening at Anzac, between Chard and Fort McMurray, for Metis children whose parents lived along the NAR line. We would board at the dorm and go to a public school nearby.[8] To get to Anzac, we would board the train, stay for two weeks and then come home for a weekend. I had no idea what this place would be like; I only knew I had to get away from the town school. And just as I had demanded to go to school in the first place, I pushed my parents to let us go to Anzac Dorm. Even now it hurts me to think of the loneliness, the powerlessness and the emptiness my parents must have felt, watching us moving away from them.

At the tender age of 13, I boarded the old NAR train on my way to Anzac. For more than a decade I was to board that train over and over again on my way somewhere in pursuit of "higher" education. For more than a decade I was to visit my parents only for short periods whenever economically possible, and then to take that train again away from them. It was never without enormous heartache. I still remember standing at the back of the coach waving goodbye to my mother as she stood on the tracks waving back. I would watch her until the steel ribbons blurred together by the distance and by my tears. I knew she was crying too. And I remember the joy of arriving. The train could not go fast enough (and it could not – it barely mustered 20 miles per hour). Finally, we would creak and rumble into Chard. My parents would be standing by their cabin, waiting, hoping. When they could determine it was really me coming towards them, my mother would break into a little jog, hesitating, then running, to greet me. And she always had such delicious food ready for me. All too soon there would be the devastating pain of leaving them again. I remember it all, still, as if it were yesterday.

Each time I took that train away from them I was not only leaving a family and a place I loved so much, I was leaving a culture, a familiar way of life, for a world that was, initially, foreign, frightening and, at times, excruciatingly lonely. With each train ride the distance between my two worlds grew, not only in miles but in ways that no words in English could ever adequately describe. What kind of a society forces families into such heartbreaking, no-win situations?

The overused and flimsy phrase, "cultural differences," comes nowhere near describing the tidal waves of changes that I, my family, and my ancestors have undergone. The real difference between Native peoples and other Canadian people is no longer cultural so much as it is political. Native cultures have been inextricably related to lands and resources; Euro-Canadian culture continues to invade these lands and resources, pulling the ground from under Native cultures, creating a power/powerless relationship that generates results immensely more profound than mere cultural differences could ever create. To speak of cultural differences as if there is a balance of power is to hide the truth of colonization.

The history of colonizing Native peoples in Canada may best be understood as the ebb and flow of an ocean. There was the initial tidal wave of the fur traders, missionaries and disease. The nature of this wave was such that Indian peoples could, for at least two centuries, stem, redirect, even dam the intermittent tides. Then there was the crushing wave of Confederation and "the national dream" – the building of the railway. Already weakened by disease, demoralization and the growing loss of economic independence, western Native peoples could not withstand this rush. Indians were forced into treaties, residential schools and reserves. Metis were forced out of the Red River area and left landless and marginalized throughout the prairie provinces. Remarkably, both Indians and Metis endured, and even regrouped, when they were left largely to themselves during the low tide between 1890 and the 1950s.

The third tidal wave, which continues to affect my generation, took place soon after World War II. This wave was the modernization movement, in which various white agencies seemed driven to whip Indian and Metis into white, middle-class, "ordinary" Canadians. This is the wave in which governments confiscated or restricted the trapping, hunting and fishing areas and resources that Native peoples loved and used. This is the wave that forced families between town schools and trap lines.[9] This is the wave in which police unabashedly picked up the most vulnerable Native people from Town streets, and in which social workers began "scooping" children away from their homes.[10] This is the wave that made our village crouch when townsmen came, sometimes striking with brutal rapacity. This is the wave in which disorientation, grief, fear and internalized rage grew among us.

And this is the wave I was born into, a wave that has haunted my heart and influenced my research and understanding of the human being as the oppressed and as the oppressor. The late 1940s to the 1960s was the tidal wave of the town – in which, like headlights of a car in the night coming closer and closer, the town loomed larger and larger. It was not just one town; it could be any town, anywhere in Canada. Town consisted of "white" people who spoke English with various accents: French, Anglo-Saxon, Ukrainian, Syrian, Chinese. To us, they were all white and they owned and ran everything. Restaurants. Stores. Offices. Schools. Churches. Hospitals. Rooming houses. Barrooms. Jails. And even the very corners of the streets we walked on. In Cree, we called them *ooh-gu-mow-wuk* (the governing ones).

Going to town was a major event, for in the 1950s we went only occasionally. For me, it was almost always a very unpleasant experience. *Ooh-gu-mow-wuk* stared and glared at us. Sometimes they called us names, like "squaws" and "bucks." Sometimes they yelled at us, "Go back home, dirty Indians."[11] And sometimes, my parents stayed to visit with their friends and relatives on the streets, in secret wine circles, or in barrooms because they had no access to the recreational and tourist facilities in town. We, the children, waited in movie houses, looked at comic books in cafes, or, if late into the night, waited vigilantly in hotel lobbies. Sometimes fights in barrooms spilled out onto the street – then, to be sure, there were the police. In the 1950s, there were few fights for there was little excessive drinking – but there would still be the police. Many times I saw police roughing up and/or picking up Native people, among them my uncles, my aunties, and even my mother. Years later I was to learn, with horror, that there were times when the police picked up defenseless women just to assault them!

If we did not go to town, the Town came to us. The presence of the priests is a good example. Wherever the Metis went, the priests went. They carried their portable god and confessionals. Priests functioned as catechism enforcers, baptizers, and buriers of the dead. I do not have any happy memories of priests. I remember them as austere-looking, authoritarian men with big dark beards who dressed in black. They taught an extremely simplistic version of heaven and purgatory, as if they were afraid we would fathom the contradictions of theology. They would pop in unexpectedly once or twice a year demanding confession, while my mother scurried to feed them. I especially remember one priest who, holding hands with my 15-year-old cousin, led her into the woods. I asked my mother why he carried such a big flashlight in the front of his pants! In retrospect, I wonder why no one stopped that priest.

For all the times and ways priests controlled Metis' lives from the Red River days up to the 1950s, their presence is almost nil today in the Lac La Biche area. When my family needed spiritual support and nurturing friendship during my mother's eight-month illness in 1981, no priest or other Roman Catholic representative ever came to us or stood by us. The priest who performed my mother's last rites and burial was and is a complete stranger to me and my family. Other friends and caring people stood by us, knowing the sorrow of the passing of seasons, and the sorrow of my gentle father, my brothers, my sister and I, and of the grandchildren.

Town brought disease. Throughout the first half of this century, thousands of Native people were felled by T.B. My community did not escape. People with advanced T.B. were shipped off to Edmonton, and often their bodies were shipped back. We had no money. We spoke no English. Edmonton may as well have been Russia, it was that inaccessible to us. Even the town hospital was inaccessible. It was only in the late 1950s that municipal health workers discovered our hamlet (which is only six miles from town) and started to immunize children against T.B. and polio. By the time I was 10 years old, I had lost more relatives and neighbours than an average white person will ever lose in a lifetime. What emotional and ideological havoc all these deaths must have wreaked on us. What questions and doubts the medicine people must have had about their knowledge and their Cree and

Christian gods. We, the survivors, walk in grief for much of our lives. There are ever new diseases that stalk our communities.

Then there were the storekeepers in town, and Town storekeepers in each hamlet. Storekeepers probably had the greatest power of any whites who had a connection with us. They acted as post office workers, bankers, translators, and managers of our family allowance, old age pension and pay cheques. In the 1950s and much of the 1960s, there was no social assistance, but the storekeepers acted in the manner of welfare agents. They kept the accounts, doling out credits against debits. They determined the price of goods, furs and berries. They watched us like hawks when we shopped in their aisles.

In this era, Native people, including my parents, never fought back. They tolerated the stares, the dehumanization, the violence, the price-fixing. One time, I challenged the books of an old-timer, a storekeeper who was always very friendly, accepting of, and dependent on his Native customers. He was buying blueberries from us and his arithmetic did not match mine. I exposed the discrepancy and made him pay us the correct amount, but my parents were mortified –not at him, but at me! "*Keyam, keyam,*" they ordered me. *Keyam* means, among other things, let it be – don't rock the boat. Don't question. Don't challenge.

My parents were reflecting centuries of colonial conditioning: fear and obey *ooh-gu-mow-wuk*. The flip side of this can be found in missionary and fur-trade journals in which colonizing Europeans assumed governing positions and considered any Native expression of independence or resistance as "haughty," "impetuous" or "arrogant."

Quite early in childhood, I became aware of the serious gaps between the world I was born into and the world of the Town with which we had to deal. It is not surprising that a large part of my life has been focused upon trying to understand and build bridges of communication between these two worlds. For me, formal education finally formed the channel through which I could articulate my many worlds. I must say, however, that who and what I am today has been despite, not because of, the school system.

From grade one onwards my student life has been filled with discomfort, loneliness and anger. Before I knew about racism in Canada, I experienced shame and alienation from teachers and textbooks that portrayed Indians as backward savages. And of course, the Cowboy and Indian movies and the attitudes of Town did not help. Yet I knew that there was absolutely no connection between such biased portrayals and the consummate humanity of my parents, brothers and sister, my *nokom* (grandmother), my aunts and uncles.

But what does a child do when she knows from a place that had not yet been "documented"?

Later, as I pursued "higher" education I soon discovered that university textbooks presented Indian and Metis peoples in as distorted and insulting ways as the elementary texts had done. The racist theme of the myth of Indian savagery was ever-present. Indian culture was described as "primitive" and "simple," Indian society as static.[12] And of course I knew that there was nothing simple or static about the world my parents or I grew up in. Today, as an historian, I document what I have always known.

As I said earlier, my going to school presented numerous complications for my family. It also presented problems for me. The deeper I moved into the education system and into the white world, the more I found myself encountering conflict: with my family, with my new white friends and acquaintances, within myself. The longer I stayed in school, the less my family knew me. The more I knew white people, the more I became aware of their profound lack of knowledge or appreciation of my background.

Throughout my elementary and high school years I heard many racist comments. Travelling in buses or trains, sitting in classrooms or in cafes, I would hear comments about "Indians" wafting mean and dirty. There was nowhere I could go, nowhere I could be, without hearing words about "Indians." Stupid words. Incredibly insulting words. It was as if Canadian whites were given some divine injunction to prattle incessantly about "the Indian problem," as they put it. I became aware that I was part of a group that was "open season" for anyone's misjudgements and slurs.

As a child, I never spoke up in classrooms or in playgrounds. As an adolescent, I felt shame and confusion. But in my late teens, I began to speak out. I began to talk back to teachers, missionaries, farmers, bus drivers, train conductors, cab drivers. To those whites I considered friends, I made special attempts to explain. Years later I came to understand that, like many Native individuals before me, I had been forced into the position of being an apologist for "my people."[13]

At the age of 19, I started what has become my career: the university. In several classes, but mostly from reading on my own, I learned about colonization, racism, slavery and poverty. I read Harold Cardinal's *The Unjust Society*, and could identify with nearly every page.[14] Finally a Native person had articulated what I had been experiencing! I came to understand that our economic poverty and marginalization, our landlessness and our fragmentation, and all the hostility and stereotyping around us were neither accidental nor isolated, nor were they due to some "cultural difference" or innate deficiency in us. Racism and injustice, deeply entrenched in all major institutions, tore our communities apart and broke people down. This oppression was rooted in a racial, religious and patriarchal ideology that claimed that whites were civilized and their manifest destiny was to enslave Blacks and overtake Indians, both of whom were considered savage. In Canada, racism was and is the foundation and the justification for colonization.

Institutionalized oppression was an earth-shaking concept for me. For years I, like my parents before me, had been conditioned to fear and obey *ooh-gu-mow-wuk* and to *keyam*. All our lives, priests preached the acceptance of one's "station" in life; evangelicals preached personal sin as the cause of all grief. My parents explained disease and misfortune as a manifestation of "bad medicine." Life was a matter of fate and personal stupidity. In addition to all this, I was indoctrinated in grades seven to nine by well-meaning Mennonites at Anzac Dorm; I was taught to adopt the Beatitudinal posture of meekness and of forgiveness and prayer for those who would devastate us. At the Prairie Bible Institute in southern Alberta (where I took grades 10 to 12), I was brainwashed never to question, never to challenge. There, medieval rules were equated with godliness. And on our town streets, Pentecostals yelled: "Prayer moves mountains," and "take it all to Jesus."

I was born into a whirlpool of *keyams* and karmas. But I was born asking. I was born, as poet Joy Harjo writes, "with eyes that can never close."[15] Even when blindness struck me in my early teens, I saw – at home and in Town – what no one wanted to see. As a child, in the safety of my own home, I asked and challenged incessantly. In elementary school, terrified of my peers and teachers, I was cowed into deadening silence. As a vulnerable teenager, desperately in need of a framework to live by, I clung to religions that had simplistic "answers" to life.

Discovering earth-shaking concepts usually changes a person. Moving away from the concept of the "personal" to the "sociological" was, for me, a revolution. Learning that poverty and other problems in my community were due to some traceable oppressive processes was for me liberation from shame and confusion. I became politicized. What was more, I was politicizing on at least two fronts: as a Native and as a woman. The early stages of decolonization entail much anger. I was as angry about the subjugation of female persons in my hamlet, and in my town, and in churches, as I was about the oppression of Native people. I was shedding innocence and layers of myths, leaving patriarchal and paternalistic "friends." I was taking on new theories, pushing past boundaries. I soon found myself confronting people who made sexist or racist remarks. I lectured to my family and relatives, on one hand about racism in Town, and on the other about sexism and the sexual offenders in our communities and towns. I was explaining issues to whomever would listen and, incidentally, even educating professors along the way.

Clearly embarrassed, my family tolerated me. My other relatives avoided me. My real friends said little. The "ordinary Canadian" whites reacted with disbelief, defensiveness and shock. I had become the Uncomfortable Mirror. What no one understood was that I was in a revolution of many layers and there is little that is comfortable or "quiet" in such a revolution. I also soon discovered that there is nothing easy about trying to educate either the oppressed or the oppressor. Nor is there anything particularly angelic about either group. Both are afraid of self-inspection and change. The familiar is safer than the unknown.

Meanwhile, I pursued life at top speed as only a healthy person in her twenties can do. Quite by accident, I got into journalism, writing and lecturing. At the age of 20, I had a major essay published in a college paper and republished in a Native newspaper. At 21, I found myself lecturing to an audience of 2,000 at a church conference in the United States of America. At 23, I travelled across the United States, visiting Choctaw, Sioux and Navajo reservations. Feeling like John Steinbeck in search of America, I experienced that hot, sticky summer as one of tremendous personal growth.[16] At 24, I became a published author. Because my book, *Defeathering the Indian,* was (and is) categorized as a curriculum guide, it was never widely advertised.[17] Even so, it was given considerable media and public attention. This initially flattered me, but I soon found myself retreating.

Something about the pace of my process frightened me, and much about public reaction frustrated me. I went back to university and, after receiving two master's degrees (in religion/peace studies and in history), I began a teaching career in Native studies at the University of Manitoba. I have been teaching there since 1977. I have pursued scholarship and teaching with the same incisive passion and exuberance I've explored my different worlds. And here too, I've found myself confronted with many contradictions, ironies and resistance. For what does a Native woman scholar do when she has had to "master" the very authors and materials that have always left her with the knowledge that they "see," but they do not see?

How incredulous I was to read the fathers of anthropology, psychology, socialism, sociology, history, political science and the great religions, and discover that much of their theories on human development are premised on patriarchal, ethnocentric and ill-formed notions about so-called "primitive people."

In the same vein, how maddening it has been for me to read "classics" such as *The Plains Cree* in which David G. Mandelbaum essentially chops Cree culture into disparate pieces of "primitive" tools.[18] Equally maddening are the assorted manuals for nurses, police and teachers for "Native awareness days," which reduce Indian culture into a pathetic list of seven or so traits.

How enraging it was to hear a colleague in history describe Indians as having a "hand-to-mouth" existence. What could a white, middle-class, male urbanite know about the nuances and genius of being Native living in and off the land? Reading "classics" and an assortment of biased archival materials, he formed his eclipsed view of Indian existence. Like so many others, he assumed the authority of white authors, passing it on as fact.

How eerie it has been to referee and comment on a problematic missionary journal of the 1820s, describing, among other things, the shaking-tent ceremony, and to know that my grandfather performed the ceremony and my father was healed through it.[19] My friends still participate in such ceremonies. What could I say to those white colleagues who treat this as a remarkable archival find?

Sometimes, my feelings of being flung across the ages are highlighted in the most memorable of ways. In the summer of 1977, my mother and niece came from Alberta to visit me. In so many ways, it was a very important visit. It was the first time Mom, a woman who had travelled centuries in her lifetime, had had the opportunity to travel miles from her home, the first time to come to my world. Unknown to us, it was the last time she would travel in full health; in but a few years she would embark on that journey of no return.

Among many good memories I have of this visit, one incident stands out. We visited the Manitoba Museum of "Man" and Nature, where there was a display of a northern Native campsite and its attendant cultural tools. In an instant, Mom recognized everything, and her whole person beamed. With great animation, she began to identify each tool and to explain its usage. She described, for example, how specific moose bones had to be shaped and honed with precision so that moose hides could be scraped without damage. She went on at great length in Cree to detail the technologies of her world. My niece and I stared at her in wonder and in pride. At times white audiences formed around us. I found myself interpreting to them parts of my mother's impressive lecture.

Besides the fact that we rediscovered my mother as the great orator, educator and walking encyclopedia of culture that she was, the significance of this episode is how poignantly it illustrates the gaps in experience and knowledge between academic perception and Native reality. What academics and other members of white society have filed away as "artifact" or "historic," my mother (and all our family members, for that matter) knew and used in everyday life. My mother, who did not ever have the opportunity to read English, experienced the museum display as an affirmation of her living culture. She would have been astonished and amused had she been able to read the descriptions, which dated the materials as prehistoric.

I was not amused. I have walked, feeling cold and lonely, in Canada's archives, libraries, cathedrals, martyr's shrines, museums and forts that venerate priests and settlers at the awful expense of Indian and Metis peoples.[20] I have cringed each time I come upon an historic site, a tourist shop, or Parks Canada's pale plaques. I have noted that at every important juncture and place in my life or in my family's life, our culture and perceptions have been either chronologically misplaced, fragmented, belittled, infantilized, denied or disagreed with by the vast majority of non-Native Canadians representing all walks of life. I should say, though, that particularly in history and anthropology, academic perceptions and language have changed dramatically since the mid-1970s. I believe that the development of Native studies as a discipline in a number of universities has influenced the changes. However, the positive and intellectually exciting changes that have taken place in some scholarly circles have not yet touched the public or the media. By and large, the public and the media have continued to indulge in outdated views and hackneyed stereotypes about Native peoples.

Stereotypes are created by those in power in order to maintain their position in society. Stereotypes about Indians abound in archival and contemporary materials, and have been repeated over a span of four centuries. We have all been shaped to view, and therefore to treat, "Indians" in a distorted way. In fact, stereotyping is so prevalent that I, as a Native and as a woman, have often felt it was not safe to walk our streets, to ride in taxis or trains, to go to a hospital or to meet a police officer alone. I have not felt safe in my own community. I do not say these things lightly. There are hair-raising examples of how far racism and sexism has been carried. For example, the image of the sexually loose "squaw" renders all Native girls and women vulnerable to gross sexual, physical and/or verbal violence. Hollywood's portrayal of the good cowboy on guard against lurking savages renders all Native persons vulnerable to white fear and hatred.

Given that our violence-crazed cellulose culture feeds on the degradation of women and of Indians, it is conceivable that Betty Helen Osborne was savagely murdered because she, a "squaw," had dared to resist white male sexual attacks.[21] In the minds of the "good boys who did bad things,"[22] it is not the place of "squaws" to resist white power, especially power snakily connected to male ego.

Similarly, it is conceivable that J.J. Harper's death in Winnipeg was triggered by cowboy-conditioned reflexes.[23] A male Indian in the dark is perceived as dangerous and aggressive, especially if he dares to talk back or to tussle with the powers that be. The tradition of seeing Natives who resist as rebellious and out of their place goes far back in history. The arrogance of oppressors is, of course, universal.

We know that the oppressor can be conditioned to be callous and inhuman by the very dehumanizing stereotypes he creates. Over time the oppressed internalize these stereotypes. What may happen to Native boys and men who, along with being exposed to pornography, internalize the view that Native girls and women are "squaws"? What may happen to Native persons who grow up with comics, textbooks and movies that objectify Indians as wild and violent? The phenomenal growth of violence in Native communities in which females of all ages are the most obvious victims is an indication of what is happening.

And what may happen to a society that tolerates all this racism and layers of sexism? I believe such a society becomes inured to injustice, evil and dehumanization. The recent hero-ification of sexual "offenders" as "victims" is a stunning example of how low our valuation of human dignity has plummeted. And in the case of Natives attacking Natives, it is a form of racism for Canadian lawyers, judges, doctors, nurses, therapists, child welfare workers, and other social- service workers, to be passive and silent while the oppressed oppress the oppressed.

I know there are many of us from all walks of life who care. I know, too, that those of us who have raised these unwieldy and painful issues risk censureship. Neither white nor Native Canadians seem ready to deal with racism or sexism.

Only recently have I begun to discuss violence, especially sexual violence, in my classes and in my public presentations. I have been stunned at the speed with which I have been labelled, lied about and psychologized. But again, I can no longer be silent. I come from a long line of silenced women who have been victimized, as if war had been declared on their persons. My *nokom*, my mother, my aunties and my sisters of many colours across this land have been victims of violence. All kinds of violence. Perpetrated by all kinds of boys (yes, boys) and men. From grandfathers, stepfathers, fathers, brothers, cousins, sons and nephews, and strangers. From pedlars to priests and police. From poor men on Main Street to rich men in business suits. There is also violence by and between women that must be addressed.

But where is the outrage? Who grieved and raged for that fostered 14-year-old Indian teenager who was raped 17 times at Lac Brochet, her place of origin?[24] I was rendered speechless when a prominent woman in government sat in my living room during elections and actually tried to justify the actions of those rapists. I believe she thought she was showing openness about "cultural differences." The members of original Native cultures considered rape shameful and unmanly. Besides, at what cost do we accept or excuse human behaviour in the name of "culture"?

I have seen enough. I have heard enough. I have read enough about the human condition (including some very naive and irresponsibly liberal criminology studies by white, middle-class men who clearly know not what they write). I know enough not to entertain naive or bleeding-heart notions about the nature of man, whether he is the oppressor or the oppressed: at the bottom is the woman or the girl.

Recently I was invited to address a federal Human Rights Commission "hearing" on the place of minority women in society. I raised the issue of violence and suggested that the commission work towards persuading the United Nations to list rape as a crime against humanity. A number of the commissioners were clearly uncomfortable. After all, had they not asked me to speak (softly, apparently) on racism and "cultural differences"? Were they surprised to hear that violence/oppression of women is not a "cultural difference" but a universal human illness? And why is it that a problem global in scope continues to be called "deviant" by so many sociologists?

Later it came to my attention that at a dinner hosted by the Human Rights Commission, one of the commissioners labelled me "radical." For two decades now I have been chasing down and debunking stereotypes. I have learned that for every image I have "defeathered," another one has popped up. Once I was "disadvantaged"; now I dare to be a "radical." Should not a human rights officer know all the ingenious ways whites psychologize Natives, and men censure women? This is the nature and function of stereotypes: as long as a power struggle exists between peoples or between the sexes there will be new convenient stereotypes for those in power.

Stereotyping, labelling, blaming, denying, censuring or psychologizing are all patterned responses in a colonial or patriarchal society.[25] Just as Native people are the Uncomfortable Mirrors for white Canadians, conscious women are the thorns in the flesh in a sexist society. And just as very few people want to see the underbelly of Canada, fewer still care to look into the caves of men.

It has not been easy to be framed an uncomfortable mirror. It is not easy to hear about "the Indian problem" everywhere one goes, or to see stereotypes almost everywhere one looks. It tests my patience to be baited, excessively challenged or branded. I have had to live with the echoes of my own words, even the echoes of my research and analyses, because no one could receive them. This disheartening and lonely place is exacerbated by the fact that there are not many Native writers or scholars with whom to share.

Educating for change is exciting but exacting. While preservers of tradition and the status quo can assume authority simply from their positions, seekers of change must always "prove themselves." And resistance can wear out a person. My bones know the places where my soul has been scorched.

So sometimes, just sometimes, I do wish I could stay with the fence-sitting side of Canada. I wish I could teach only statistics so that my students would stay sleepy, or simply tell jokes so that my audiences would keep on laughing. Sometimes I wish I could "tone down" the fire in my voice that aggravates those who want to hear a demure Indian princess. Could I write poetry without politics? And why do I not dress more traditionally? At times, I wish I could "live and let live," tolerate the moral majority, accept everybody and, as some have chided, "understand that we mean well, we are all human, be accepting, be bigger than us." I wish I could be satisfied with mediocrity and, of course, sincerity. I wish I could be happy just being nice, being with my nice friends talking about nice things, going to board meetings and church or believing in karma. If only I did not expect so much from others, or from myself. I wish I could believe in feasibility studies, inquiries, conference resolutions and royal assents. Maybe I could be a yuppie, or even an "ordinary" Canadian. I know my bones would like this very much. I wish I could dance for Wisakehcha with my eyes closed.[26] I wish I could say *keyam.*

But I was born asking, and with eyes that can never close. The real wishing I do entails the transformation of people and of society. But how shall we transform the oppressed and the oppressor? And upon whose shoulders, whose consciousness does the task of transformation fall? I cannot trust ideological formulas. And I cannot be satisfied with conformity. I have known the shadows. I have heard the voices crying in the night. I have seen the sleeping. I know

the sorrow of the poor
the sorrow of woman
the sorrow of Native
the sorrow of the earth
the world that is with me
in me
of me.[27]

I have been flung across the ages – and I have been the one to take the train, to ride the tides, to learn English, to cross the chasms. But who will know my world, my mother, my Cree?

Through the Fog:
Looking at Academia

Rosemary Brown

I recently completed a year as a full-time professor of women's studies in the Ruth Wyn Woodward Chair at Simon Fraser University. That year gave me an opportunity to observe at close range the trials and tribulations, as well as the joys, of academic life.

My first observation was that the pursuit of feminist goals is the concern of a very small percentage of the people who make up the university community. Most of the women on campus, students as well as teachers, are not openly and actively supportive. The brunt, almost the entire load, is shouldered by a few women who are stretched so thin that their health and their sanity are at risk. The same women who teach the courses also sit on the committees, do the research, importune administration, and do whatever has to be done to introduce, protect and sustain the inclusion of the study of women's condition in the academic curriculum.

I observed that for women on the campus the obstacle was not so much a "glass ceiling," through which they could see but not go, but rather a thick, deep fog, which shrouded and hid an impenetrable wall of closed minds.

In 1987, when I was invited to participate in the National Symposium on Post Secondary Education, I explored the relationship between women and other disadvantaged groups with the universities where they taught and studied. I learned that the situation that existed at Simon Fraser was not unique. Indeed, it seems that most post-secondary institutions cling to the medieval concept of a university as a self-constituted community of teachers and scholars licensed by the pope or emperor or king, to confer degrees and enjoy certain privileges and immunities. Those universities that have evolved to the twentieth century have re-defined their role so as to link it to corporate needs and corporate funding.

Because the study of the condition of women has proven not to be a priority either in medieval times or now, the conservatism of university boards and bureaucrats has stymied all attempts to expand the curriculum and structure of their institutions to meet feminist criteria. Simon Fraser University began developing a women's studies department in the very early seventies, but did not actually achieve a tenuous skeleton of a department until the eighties. Yet Simon Fraser University found itself well ahead of the University of British Columbia and the University of Victoria. On the other hand, because of its links to industry and to corporate funding and interests, in just a few short years the University of British Columbia established its Department of Asian Studies, a far younger area of study; the department enjoyed a firm and rich position as the pride and joy of the University of British Columbia, and was constantly bragged about by the president.

At the same time, the challenge to the legitimacy of studying the condition of women continues to be masked by the chronic shortage of funding that all universities are experiencing. The efforts by women on campus to build and expand feminist teaching, research and study is indeed hampered by the fact that expenditures on universities as a percentage of the gross national product has declined from 2.04 percent in 1970 to 1.33 percent in 1985 and 1986, resulting in depreciation of research equipment, erosion and decay of library holdings, decrease in student services, and regression of employee salaries. Rather than recognizing the problem of underfunding, some government departments at both levels have been looking at the possibility of trying to select particular programs within the university for special funding – the temptation to pick politically glamourous university programs for special funding is great.[1] Because women's studies is not politically attractive nor "glamourous," its funding has been erratic, picayune, and fragile at best.

Another observation that I made concerns the absence of both power and influence on the part of women to advocate, to protect, and to nurture feminist interests in the university. The small base of support for feminist ideas and study in the academic community that I mentioned earlier, when coupled with the powerlessness of its advocates, leads to results that are predictably discouraging. A survey conducted by the Dalhousie Faculty Association, released in February, 1988, revealed total and complete absence of women in the ranks of senior academic administration, including the positions of president, vice-president (academic and research), assistant vice-president, deans and advisors to the president. It found that 73 percent of male staff and only 59 percent of female staff had tenure; it also found that 37 percent of males and only eight percent of females were full professors. These statistics vary insignificantly from the 1973 findings of a similar survey conducted at UBC, which also found women absent from the top decision-making ranks. Consequently, because women are clustered at the "importuning" level of the power structure, we find that the process of initiating, introducing or expanding either curriculum or course development in women's studies is slow, difficult and often unsuccessful. We are reminded by William Ryan, in his book entitled *Equality*, that institutions of learning are really ideological instruments for teaching by endless example and repetition that individual human beings are all different and, in particular, the major difference is that some are superior and others inferior as a consequence of their different internal qualities.[2]

Historically, universities were developed for the benefit of privileged intellectuals – they were not intended to be instruments of change, but rather were protectors and perpetrators of the status quo. Strong concrete barriers to protect and preserve them as institutions to educate the powerful and rich male decision-makers and trendsetters have existed since their inception.

The existing structure of our society is designed to keep women out and down. We are let in to the system on the condition that we abide by its norms. Seeking to re-structure post-secondary institutions so that they respond to feminist ideology cannot by any stretch of the imagination be construed to be abiding by the norm.[3] Like other racial and cultural groups that are also attempting this reformation, women are actually trying to prod a ponderous bureaucratic dinosaur into thinking and acting in ways alien to its genetic heredity. Wiser heads than ours wonder at the challenge that we as feminists have taken on in this instance, and at the enormity of the task in which we are engaged. However, desperate times call for desperate measures. If we do abide by the norms that society has assigned to us, then the lives of most women will remain what they have always been: a cycle of dependence, forced labour, forced sexual access, forced reproduction. And the position that some of us have moved up and out of, at least in some way and in some part, will be filled by another woman. Thus ensuring that women will be used and used and used until we are all used up. "Women will be born, degraded and die."[4]

The challenge for feminists in the academic community continues to be to have and to maintain a realistic appraisal of their goal – namely, to redesign a powerful cultural indoctrination. And the most painful part of this challenge for women is to recognize and admit that limits to our power and influence do exist. We must scrupulously measure the effect that our efforts have on our institution; we must also analyze the potential of our institutions for significant restructuring. As laudable as optimism is, grandiose and exaggerated goals lead to disappointment and self-doubt – and the sustained and futile banging of our heads against an immoveable object contributes inevitably to burnout.

The other thing that struck me about the family of academic

feminists (once I got past their hollow-eyed exhaustion) was not just the extent of valuable research or study that they were conducting, but also how much information they kept clasped to their bosoms – while female politicians, community activists and other women involved in the liberation struggle remained unaware of and deprived of such information.

Throughout my political career, as an advocate for women's issues, I had always maintained a loosely knit network with women in many different walks of life. I had assumed that I was reasonably abreast of changing issues in all areas of study. After just a short time as a member of the university community, however, I came to realize that, in fact, the pieces of information that I had been receiving from my network were only answers to questions that I posed, while information about the new and changing developments in relevant fields of study were not reaching me. Perhaps it was assumed, erroneously, that if I did not request information on a topic, either it was of little importance, or of little interest and value to me in my work. "Why was that?" you might ask. Well, the answer, I suspect, is that academia is a closed community of scholars who publish in the journals of their own disciplines, attend and give papers at conferences, symposiums and conventions of their own professions, talk to each other, and create networks with each other. Unless one happens to be a student or a teacher in a particular discipline, much that is discovered and known in a particular area remains closed to people on the outside.

"Ivory tower" is a title that has been well earned. Feminist scholars do tend to be more open about their work than scholars in other areas are because their work touches on the daily lives of women. They are also members of a particular academic family, and interact extensively and often exclusively within that enclave. As a result, they may work almost exclusively to raise the consciousness of men and other women within their own discipline and not reach out to influence persons in the world outside their field. An example would be the debate surrounding ethical and moral dilemmas posed by reproductive technology. This debate has just begun and is ongoing – yet the question must be posed as to how well-informed the elected women in Parliament and the provincial legislatures are to put the case effectively and accurately before those august bodies, and to truly represent women's concerns. Let me assure you that advisors to government or to the opposition are not present when the tough fights take place inside the caucuses – and for women to have uninformed or ill-informed representatives in that pressure cooker doing combat against 2,000 years of prejudice and ignorance is, in my opinion, not only irresponsible but also dangerous.

Margrit Eichler, Nancy Morrison and a number of women's groups have called for a royal commission on and public discussion of this issue before any legislation is imposed on the country – our government chose not to respond to this request. It went to an election instead, and launched a campaign during which, because of the compelling nature of the free-trade debate, the issue of reproductive rights was not raised. It is possible that the subsequent decision to establish a royal commission was aired, debated and thrashed out inside the government caucus; no doubt future decisions on reproductive rights legislation will also occur there, in that predominately male forum. The question about which we must be concerned is whether the few women present in the government caucus have been sufficiently well-informed to defend us in that unequal forum, and whether the women elected to opposition caucuses have the knowledge and the information to represent us within their caucuses as well as on the floor of Parliament when such debate takes place.

Part of the push to get women into universities and institutions of higher learning was to enhance their personal economic and academic status; the other part was so that they could contribute to improving the lives of all people. Maintaining the ivory-tower concept, which supports the inbreeding of knowledge and information, defeats at least one of those original purposes.

The endowed Chair in Women's Studies at Simon Fraser University initiated a one-day workshop for female politicians in the spring of 1988. On that day, women who held elected political office at all levels of government as well as in native bands were invited to meet a group of women academics from universities and community colleges in the lower mainland of British Columbia for a mutual exchange of information. It was a tentative attempt to help women politicians scale the ivory tower and learn about some of the study and research being done there, while allowing women academics to learn more about the issues that concern politicians. Serendipitously, an added benefit of the workshop was that it gave the politicians an opportunity to form networks with each other, to meet as sisters rather than as political antagonists. And it allowed all of us to discover that, quietly and without fanfare, over 500 women in British Columbia were holding elected office, most at the municipal level. Many of the women were committed to a long term of political service.

At a Canadian Association of University Teachers conference in 1988 I raised the issue of the weakness in the chain of sharing information among women on both sides of the academic fence. At that time, it was explained to me, and I accepted the information as true, that academics lose status within their own disciplines whenever their work is seen to be commercialized, common or ordinary. It was explained to me that if women wanted to progress within their disciplines and to be respected by their colleagues, they had to observe the rules of academic "exclusivity" and isolationism. Ambitious women academics, therefore, could not run the risk of having their work perceived as "ordinary" and easily understood – this would reduce its value among their peers and by the seniors who make decisions about status and tenure in the university. I was reminded of the experience of David Suzuki, a highly respected geneticist (and Canadian Booksellers' Association author of the year in 1990), who suddenly found the quality of his research and his work being questioned once he began to discuss it in lay language that could be understood by non-academics. The practice of building an intellectual aura around academic work is a protective device that has more to do with survival within the academic community than with a wanton wish to be secretive. Therefore, feminists in academia are challenged to find ways to channel information to those women who influence policy decisions, as well as to the larger community of women. It must be done as part of the ongoing process of raising consciousness and, somehow, in such a way as not to lose the respect of their colleagues nor their place in the pecking order of the university community.

As a result of my own experience in facing the challenges and dealing with obstacles during my years in politics, I have come to the conclusion that the strongest ally that feminist academics have in facing their obstacles rests in the fact that it was the co-operative effort of women in the community with women in academia that resulted in the development of women's studies as a legitimate discipline. The power of this union should never be underestimated nor ignored. Indeed, the most effective pressure that a group can bring to bear on an institution is through the community; so it is quite possible that any further change in post-secondary institutions will come about only when there is more community outcry.

However, as long as negotiations between feminists and their institutions are conducted in secrecy, there is very little that the women's community can contribute to the endeavour. I am a firm believer in the effectiveness of indirect application of pressure. In this instance, wider dissemination and discussion of the reality of academic life and work is clearly mandatory to the process.

For feminists who work and learn in post-secondary institutions, each attempt at change should be approached with the same precision and detailed planning as one puts into contact with government or one of its bureaucracies. The extensive involvement of the women's network in the planning, strategy development and implementation of these changes would ensure that pressure from inside the institution will be complemented with pressure from outside, thus making it easier for the institution to hear and appreciate the seriousness and legitimacy of the demands.

Sexual Harassment and Life: Just the Beginning

Marilyn MacKenzie

We have new terms like sexual harassment (which ten years ago was called "life").[1] *Gloria Steinem*

It was a cold January evening in Winnipeg, in 1982, when Gloria Steinem spoke those words at the University of Manitoba. I am not even sure I knew, for most of the women at the University did not, that the President's Advisory Council for Women (PACW) was actively working on sexual harassment policy and procedures for this large prairie university.

I was a sessional field instructor for the School of Social Work at the University, living with the constant fear of being "cut" from the budget. This was not a career one could count on. My children were reaching the age when rather naturally they were becoming more independent. My husband seemed to take me for granted. I was no longer willing to be the traditional wife and mother, and I was heavy in body and spirit, uncertain of my future. It seemed I had nothing to lose by applying for the new position of Investigation Officer for Sexual Harassment Policy, so I took the plunge. I planned how I would dress and act for the interview. Being five feet tall and blonde, I knew that I would have to dispel quickly the myth about the low intelligence of blondes. I intended to be taken seriously. In preparation I thought about my personal experience of being sexually harassed and I read and re-read the University's definition of sexual harassment:

– unwanted sexual attention of a persistent or abrasive nature made by a person who knows or ought reasonably to know that such attention is un-wanted; or

– implied or expressed promise of reward for complying with a sexually oriented request; or

– actual reprisal or an implied or expressed threat of reprisal for refusal to comply with a sexually oriented request; or

– actual denial of opportunity or an implied or expressed threat of denial of opportunity for refusal to comply with such a request; or

– sexually oriented behaviour when it has the purpose or effect of creating an intimidating, hostile or offensive environment in which the student or staff member studies or works.[2]

Beginning a new position and a new phase of my life was exciting and terrifying at the same time. I was not familiar with the people or the system, and I lived with real insecurity about what they wanted me to do and what I needed to do. While the title "Investigation Officer, Sexual Harassment Policy" might sound impressive, it could be viewed as only a token position put in place to appease women but with no real potential for effect. In the six years prior to my appointment, there had been only four instances of sexual harassment that had come to the attention of the administration of the University of Manitoba. Some of us suspected there were likely many more undisclosed.

I took a deep breath and dove in, beginning with publicity. My daughter and I designed a poster and brochure for campus-wide distribution and put the policy and procedures into a matching folder for early identification and accessibility. These were sent out to every faculty, union and significant group on campus. At the same time, I negotiated for an office. This office could not be in the Administration Building next to the president and his vice-presidents, nor could it be located in or connected to any one faculty. I wanted to be autonomous, in a neutral setting with easy access for all, including handicapped people. After consideration of various alternatives, I finally settled on a large, informal setting located in a discreet back corner of University Centre (the students' union building), in the centre of the campus. The office is conducive to both informal mediation and structured investigation. It is bright and sunny, with room for all parties to have their own space in the presence of the opposition. I knew that the environment was important, and fortunately, I received the financial backing to create the type of setting that would best facilitate some often difficult processes.

A second step was for me to reach out personally to the University community and to the public. This involved interviews with the media, speeches to university groups, and in-depth educational workshops for potentially vulnerable groups on the campus. In the past five years, I have participated in hundreds of media interviews, workshops and speeches both on and off our campus, and presentations at conferences here, at other Canadian institutions, and in the United States.

The position was half time at first, the rationale being that, up to that point, there had been very few reported cases of sexual harassment. Within the first year of my appointment, I handled 21 complaints. Some University officials felt that this number was extremely high and reflected the University in a negative light, while others believed this represented only the tip of the iceberg. Reactions ranged from, "Twenty-one cases is far too many, so how can we get this problem under control?" to "Only 21 cases for 24,000 students and close to 4,000 staff – how can that be? What are you doing to try to get the other hundreds to come forward?"

According to the literature, between 20 and 30 percent of all women students have experienced sexual harassment. A survey we conducted at the University of Manitoba in 1988 indicated that the figure for harassment of females (undergraduate and graduate) was 15 percent.[3] While 15 percent was lower than expected, it means that in 1988 approximately 1,800 women experienced sexual harassment on our campus. Other studies have indicated that between 36 and 70 percent of women in the workplace are harassed.[4] According to a 1983 Human Rights Commission survey, 49 percent of women and 33 percent of men experience sexual harassment on the job.[5] These studies clearly indicate that sexual harassment is a major issue in our society. Sexual harassment violates fundamental rights, personal dignity and personal and professional integrity. It is a serious offence against individuals and society generally. If individuals or a group of individuals believe that they have been subjected to sexual harassment, they should take direct action, such as making their unease and/or disapproval known to the offender and consulting with the investigator or the appropriate administrative officer.

Part of my work is the handling of actual cases. This is the most exciting/fatiguing, challenging/depressing, rewarding/thankless part of the job. The situations have ranged from innuendo, joking, leering and staring, through to touching, stroking, brushing up against, fondling and sexual assault. I have encountered students harassing students, faculty harassing students, students harassing staff, staff harassing faculty, faculty harassing staff, faculty harassing faculty and staff harassing staff. It is all out there, happening daily and, like incest, it cuts across all walks of life. Each case is unique, and yet in many ways all cases are remarkably the same.

Inevitably, the victims or complainants are reluctant and nervous about coming forward. In many cases they are extremely vulnerable, for example, international students or single-parent support staff. They usually have endured the harassment for some time and only finally disclose it out of desperation. Like other victims, they are worried they will not be believed, have already started blaming themselves for at least part of the behaviour, and question whether anything will be done to help them. Initially, my main goal is to assure them that they will be listened to without judgement, in a fair and understanding way. The second most important point is to convey to them that they have some control over the process, and that they will decide how far they take the complaint. I offer my experience and authority. At the University of Manitoba, the policy is universal for all groups on campus. A first-year student will be treated with the same respect and dignity accorded a full-time tenured faculty member or an administrative director. There are no separate procedures for one group or another. This is a major strength in establishing the credibility of the policy with the various groups, especially with the unions, on campus.

Whenever a person lodges a complaint, an assessment of the situation is begun. First, it must be decided whether the alleged behaviour would constitute sexual harassment as defined under policy. One of the first avenues explored is the possibility that the person can handle the situation informally by herself.[6] This is a lovely idea but one that is not usually realistic. For the most part, speaking out is difficult: the key factor in sexual harassment cases is the imbalance of power. As one woman stated, it's not easy to say no to your boss and keep his ego intact. Nor is it easy to say no to your professor when he seems to hold your grade in his hand or has a strong voice in your recommendation for graduate school. These are the kinds of dilemmas complainants are faced with, and these are the reasons that so many endure the harassment for so long before they finally come forward. We will never know how many others resign from their jobs, drop courses, or discontinue their education. We suspect there are many.

When a person believes herself to be sexually harassed, an informal or formal complaint may be lodged with either the Sexual Harassment Officer or the appropriate administrative officer. One type of informal solution that has worked well in some cases has been the "letter" technique. This letter is sent by the complainant herself and has three parts. First, it outlines exactly what the behaviour was and when it occurred. Second, it states clearly how it made the person feel (for example, upset, humiliated, angry). Third, it requests clearly and directly that the behaviour stop immediately. We recommend enclosing a copy of the policy and procedures, registering the letter, and sending a copy to the Sexual Harassment Officer.

Although a letter can work in certain cases, many complainants cannot bring themselves to write such a letter, for fear of retaliation or reprisal. Even though there is a retaliation clause in the policy, many lack belief in this protection.

Another alternative is for the complainant to approach the respondent with a witness to demand that the harassment stop. Generally speaking, informal resolution is preferable to formal investigation.

The formal process of investigating complaints is much more involved and can take many hours, days or weeks. Initially, the procedure is the same, beginning with an assessment to determine whether the alleged behaviour is sexual harassment. Once the assessment is completed and a decision to lodge a formal complaint has been made, the specific procedures outlined in the policy are followed. The complainant must sign a written statement about the alleged behaviour and ask for the assistance of the Sexual Harassment Officer in the resolution of the matter. She may also seek legal counsel. It should be noted that university policy provides for disciplinary action toward the complainant in the case of frivolous or vexatious complaints. To date there have been no such cases.

When I receive a written complaint, I call the offender's unit head, that is, his dean, director, boss or manager (almost all of whom are male). Together, we interview the complainant and then the respondent. The respondent is informed of the seriousness of the complaint and is told that he may bring a member of his union with him. At the first meeting with the respondent, he is shown a copy of the complaint and asked if he wishes to respond verbally to any or all of the allegations. Reactions vary from denial of even knowing the complainant through to tentative admission of guilt. If there are witnesses to the alleged incidents, they would also be interviewed by the manager and myself.

The respondent does have the right to take the written complaint away with him and to consult his union or a legal representative at any time throughout the process. If the respondent's version of events is different from the complainant's, he is asked to put his statement in writing.

A thorough investigation of the entire situation is lengthy and complete, and includes statements from witnesses for both sides wherever applicable. In many cases, credibility of witnesses will ultimately become a factor. If guilt or partial guilt is not admitted, then a judgement must be made as to who is more likely to be telling the truth. This judgement will be based on consistency of evidence, reliability of witnesses, and knowledge of human behaviour. Then the unit head must decide on and initiate an appropriate course of action.

The course of action can range from requiring the respondent to apologize either verbally or in writing; sending the respondent a formal letter of reprimand; implementing a suspension (for example, for four, six or twelve months without pay); effecting dismissal; or, in the case of students, expelling the student. These decisions are the responsibility of unit heads and are often very difficult to make.

If there is a disciplinary action and the respondent feels unjustly treated, he has the right to grieve the action under the collective agreement of his union. If such a grievance is denied through the first, second and third stages, the respondent has the right to go to arbitration for an impartial hearing of the facts.

If a case goes to arbitration, it can be financially and emotionally costly for all those involved.[7] Our first such case lasted two full weeks with ruthless cross-examination of the complainant, respondent and witnesses. There were times when the process was so difficult that proceedings had to be interrupted in order to allow the complainant to compose herself. Her moral character was questioned, the policy and procedures were questioned, and my credibility was questioned. The outcome was that the arbitrator found that the disciplinary action was fair and just, and that due process had been followed during the investigation. While a major victory was won, it was a painful process. When the complainant appeared on a panel at the Fourth Annual National Sexual Harassment Advisors' Conference in November 1988, she stated that although the arbitrator ruled that she had been the victim of "sexual harassment of a particularly heinous sort," had she known the extent of the ordeal she might not have laid a formal complaint. However, she did feel vindicated, and hopeful that sexual harassment policies will work for women.[8]

The National Conference of Sexual Harassment Advisors (NCOSHA) was established in 1985 by sexual harassment advisors who met at an ombudsman conference. NCOSHA's mandate is to organize an annual national conference about sexual harassment issues for Canadian university and college sexual-harassment advisors and policy-makers; provide a national forum for the collection and dissemination of scholarship and research about sexual harassment in post-secondary institutions; and provide for centralized mechanisms for the collection and distribution of sexual harassment policies, procedures and statistics. We work together toward the goal of eliminating sexual harassment. Sexual harassment is not fair and it will not be tolerated. The first NCOSHA conference was held in Toronto in the spring of 1986, the second in Banff in the fall of 1986, and the third in Montreal in the fall of 1987.

I chaired the fourth conference in Winnipeg in 1988. Presentations included an overview of sexual harassment, an experiential workshop involving actual cases, a review of models for dealing with cases, and a panel of people at the University of Manitoba who had had experience with my office. It was on this panel that two complainants described the pain and anxiety they experienced as victims of sexual harassment. As I heard them relate their experiences, I was proud to have been part of the system that did not brush the incidents "under the carpet," or trivialize them as minor annoyances that women experience at some time or another. Sexual harassment is an affront to human dignity. We became angry and upset over the trauma that victims experience. Many felt anger too, at the lack of interest shown by their own institutions. This was healthy anger, mobilizing energy for action. Participants from all over Canada, and the media, were interested and concerned about sexual harassment, and politicians in power said publicly that harassment is not just or fair. We moved toward our long-range goals of justice and equality for all.

There are still days when progress is hard to see, so on those days I re-read a letter from a former student:

You have helped me in more ways than you know. I am able to say no thank you, and not feel guilty or mean. I felt good that I hadn't become submissive or a man-hater.

One time in our office, with my co-workers present, he put his hands on my shoulders from behind me. I said in a friendly but firm voice, "Hands off the goods." I had to say it twice. He didn't touch me again after that. I thank you for teaching me how to do that with confidence.

In November of 1988, I was particularly sensitive about female-male relationships in the office. I couldn't figure out why, because nothing significant happened. Then, I realized that it was one year since my incident on campus. I'm not sure I understand it, but I suppose it is similar to some families who feel sad and mourn on the first anniversary of a death. It just happens.

I am moving on to a much better company now. Again, I will be their first female. It is a medium-sized company (about 100 people). Its upper management is entirely made up of men. They do not have many of the special services offered by many big companies, so I don't expect them to have addressed sexual harassment in any special way. I'll find out when I get there. In any case, I feel confident that I will be able to handle most situations, should the need arise.

I wanted to write to you after each of my affirmations during the year. Each one made me proud of myself for taking charge. I didn't write, but I hope that this letter gives you a smile to start the new year.[9]

This letter certainly did give me a smile and encouragement to run another mile.

My daughter is now at university. I feel confident that she will not tolerate sexual harassment in any form. I know that she will reach out and help someone else come forward without fear of reprisal, should the need arise. I feel happy that my teen-aged son is a warm and sensitive human being who truly cares about other people, and who is not ashamed to cry. I know that in some ways he is vulnerable, but I am confident that he'll be able eventually to surround himself with others who think as he does. I know they both will contribute to making this world a better place to be.

As for me, I have learned to be a single parent, independent, and in charge of my own life. I know what it is like to have to work for a living in order to pay the mortgage. In some ways I now have a lot more sympathy for men, since they traditionally have carried the wage-earning responsibility for the family. At the same time, I am often outraged by the way men treat women in our society.

I have also learned that you can be all alone in front of a blazing fire, and yet not be lonely, or be surrounded by many people and feel alone. I know that I do not need a man to validate my existence; at the same time it is important to me that my lover really knows who I am.

Finally, I have come to believe in myself as a person and as a professional capable of influencing change and at the same time able to change. Each day I wake up and wonder what I will encounter, to whom I will talk, and whether we will win or lose. I know that what I am fighting for is important and worthwhile and that in some small way, perhaps, I can make a difference. As I cross the threshold into middle age, I have never felt more energized, more determined, or more committed to living the changes.

Eve, Lu-Ann Lynde and Carol Rose

Walking the Motherpath

Carol Rose

For over 15 years I, like many women involved in the Judeo-Christian traditions, have been trying to reconcile my spiritual practice with my feminist convictions. While I believed that scripture may well have been divinely inspired, I realized that the interpretations and legal doctrines drawn from this "divine source" were, at best, misunderstood and frequently biased.

I also understood that all religions seek to impart wisdom or knowledge by choosing teachings that they believe best illustrate their understanding of the world and how it should operate. Thus all religions select stories, parables, poetry, psalms and laws in order to preserve a particular world view. In this sense Judeo-Christian traditions are not unique. They too have undergone a selection process – a process begun long ago – that organizes and chooses what to include and what to discard in order to maintain its notion of reality.

I realized, too, that the selection committees were composed of wise, often charismatic, leaders and spiritual guides who knew the limitations of the printed word, though they chose to include them in their holy books. They were great teachers who could see beyond the "word." They were, themselves, "the word"; they could create meaning based on life experiences. Their oral teachings gave clarity to what the printed word could only suggest. Thus, I felt certain that if women would just educate themselves, both to the written and the oral lore of their traditions, they would discover truths therein that would enlighten and delight both male and female devotees.

In addition, I was convinced that, like all ancient traditions, there was a treasure house of oral teaching that had, for a variety of reasons (not the least of which was the printing press) become lost, or unavailable, to the contemporary seeker. I hoped, as women studied the various commentaries and additional writings, that myth (in my tradition called *Midrash*) would become their doorway into this lost oral tradition; that their eyes, if not their ears, would come closer to unedited, creative insights into scripture. Since Midrash contains many possible interpretations (all presented non-dogmatically and often side by side on the same page) the reader could sort through this raw material and, as tradition allows, could begin making educated choices about which interpretations to accept and which to discard. I hoped that their study would lead them to oral teachings that contained examples of the contributions and the divinity of all those created in the image of the Creator.

What I failed to acknowledge, however, was that, in the majority of cases, those who served as the codifiers or the interpreters of these teachings were men. These men, who were recognized either for their wisdom or for their personal piety, served as the "teachers of truth" – and they perceived this truth based on their orientation as men, or on the teachings that they themselves had received from other men. Men continued to be the authoritative interpreters of text, despite the inequities that many of their teachings perpetuated.

This became clear to me, very dramatically, in 1987, during a workshop on myth and ritual. As part of the preparation for the ritual I was to conduct, I examined Biblical readings about the lives of the Matriarchs. While what I found in the traditional rendition of the text did not surprise me, it was the commentaries, the mythic interpretations, that disappointed me most profoundly. Suddenly I was face to face with the limitations of not only the written presentation of these women, but also with the oral teachings that had been preserved. It was then that I truly "knew" that study alone would not provide me with the answers. Studying meant looking at and understanding the available material, whether written or oral, as it had been handed down for generations. Regardless of the greatness, the genius or the inspiring quality of these teachings, I now saw them for what they were – selective in their entirety. They were representative of a world view that had an investment in maintaining the status quo, both in terms of human relations and in terms of the ways men and women could relate to the Creator. This brought me to the edge of learning. I felt that I could not escape the patriarchal emphasis in scriptural reading, nor could I ignore the equally patriarchal interpretations of that holy text.

This was an awesome moment – one that left me feeling quite alone. I was alienated from the very tradition that had guided my life until now. It was as though I had climbed a high mountain and was standing at its very peak, knowing that there was nowhere further that I could go. Then I remembered a line from the Bible that was addressed to Abraham and Sarah as they started out on their journey; it was a line I felt certain was appropriate for all who set out on a new road: "Go from your land, and from your kindred, and from your father's house, to a land that I will show you."[1] I felt that I had, indeed, begun moving out to an unknown land, a land that required leaving all that was familiar behind. In reality, I had made the decision to leave "my father's house." But where was I to go now? I needed models to guide me as I took my first steps along this uncharted course. So, as part of the ritual that occurred in the workshop, I decided to construct a house, or tent, of my mothers. Perhaps there I could find direction. Perhaps the mothers of my tradition could offer me guidance.

To quote Hallie Austen Inglehart, "it is a well-known psychic axiom that if you begin to act as if something were true, it becomes more possible."[2] So, I tried to imagine what the tent of my mothers would be like. To my surprise, the more I began to trust the "as if" process, the more I began to "see." Suddenly, my newly built structure (made of a prayer shawl and four poles) became real, and I found myself in the presence of the Matriarchs: Sarah, Rebekah, Rachel and Leah. To make these Biblical women visible to the other workshop participants, I stationed four of my friends at the corners of the tent. They became the physical representatives of these mothers. Since what they had to say was, as yet, unknown, I had to find words to put into their mouths. I tried to recall all that I had ever learned about them, and I acted as if I understood them – their thoughts, ideas and feelings. Cautiously, I began to trust my own interpretive abilities so that I could become their storyteller. Yet, this terrified me. Could I really "know" them well enough to speak on their behalf? Would my presentation of them be accurate, as accurate as the Midrashic interpretations of the past? Is this what it meant, then, to leave the patriarchy, to leave accepted renditions of the "Source"? Is that what it really meant – to delve into these teachings as a woman and to take responsibility for the re-telling of the tales from women's perspective? I recalled a line from a favourite book: "Our ancestors created these tales in order to give their descendants the best information/education available at that point in human evolution. The storytellers of today must do the same."[3] This became my inspiration. I was determined to continue the process, to go on with the journey to the tent of my mothers. I believed, more strongly than ever, that examining the Matriarchs' lives would help me find models for my new life course. Perhaps it would also serve the lives of other women as well, providing them with images that could guide them in their journey.

The workshop ended, but the experience of the ritual lingered in my memory and in my imagination. Often when I thought or read about the women in the Bible, I realized how much "bad press" they had received. Frequently, I heard the words of friends and mentors pounding within my heart: "What we need is redemptive Torah, women's Torah.[4] We need to find creative ways of looking at text, using our own life experiences as guide posts. We need to see these women in the context of their time, but we also need to see them at the centre of their own stories. They must become the main focus of the tale. We need to do this as women and as a nation."

The task was suddenly much greater than I had imagined (though certainly I was not the only one considering it). It was not simply a matter of finding positive kernels in the existing material. Even acting as if we knew the Matriarchs imaginally was not sufficient. What we had to do was shift the emphasis of an entire body of history to include women. In a literary sense, we had to emulate Marion Zimmer Bradley's *Mists of Avalon*.[5] What made it so complicated was that we were trying to do it with so-called sacred text – with traditional text respected for its continuity. And we had to do it as "insiders," as those who felt directed and commanded by the wisdom of the past. I was suddenly aware of the enormity of this undertaking. It required so much work. It probably would have been easier to turn my back on the whole thing at this point. Yet I knew that turning my back would be as impossible as trying to live as if I had never had this experience. The truth was that I had changed, and the task could simply no longer be ignored. The workshop was a catalyst for a major shift in my life journey. It crystallized the importance of bringing women's lives, past and present, into focus. It seemed that I had been one of the women chosen for the task, and now I had to find appropriate ways to respond.

I began reading more books by women, about women. I started attending workshops led by women that dealt with the issue of women and spirituality. I wanted to learn how other women, from other traditions, integrate spiritual practice into their lives as feminists. I participated in rituals designed by women, and I felt how powerful these were. I began to understand, in the words of Diane Mariechild, how rituals "are a stylized series of actions, whether physical or mental, that are used to change one's perceptions of reality, [and how we] create in the microcosm what we desire in the macrocosm."[6] I saw that when women take hold of ritual and story-telling processes they change the ways they view themselves and the world. I knew, then, the importance of ritual as a means for changing not only self-perception, but also the very essential function of ritual as worship: the worship of a creator who is whole and balanced.

What I learned from reading, as well as from the women I met, was that we were not trying to gain expertise in ritual and myth in order to duplicate the imbalance of patriarchal culture, but rather we were struggling to rid ourselves of the limitations that this culture had imposed. We were searching for ways of "being," for ways of relating to our creator and to all of creation. We were trying to deal with our sense of spiritual isolation creatively. Many, like myself, looked to the lives of ancient women, seeking precedents for our own experiences.

Some began writing – liturgy, poetry, songs and commentaries – always striving for more egalitarian language and interpretations. Others created new rituals, often grafting these on to life-cycle or seasonal celebrations. I, too, designed rituals, especially those related to women's rites of passage. The most powerful of these, perhaps, was a naming ritual designed for our daughter, Adira.

In collaboration with my husband, Neal, I tried to mark the arrival of our beautiful female child with a sense of holiness and communal joy. We focused the ceremony on the naming process, choosing names of power and meaning that, we hoped, would guide her toward a personal relationship with her creator. Throughout the ritual, we emphasized the relationship of her nation, indeed of all nations, with the feminine facet of the Divine, the Shekinah, or God Immanent. To help us usher Adira into this consciousness, we gathered together a quorum of 10 women, who formed a "chain of love." Each woman held the infant in her arms and blessed her, passing her to the waiting arms of the next, symbolically moving her from the outside to the centre. At the end of the chain, there was a woman seated upon a special chair. This was the seat called "the throne of Miriam the prophetess." There, Adira's godmother awaited her in the guise of the prophetess Miriam. Placing our daughter in the "lap of Miriam" we hoped would give her grounding. She would become the godchild of a wise one, of a woman of vision, of leadership, of clarity. She would be taught by her to dance and to rejoice. She would become the daughter of all who witnessed her naming, of all who saw her divinity and strength. She would be reborn into the community of Israel, with the help of Miriam, the midwife of the nation.

While the creation of rituals (centred around specific events) was highly significant and rewarding, my own life work became increasingly more directed toward Biblical women. Often I would dream, and when I awoke, I would write "Midrashic poems" about the women who had visited me in my dreams. The poems seemed to be coming from a source within myself; their creation seemed inevitable. I would discuss these women with many other people, trying to learn as much about them as possible. Eventually, I began envisioning them as a set of cards. I chose to trust my dreams. I began searching for an artist who would help me shape the images of the women who appeared in my dreams and inspired my poetry. I approached Lu Ann Lynde, a friend and colleague, educated in the Christian tradition, and together we worked on the *Motherpath Deck*. It was terribly important that the artist, too, be a woman committed to the positive representation of the Matriarchs. It was clear that much of our work was being directed from the "inside." We would often sit and talk about what we "knew," then we would separate for a few days, or even weeks. Regardless of the differences between us in our previous talks, when we got together again the illustrations and the poems matched.

The cards are the result of our "Midrash making"; they have become a vehicle for making the lives of our foremothers available. They are my response to the challenge of remaining faithful to my tradition while at the same time making changes from within. They have become a significant tool in the workshops that I facilitate. All of the women represented are portrayed in their fullness; they are neither overly weak nor unrealistically powerful. They are individuals; each has her own integrity and uniqueness. Our hope is that women will look at them and see reflections of their own life issues mirrored therein.

In my workshop entitled *Walking the Motherpath*, I use the cards and a variety of exercises, beginning with an examination of what we have been taught in the past. We discuss the images of women that we have been carrying, and we create a ritual to restore our vision. Then, free of fear, we look at the lives of our Biblical mothers and, indeed, at the lives of all those women who have influenced us, and we put forward our own intuitions. The hope is that we will create a new oral tradition, one that is inclusive of the contributions of women and, therefore, healing. In her book *Woman Spirit*, Hallie Austen Inglehart nicely summarizes the importance of this process: "We grew up believing that we didn't know anything – that our teachers, bosses, leaders, and spouses knew better. But now I know better – we really do know. All I have to do is look inside myself and to other women, and trust us and what I have intuited and known all along. And the world badly needs our ideas and our ways of being to regain its balance."[7]

The balance Inglehart speaks of demands that we include myths by and about women in creating this new tradition. We must tell new stories about lives of capable, strong and inspired individuals. We must include stories that present women and men honestly, and that illustrate their relationships, their frailties and their importance in the divine scheme. In addition, traditional images of the feminine facet of the divine need to be reintroduced. Images of the One who is called Goddess, or Shekinah, or Sacred Mother, need to become part of our reality. For regardless of what She is called, it is She whom we search for as we struggle toward wholeness. She is our access, the Holy Immanent that mystics of all traditions tell us we can know and call upon in our daily lives. It is this image, perhaps more than any other, that women have brought to consciousness as they find their way in contemporary spiritual life. For when we enter the tent of our mothers, we enter the traditional dwelling place of the Shekinah, the divine feminine abode. It is there we encounter a more complete metaphor of the Holy One. Insofar as we are created in the image of this being, we meet a more whole image of ourselves as well.

In the traditional myth, the Shekinah has been banished. She is forced to wander with the people as they work toward redemption. Who but women could have taken us so close to the truths we must face in order for this redemption to occur? It is from the lives of women that we learn what it means to have a part of ourselves in exile. But there is great danger in recognizing this truth. There are many who would rather not see. In the context of the Judeo-Christian traditions, many of the inroads made by women continue to be labelled "pagan." However, if paganism is understood as the worship of a single aspect of the divine, then it is the traditionalists who need to re-evaluate what is being perpetuated in the name of religion. "Ignorance about women and women's culture perpetuates women's powerlessness and men's imbalance."[8] The earth and her creatures cry out for an awareness that will nurture and make whole. The religion of exclusivity can lead only to further separation and divisiveness. The stories of the past must be retold, tempered with the wisdom of the present, in order to bring healing to the future.

Touching the World Gently –
Through Feminist Theology

Shirley Kitchen

We gather as women in a religious community to tell our stories, to name our world, to transform the culture in which we live. We leave behind us the norms and preferences of female behaviour as described by others. There are differing points of view on how to define feminist theology. Some people would like to reconstruct our religious past, others would like to throw it out. Some of us are trying to create new traditions, new symbols, a new language. In any event, the definition of self and world comes from being aware of the history of that world and how we have lived in it.[1]

As a religious feminist, I see now not only how my institutionalized Christian background betrayed me as a woman, but how I can look for alternate world views that incorporate systems that are not hierarchical and domineering, that value a pluralistic approach to living together, and are mindful of the world around us. I now have a place to speak. Hearing other stories, I know my own experiences are real. I am able to worship, to create my own rituals, to find my own medium of expression. I give thanks. It is both comforting and exciting to feel at home in my world.

The journey to my present awareness began in the 1960s. Like many women at that time, I was primarily a wife and mother. I loved my growing children with an intensity previously unimagined. They taught me joy and commitment and wonder at a level beyond any other experience. But there was an empty space that followed me around like a cartoonist's balloon, waiting for something to be written in it. I wanted more. I thought there was something wrong with me. I blamed myself for the wanting. Gradually, through the women's movement, I became aware that we, as women, are taught to "view happiness and contentment within restrictive and limiting contexts."[2] We learn to live by the definitions of others, to serve, to be loyal and to put others first. Society did not take into account my personal needs, aspirations and ambitions. No wonder I felt alienated. And guilty.

As part of my daughter's education, I enrolled her in the Sunday school of my childhood denomination, and started reading the educational material prepared for both children and adults. It did not speak to me. How could an ancient account of men with their mores and values be relevant to me, a modern woman, and to my female child? It was as though I did not exist. "It takes a leap of faith to believe," I was told. I struggled with the words "faith" and "heresy." And still I felt excluded. The feelings of alienation and invisibility became so strong that one day when I went down to the church basement to pick up my daughter from Sunday school, I was afraid I would not recognize her, or that she would be unable to see me. I removed her from Sunday school. My questions about personal salvation, transcendence, original sin, omnipotence, sacrifice, self-abnegation, obedience were unanswered, even rejected. I was silenced.

Almost 10 years after that, Mary Daly wrote that "the believer is often commanded to assent blindly to doctrines handed down by authority (all male). The inculcation of anxieties and guilt feelings over 'heresy' and 'losing the faith' has been a powerful method used by institutional religion to immunize itself from criticism. Women especially have been victimized by this."[3]

I joined a liberal religious church whose congregations covenant to affirm and promote, as one of their principles, a free and responsible search for truth and meaning.[4] In 1983, a group of about 15 women within the church decided to meet on a regular basis.

While most of us participated as individuals in fundraising, cooking for church suppers and/or visiting the sick, we wanted something else from the group. After two formal objective setting meetings, we decided to leave our goals and definition of our needs open-ended, trusting that the urge to get together with other women was so strong that we would define ourselves as we went along.

One of the first decisions we made was about how the group was to be organized. The administrative positions, including that of facilitator, would be rotated. Our decisions would be made by consensus whenever possible. Since one of our guiding principles was the affirmation and promotion of the inherent worth and dignity of every person, each individual opinion was listened to and considered. If we could not reach consensus, we would accept rule by majority. Not everyone was comfortable with these decisions. Some were afraid we would be deadlocked forever in discussion. But this has not been the case.

The rotation of the facilitator's role has, perhaps, been the most rewarding factor operating within the group. People who are ordinarily shy and hesitant to speak now lead discussions, prepare material for opening and closing meetings, and bring personal contributions such as music or readings to the group.

To enhance participation and ensure confidentiality, we adhere to the following guidelines:

– We speak in the first person, for example, "I think or feel this."

– Personal statements are taken at face value. There are no statements of judgement, such as, "You can't possibly mean that!" or, "Tsk, tsk."

– There are no right answers, only many possibilities.

– Each person has the opportunity to be heard and the right to be listened to.

– Advice is given only if requested.

– What is said within the group stays within the group.

– We are all responsible for what happens within the group. If I do not like the topic proposed for discussion, I am expected to say so. If I am not being heard, I say so. If I am being judged, I say so.

The continued use of these guidelines has given us a sense of trust and has led to a level of freedom of speech that is so therapeutic and powerful that the high energy of the group is often noticed and commented on by people who are non-members. The longer I work within the group, the more I realize how "right on" were our instincts to gather and to leave our goals open to definition.

In our particular approach to human relations we empower each other through encouragement and personal support. This approach offers an alternate view of power in operation, that of "power from within" instead of "power over." Power from within allows us to act on our own behalf, to contribute to our own sense of being, to participate directly in defining ourselves and our immediate world.

Definition of self and the world began for us with a series of presentations researched and delivered by individual members of the group. The topics chosen arose out of personal interest and included an examination of how women are portrayed in the media – in magazines, on television and even in modern poetry. We discussed self-care and ways to influence our treatment by the medical community. We told stories, defining spirituality for ourselves. From personal presentations we moved to a more structured curriculum of reading, designed to create bonds among women. Through novels we were introduced to female power, humour and wisdom. We read about women's life stages and transitions, about cultural conditioning, about relations between mothers and daughters and with men.

We saw how women struggle toward survival and independence, and we began an examination of symbols in our lives.

At this time we committed ourselves as a group to do a worship service in the church. We decided to develop the idea of the touchstone: that which tests us, serves as a standard, or marks our lives in some meaningful way. I took along my soapstone carving of an Inuit fisherwoman and introduced her as one who, like me, actively supports and feeds her children. We were beginning to form connections with other women, seeing our commonalities, and our differences.

Our recent study sessions have dealt almost exclusively with theology; that is, how traditional Western religions have affected us as women, and how we as women are responding, moving toward our own religious practices. For some people, these journeys mean making changes; for others, it means discarding religion from their lives or considering goddess-based, pagan or wicca traditions. Many of us are creating our own rituals, symbols, myths. We are beginning to understand how profoundly we have been influenced by Biblical descriptions of women and men. My realization of the effect of these teachings came slowly. But one day I knew with sureness that "Judaism and Christianity are sexist religions with a male God and traditions of male leadership that legitimate the superiority of men in family and society."[5] I realized the enormity of being defined as secondary, inferior, lower on the scale. The fact that for centuries women were not seen as persons still defines our day care, our paycheques, our pensions, the value of work done in the home and in the marketplace, and affects how we feel about ourselves.

Within our group we spoke of how we were not being listened to at work, of having our suggestions frequently picked up and presented by men as original to them, and acted upon apart from us. We spoke of our anger and frustration at having our ways discounted until I, for one, could respond to the accusation of being bitchy by saying, "Some people still define anger that way. I see my response as legitimate in this situation."

Self-blessing rituals, in which we named our body parts, took them, for me, a rural-born woman, nurse and mother, out of the realm of the unmentionable. We spoke of childbirth. I openly, no longer secretly, rejoiced in the part my body had played in bringing new life into the world.

The stories we shared imparted a sense of reality to my life that I had never before experienced. I began to pay attention to my feelings, regarding them as genuine and appropriate even in situations where previously I had dismissed them, telling myself I was out of step, or out of line, or neurotic.

The process of changing our perspectives involved the use of drama. We re-wrote and enacted the story of Genesis, with Eve in the leading role, created by the Goddess in her image. We followed Eve and Adam through part of their life cycle. Eve was dominant and aggressive and made her own way in the world. At the birth of a girl baby, all the players and the audience blew whistles, threw balloons and danced wildly in celebration. We portrayed a man, struggling to be a "good" homemaker, seeking help in his frustration and feelings of alienation only to be told by a female professional that he had "vagina envy" and that he must go home and try harder. The play was both funny and sobering, ringing true for those of us who grew up under Freud's influence. Watching it, we knew that the psychological and social positioning of women and men through religious sanctioning is unacceptable to us.

Coming to terms with my Christian background meant dealing with the myths, symbols and rituals of Christianity in ways other than re-writing the story of Genesis. I do not feel friendly toward nor accepting of a god that was created out of an hierarchal system that subjugates women, but I yearn for the transcendence that some derive from the story of Creation. I yearn for meaning beyond everyday existence. It may be important for some people to have the symbol of Jesus as the incarnation of the divine in human beings, but the feminist tendencies in me are more comfortable with the idea of a woman walking beside her son rather than kneeling before him. The question that arises after the rejection of a god is, "What does one worship?" The answer I am at ease with right now is: I worship in the sense that I pay honour to that which is worthy of attention. For me, this is the state of being, with its mysteries, wonders and inter-relatedness. The symbol that best represents this state is a spiral created out of play dough in a study group on symbology, or drawn by six women on a newspaper sheet using every colour of the rainbow. A spiral allows me to think of life not as a linear progression, but as movement in ever-increasing encompassing circles. This is consistent with my own experience that life events repeat themselves and, with repetition, grow deeper in meaning and substance.

We open and close our meetings with candle lighting, and incorporate it into original graces or blessings. The light of the candles symbolizes warmth, light and knowledge. Water is an important component of our self-blessing ceremonies, and drunk with wine it is a symbol of community. At interprovincial and international conferences we acknowledge the linking of geographical areas by mixing water brought from flowing rivers as a symbol of unity and strength among delegates from various areas. In the tradition of wicca, I have participated in chants, voicing in varying tones the names of those present so that the whole is harmonious and blended.

Symbols are important to me; without them I can easily slip back into the state of dependency and powerlessness I experienced within the patriarchal religion of my early years. The most powerful symbol, for some, would be a female god. I have taken part in discussions on what life would be like if a goddess were the main religious symbol. Would our intellectual capacities be recognized, our opinions sought? Would our child-bearing capacities, as well as menstruation and menopause, be honoured, celebrated? Would our daughters grow up with positive self-images, and be accepted by the world? Would our mothers be respected, revered as wise counsellors, able to make decisions and act on them independently?

My personal search for an ultimate symbol goes on. And there are other questions. Are there symbiotic relationships in nature that could lead the way toward harmony, that would serve as a model to replace our current one of confrontation, antagonism and competition? Defining my own theology through feminism has made me aware of the connections between the struggles for freedom of worship, for peace and for the preservation of our planet. My voice has been added to those of others who are trying to save our world, to touch it more gently.

The silence imposed upon me as a woman has been dispersed.
I write my own captions.
Blessed be.

Conquer this Earth and Subdue It

Shirley Kitchen

C   the bush appears silently
O   overnight
  N   an underground searching for life
  Q   the parent slivered by winter ice
    U
     E   lilac bushes can be trained
      R   my neighbours say
          eyeing the creeping growth   mindful
          of their raspberry canes

T   I approach the slender sprouts
 H   philosophically
  I   in a civilized environment
   S   I explain to them
          unchecked growth is not allowed

          reluctantly I attempt to pull the shoots
E   from the soft earth   they are tenacious
 A   firmly rooted
  R
   T   visions of sculptured beauty   a perfect globe
    H   lead me to try again   this time
          with the hacksaw

          the tendrils splinter   grinding
A   nerve ends in my jaw
 N
  D   I grab the axe   a swifter approach
          to death   it cuts more cleanly   the blows
          thud along my rib cage   the blade
          shears my knuckles   blood mixes
          with the sap

S
 U
  B   I sit to staunch the flow
   D
    U   small brown twigs reach for my ankles
    E   straighten my spine
          tiny green buds caress my eyes
I   sprout from my lips
 T   my roots sink into the earth

Giving Birth

Katherine Martens

It was a mellow September afternoon in 1962 when I came home empty-handed from the hospital after my first baby was born. I looked up at the blue sky knowing that the things I had not faced in the birth and death of my child would have to be faced some day. Avoiding that task has taken up a lot of my energy for a long time.

A series of health problems forced me to take up my pen to write. In the process of seeking a kind of health that goes beyond a mere absence of disease, I feel I am giving birth to myself. I have faced deeply buried anger. As I tell my story, often tears fight with anger for the upper hand. Twenty-six years have not brought composure and distance or objectivity. A birthing experience is never forgotten. A year ago, although I was not consciously aware of the twenty-fifth anniversary of our baby's birth and death, I became very anxious and suffered stomach pain; that is, until I was able to therapeutically relive and resolve some of the pain.

On September 11, 1962, I was in labour in a Toronto hospital. Labour had begun when my water broke the night before. We were clocking contractions at five-minute intervals when we called the hospital and were told to come in. In the hospital my contractions slowed down while I went through the admitting procedure and was prepped. Prepping consisted of an enema, the shaving of my pubic hair, and a rectal examination. Then contractions began again. Even before the prepping I said good-bye to my husband, who was told to go home and wait for a call from the hospital. I will never forget how alone I felt after he left. It was rare for a husband to be allowed to stay with his wife during labour, not to mention delivery, and my request for him to stay was refused by hospital staff. I was not a fighter at that time. None of the nursing staff, and certainly not the doctor, stayed with me longer than they needed to to accomplish a specific task. Our families were miles away, on the Prairies.

What I remember of the next few hours is my desire to walk around or change my position. I was told to stay on my narrow bed. The loud cries and calls from more vocal birthing mothers shocked me, and I wondered if I too would feel like screaming after a while. Somehow, I felt they should be more stoic and placid. There seemed to be a parade of strangers who were entitled to poke and prod me with as little ceremony as if I were a slab of meat. A kind, white-haired Scottish nurse who was going off duty just before midnight assured me that I should have my baby by mid-morning the next day.

At long last I was visited by the doctor. My obstetrician, Dr. X, was out of town at a conference, and Dr. Y was taking his place. Since he was in the hospital for an emergency ectopic pregnancy anyway, Dr. Y came in to examine me; he told me that I should not try to be a martyr, but should take the medication he would order. Feeling chastised, and having no one around to give me moral support, I followed doctor's orders. The medication was Demerol; its effect was that I became sleepy and my contractions slowed down and finally came to a stop. But I was a "good girl" and did not create a fuss, which meant that the doctor was able to get some sleep.

When the day shift arrived, it was necessary to start my labour again; and presto, another medical intervention was used, thus quickly turning my labour into the very opposite of the natural breathing-assisted labour I had hoped for. A drip was attached to my arm to stimulate labour, and from then on things were out of control as far as I was concerned. When labour pains started they were quite intense. Around 2:00 in the afternoon, after a Caesarean had briefly been considered, my baby was delivered. I remember feeling as if I had not really taken part in anything.

Our baby (whom we never named) did not cry, and they rushed him to the side of the room where they gave him oxygen. I suspected he was not healthy and I asked what was wrong. I tried to joke with the nurses, telling them that my mother had had 15 healthy babies, and surely I could have one healthy one. The baby had suffered brain damage due to lack of oxygen some time during the labour and would probably not survive more than 12 hours. I did not have the presence of mind to ask to see him, to demand my child and claim ownership of this damaged result of the most up-to-date obstetrical ward in the country.

Instead, I was brought to my empty room and my husband was allowed to come and see me. Later the pediatrician came and asked if I would like to see my baby. I am thankful for that. Many women were denied that basic right. At least now I know whom I am mourning when September comes and that old clutch of grief steals the colour from my face. At the time of my baby's birth and death, mourning was considered a sign of weakness, and it was important to be seen as "taking it well," which meant that I hid my feelings from others.

In what way was I unprepared for the hospital experience? I had attended a six-week course in childbirth preparation, in which hospital routines were discussed and criticized for their lack of consideration for the individual, but there were simply no alternatives to hospitals and doctors. Pregnancy was considered a pathological condition; birth was a medical event, and women in labour were expected to fit into the routine of a hospital, not vice versa. I naively thought hospitals were institutions whose routines and schedules were designed for the maximum benefit of the consumers. Ironically, in the process of birthing, women are primary producers, not consumers. When one of my sisters arrived at the hospital to deliver her child, a nurse said to her, "You can't feel like pushing now, the shift is just changing."

I had especially enjoyed and excelled at the breathing exercises during prenatal classes and had told my doctor that I hoped to use them in labour. In my innocence, I did not know that I would need the support of some other person, preferably female, who could be depended on to stay with me throughout labour. When I saw Dr. Y a few days before onset of labour and told him I hoped to use my breathing exercises, he looked at me and said, "You don't know anything about childbirth, you've never experienced it." Why didn't I get up and run as fast and as far as I could at that moment? Or failing that, why didn't I say, "And neither, Doctor, have you." I did not talk back to doctors in those days.

I have since learned to be more assertive. But, in retrospect, I have often blamed myself for not having been more aware of how women were ill-treated during childbirth – that is, until I remember that women's complaints were consistently used against them. Barbara Ehrenreich and Deirdre English, in *For Her Own Good: 150 Years of the Experts' Advice to Women,* describe the patriarchal attitudes that led up to the dark ages of obstetrics in the 1960s. "Most female complaints and, in particular, gynecological ones, were blamed on women's rejection of the 'feminine role.'" Physicians in the 1950s and 1960s viewed the following conditions as symptoms of our rejection of the feminine role: "dysmenorrhea, excessive pain in labour, menstrual irregularity, pelvic pain, infertility . . . or complications of labor."[1] I quickly gathered from my reading that any woman who complained or was too demanding in the hospital was labelled neurotic.

Recently I interviewed 58 Mennonite women of various ages for an oral history project called "Childbirth in the Mennonite Community" for the Manitoba Provincial Archives and the Mennonite Heritage Centre. I interviewed both young and old women, to get an historical perspective. The project was my brainchild, prompted in part by a desire to work through my feelings about the relationship between me and my mother, and also because I wanted to understand the reasons for the changes from home births to hospital births and from breast feeding to bottle feeding.

Some of the older women I interviewed had given birth to their older children at home, attended by a doctor or midwife; their younger children were likely born in a hospital. My sample is biased in favour of survivors; none of these women died in childbirth. Was it the fear of complications that made hospital birthing, when it became almost universal, so attractive to women? Or was it for those who had large families a welcome respite from unending housework? Or was it the insistence of the doctor? Or all of these? One interviewee remembered that she had had strong misgivings when she went for her first hospital birth; it seemed so uncomfortable to have to leave her home for what she had hitherto done at home. But many older women who had had easy home births assisted by a good, trusted midwife, or a doctor who came to their homes, were inclined to have their younger children at home too. In the 1920s and 1930s, childbirth was considered a private event that should take place at home. When a birth was imminent, the school-age children in the family were often sent off to Gramma's house without being told the reason.

At first glance, it may seem as if the young women now choosing to give birth at home are perhaps just romanticizing the past, but when I interviewed them I found that this is not so. One of the reasons some women are now choosing to give birth at home is to make sure that they will have a constant support companion throughout labour. Ironically, that may have been the same hope that inspired the women to give birth in hospital several decades ago. Perhaps they thought they would no longer have to worry about whether the midwife or doctor would arrive at the house on time. Another reason some women now prefer to give birth at home with a midwife present is to gain control over the experience and to avoid hassles about medication, anesthesia, episiotomy, position during labour, who may or may not be in the room during the birth, and supplemental feedings after the birth.

In 1935, the year of my birth, my mother, who had already had eight home births with the assistance of a midwife or doctor, drove 80 miles to a Winnipeg hospital for my birth. My parents had enrolled in a pre-paid hospital plan at Concordia Hospital so that my mother could enter hospital and have her baby the modern way. Having had so many births already, she did not have a very long labour with me, and it was only by holding me back that she was able to give birth in the hospital and not on the long drive into the city. I was the first of her children to be formula fed with a bottle, which was becoming the thing to do too.

There have been changes through the years, and some of these changes have been made on the labour floor in response to pressure from women. In one Winnipeg hospital in 1988, routine practices such as shaving pubic hair, repeated rectal examinations and enemas have been eliminated, and women are not confined to bed during labour. Husbands are not merely tolerated in the labour room, but are encouraged to stay with their partners during delivery, and medication is no longer forced on women. It seems that in the area where female nurses have some authority, that is, on the labour floor, changes have been made; but in the delivery room where, typically, male obstetricians are in charge, little has changed. The mother is still moved around from room to room as if she were a mere receptacle containing the baby, which belongs to the hospital. In the delivery room, where the majority of births take place, the bright lights, instruments, shiny machinery and a large ticking clock on the wall scream out that labour and birth are a sickness, fraught with danger. The delivery is "managed" for the convenience of the physician, not for the birthing woman. There are encouraging signs, however, in the younger generation of doctors, more of whom are women, who are willing to try new approaches to birthing.

Barbara Katz Rothman, author of *In Labor: Women and Power in the Birthplace*, claims that there is a delivery-room timetable, labour is expected to last a certain amount of time, and obstetricians are prone to intervene if birth does not proceed at a certain speed.[2] Yet each birthing woman needs to go at her own pace in all stages of labour. The woman is still placed on a narrow, high table, her feet up in stirrups, in the position Michel Odent describes as the position most unsuited for giving birth because it can restrict oxygen transfer to the baby.[3] The woman is reduced to the position of a passive patient being delivered of a baby. Episiotomies are still routine. The closeness of the mother-child bond is disturbed when babies are snatched from their mothers for immediate routine examinations and procedures.

Waking at night and hearing a baby crying down the hall in a hospital remains one of my most vivid and heart-rending memories. I was frantic, wondering which was worse, the knowledge that my child was crying and wanting to nurse, or the frustration that somebody else would finally pick her up and gave her a bottle. In either case, I was being robbed of the opportunity to mother, and I should have packed up and left the hospital. The trauma of a bad experience remains for a lifetime; there is no way to go back and make it right. Many women I talk to tell similar stories of indignity, feelings of inadequacy and disappointment.

Giving birth might have been a satisfying physical, emotional and spiritual event for me were it not for medical interventions and the absence of a constant support person. As well, the fact that I was not on my own turf interfered with the natural progression of birth. Nature is unpredictable, not always orderly, and every woman in labour has her own rhythm and pace, which is affected by strange surroundings. Even animals seek out a quiet, secluded place in which to give birth. The inner (emotional and spiritual) and outer (physical) experiences of giving birth should be intricately woven together, but the integration of the two was lost to me. For many years I could not even articulate this need; all I could remember was my depression and sadness, then a deep anger. When I found my voice, my child-bearing years were over.

Each time I gave birth to a daughter, my first thought was, "Oh, no, she's female, she will go through this (giving birth) too." Then I felt deeply ashamed and depressed because somewhere inside me I knew that giving birth, though it was hard work, could have been a beautiful, satisfying experience. True, after my first delivery, I had no more Demerol (I actually had to fight for the right to refuse Demerol each time), but I had epidurals and episiotomies. Episiotomies are routine, usually done without the mother's informed consent. The symbolism of a male doctor (active), with a knife in hand, poised over a female patient (passive), still angers me as it hurt me then. Childbirth, the experience that could symbolize most clearly the thread of life that links grandmothers, mothers and daughters, has become an alienating incident that many of us try to forget.

Childbirth could have been a challenge, a time for me to face my deepest emotions, a time to focus inwardly to accomplish a goal. (Ironically, that accomplishment would have come about by my letting go – letting go physically, letting go of fixed ideas of how things must be.) After giving birth, I tried to forget my experience and go on to other things in my life. But I continued to feel passionate about birth because it seemed somehow unfinished for me. I had allowed the act of giving birth, a rite of passage in my life, to be treated as an illness during which I went to a hospital, was medicated and anesthetized because I assumed that the hospital staff knew what was best for me and my baby.

In some ways, the stories of the older women in my history project did not differ significantly from those of the younger ones, until I listened to the labour and delivery stories of the younger women who had experienced medical interventions. Their stories were told with tears close to the surface. In the 1980s, women who felt strongly about how they wanted to give birth and did not want to fight with the hospital to allow them to give birth to their children without medication and other interventions, found midwives to attend them at home. The tape recordings of modern women who chose to have their babies at home seem to sing with happiness and contentment. The older and younger women alike valued above all else the supportive presence and care of a particular nurse or midwife. The highest degree of satisfaction was expressed by a woman whose mother was the midwife who assisted her during most of her births. At a meeting I attended of a home-birth support group, a number of women expressed the feeling that giving birth at home had empowered them.

With the advent of hospital births several decades ago, women were expected to labour on a narrow hospital bed, many were ordered not to move around but to lie in a prescribed position, attended by, at best, compassionate over-worked nurses and at worst by nurses who were judgemental, uncaring and punitive or who worked by the rule book. An example from the 1940s is the case of the couple who drove miles over bumpy prairie roads into Winnipeg, rushed through red lights to get to the hospital on time, only to have the nurse on duty push the baby back so that the doctor could deliver it.

My memories are dominated by the sense that there was someone missing. I had no continuous presence with me. When my husband stayed with me for three subsequent labours and two births, my anxiety dropped to a tolerable level. Had I had both my husband and a woman who had given birth beside me, willing to wait with me and support me, perhaps the outcome of my first delivery would have been a live baby.

Mike Samuels and Nancy Samuels, in *The Well Pregnancy Book*, report on a study of the effect of a supportive companion during labour and delivery. In the 150 cultures studied, a family member or friend stayed with the mother continuously in all but one. In most cases the midwife, grandmother and husband all remained with the woman. They found that women who had a continuous companion had lower levels of stress hormones present in their blood during childbirth because they were less anxious.[4] They concluded that high levels of stress hormone interfered with uterine contractions and slowed down blood flow to the baby. They comment that emotion affects labour; in large amounts, the stress hormone makes uterine contractions less effective and thus slows down labour.[5]

In the foreword to her book *Immaculate Deception*, Suzanne Arms states: "Where and under what conditions a woman gives birth affects the course of her labour, the normalcy of her delivery, the health of her baby, and the lifelong relationship of mother and child. Women have always felt the need to find a 'safe' place for birth, safe from harm and disturbance. The hospital, we have been assured, is that safe place. But we are beginning to wonder."[6] Women began giving birth in hospitals partly because midwives were pushed out of their traditional role by doctors. At first doctors would come to their patients' homes, but after hospitals were built, they preferred that women come to them. There is a profound difference in status between a woman who enters a hospital as a patient and one who welcomes a doctor into her home as a respected professional who is there also as a guest. Where there is no indication of abnormality, what better place is there than your own home for the birth of a new baby? It is where you decide who comes in or out, how you wish to await your baby; it is where you are in charge. Since modern medicine can work wonders in emergencies, the best of both worlds exists when there is co-operation and collegiality between midwives and doctors. The choice of some women to give birth at home should in no way be seen as going back in time. These women are making a very conscious decision after thinking through all the pros and cons of both home and hospital birthing. I am not recommending that everyone should have her baby at home, but I am advocating informed choice.

When a baby is born, the forces of life and death brush up against each other. We have grown accustomed to thinking of the hospital for both births and deaths. Yet most of the people in the world were born at home and most die at home. Is it our great fear of these natural events that has made them into medical events? In my first baby's birth and death I put my faith in doctors and medicine, but that was no guarantee of a safe outcome. I do not claim that a home birth with a midwife present would have guaranteed a living child, but the risk would have been no greater than the one I took.

Another result of the medicalization of birth has been the movement away from birth as a family affair; it has become an isolated event in which the mother leaves home to "do her thing," leaving her family to fend for themselves. Books on childbirth and child care advised: "Don't listen to your sisters and mother or women friends. Ask your doctor and take his word. He knows." The implication was that the doctor's advice was scientific and factual, and your sister's, while based on experience, could not be generalized. Dismissed as "old wives' tales," the wisdom of those with past experience was considered of no account and was termed dangerous. The result was alienation and isolation; women having babies could no longer rely on other, experienced, women, the traditional source of support and counsel. Nor, they found, could they rely on their doctor (for he was rarely available) to discuss with them their minute-by-minute concerns about breast feeding, for example. In my own case, it seems I had faith in modern science, medicine and the mind, but a distrust and fear of the wisdom of other women and of the body.

Elizabeth Noble, in her book *Childbirth with Insight,* describes childbirth as a sexual and sensual process. "A display of sexuality is not considered appropriate in a clinical setting, where shaving of the mother's pubic hair, draping of the body and restraint of her vocalizations, movements and partner contact have been routine procedures changing only slowly."[7] Noble suggests that the tension and breath-holding techniques associated with the medical approach to childbirth are part of a pattern of sexual repression. For many women, giving birth marks the beginning of an intimate knowledge and acceptance of their bodies that includes their sexuality. She advocates an approach to childbirth in which a couple go (or the mother by herself goes) beyond all structured and controlled training methods for childbirth and put their trust in the human body "thus permitting a labour to take its natural course in what is inevitably a spontaneous and uncontrollable event."[8]

I see examples similar to the role a good midwife plays in at least two other areas of life in which I have had some experience. A good editor and a good therapist are also dedicated to helping the writer or client to follow the very best that is in her. The editor and therapist are not there to take over, but to facilitate a process, not to direct and make decisions, but to patiently be with you and figuratively hold your hand while you take your quivering first steps. This model can also be applied in the process of interviewing older Mennonite women, who are reserved and not used to discussing the intimate details of their birthing experiences. Birth is integrated into their lives. When I ask them to tell me their life stories the way they gave birth to their children emerges in a natural and modest way. The younger women, whose lives are in many ways much more open, talk freely about their experiences. The very way in which the story is told becomes part of the story.

Giving birth could have served as a rite of passage in my life, a time of testing, of going to the end of my endurance by facing pain, not avoiding it, not escaping it, but going through it to the other side. Pain is relative, and some of it can be prevented by massage, touching and the constant presence of a loving person. What I had postponed during my children's births I had to make happen much later in my life while I was going through menopause. I finally learned to assert myself in health matters. I was taking medication for gastro-intestinal problems, but I was determined to wean myself of it and get to the root of the emotional and spiritual problems that caused my ill health. Step by step, I gained the endurance and inner strength to rid myself of life-long allergies and stomach distress. My program of wellness has included psychotherapy, walking, following a macrobiotic diet, reflex-ology, meditation, T'ai Chi, and touch therapy (therapeutic massage and counselling with Joan Turner).

When I began reading books about childbirth, I realized I had pushed them away for many years. I could not bear to read about how some other woman had had a lovely, unmedicated, natural birth, the kind I never had. Neither did I want to read the horror stories. So my finally reading books like *Midwifery is Catching* by Eleanor Barrington was one way of facing the pain. What a relief it was for me to read: "I wouldn't have had the courage to refuse pain-killing drugs if they had been handy. In a hospital, even my non-interventive doctor would have felt pressure to do something."[9] Yet Barrington was happy she put herself to the test by giving birth at home with a midwife and thereby gaining new confidence in herself.

I feel I have given birth to myself – and done it without anesthesia. I did the necessary work with the help of others, but not by blocking out the pain. I have faced the full range of my fears, anxieties and anger, but I have also felt the full range of the joy, passion and creativity that comes from fully experiencing a rite of passage that has the potential for life, and for death.

Elizabeth

Di Brandt

so now Elizabeth like you i have become
mother to a ghost child waking me at
night with her absent cries like yours
Elizabeth mine was a girl & you should
have seen the light this morning in her
hair its shining i lay there long after
she had gone feeling the soft damp weight
of her baby smell on my pillow the tiny
clutch of her hands a hundred lovers
after this will not be enough to ease
the ache of my empty heavy breasts the
world's great lust too little to replace
her eager lips her tiny lost embrace

tears

Di Brandt

(for Heidi Harms)

you take the tears a woman
might cry in middle age after
a lifetime of swallowing them
whole one by one gagging slowly
in the night you let them out
tenderly stroke each sob gently
into life watch them grow around
her profusely like wildflowers
or weeds sometimes they're
like a river in spring swollen
with snow from the hills or
babies without mothers screaming
themselves silently to sleep
sometimes there's such quiet
in the middle of it you think it's
over but before long you understand
that was only the sadness needing
to breathe you take the tears a
woman might cry in a lifetime
over her babies & her lost lovers
& her grief watch them spill richly
& strange to the ground not even
Solomon in his glory was surrounded
with such splendour nor are lilies
arrayed in garments such as these

already there is no going back

Di Brandt

already there is no going back
the trees curl around your
feet the air is full of messages
you miss the father in your
bones the rain falls warm
on your cheek you stand alone
at the world's edge your soul
is worth diamonds your feet
are heavy with the weight
of it which way you whisper
mother please

Healing Hands, Debra Lynn Krahn

The Look:
Women and Body Image

Lucille Meisner

She is a specimen under a microscope. Her father places his chair at the kitchen table to watch her from the best vantage point. His hungry eyes undress her 12-year-old body. She knows it and is afraid. Nervously washing dishes, she drops a glass. "Hurry up with those dishes, I have work for you outside," he mutters as he goes through the screen door, not without glancing back. He likes to see her squirm. "Wash that truck clean, damn you!" he yells as he sprays her with icy water from the garden hose. She knows he really wants to see the cold, wet clothes clinging to her firm young breasts. "Girls and women are stupid, inferior, and mostly ugly," he says. "The ugly ones are put to work. . . . That's what they are good for. Good-looking women are taken to bed." What category does she fit into? Fearful and insecure, she knows she must be ugly because she is put to work. In an odd way, she is relieved.

Growing up in an environment where a woman's worth is based entirely on appearance makes it impossible to have confidence in anything but the physical self, and that is fragile at best. One is either ugly or attractive, for use or abuse. There is not much to look forward to.

Today, as an adult woman, I grieve for the child who was me. I know she and I are not crazy, nor did we make up the painful stories of my childhood and adolescence.

Leaving a place where one is subject to abuse because she was born female means leaving only in a physical sense. Psychologically the memories and scars are taken with you. I left home, went to university and joined a women's weight-lifting club as a way to maintain my physical health and to make friends. I realized later that the real motivation was to prove my father wrong. I would be attractive and I would be independent. I am female, but I would not be "put to work" or "taken to bed." I studied diligently and worked out at the gym with dedication and discipline. I became a perfectionist, compulsive about everything. I dieted to prove that I could.

Eight years ago I first realized that what I and other women were doing daily in the gym in no way reflected a concern for our health or fitness. If it did, we would not have starved before our workouts, and eaten salads with oil-and-vinegar dressings after. What we were doing was striving to achieve the thin ideal at all costs.

We socialized with male body builders who ate "hungry-man" breakfasts with side orders of pancakes and extra toast. The men who were entering annual body-building contests would diet for eight weeks prior to the competition. For us, the dieting and "competition" went on year-round. Day after day we ate poached eggs on dry whole-wheat bread and drank cup after cup of black coffee. At 23, I found some satisfaction in this lifestyle. The compliments about my willpower, control and discipline were welcomed. Temporarily, I experienced some relief from my overwhelming insecurities.

When I was home alone I prepared breakfasts that I could not consume in public. Defiantly I indulged in the pancakes and buttered toast that I denied myself in the presence of others. I recall now that with each mouthful I felt stronger, yet weaker; comforted yet alone. Angry and confused feelings were smothered and kept in my stomach, never allowed to rise up to my throat in words that would express the hot inner turmoil that I felt. Eventually there was no amount of food that could quell my resentment at feeling continually noticed, yet never known. I still felt like the little girl at the kitchen sink.

Since this enormous effort did not seem to be working, I began to question the attitudes we held and the price we were paying to achieve the ideal body shape. I began to see myself and the other women at the gym differently. No method of weight control was too drastic to reach and maintain the thin ideal. Fad diets, fasting, Ipecac (to induce vomiting) and laxative use were common topics of conversation. Health tips focused on living with the side effects of our obsessive behaviour. Diarrhea, fainting spells, dehydration and severe stomach cramps were commonplace. But were we ever looking good. Well, almost. . . .

"Shapely" bodies and vacant eyes moved around the gym obediently, punishing and starving their physical and emotional selves under the guise of fitness and health. It took a while for me to realize that the "fitness" atmosphere I was participating in was actually detrimental to my well-being. What I took with me from that experience was a desire to pursue graduate work in feminist therapy, specializing in weight preoccupation, body image, anorexia nervosa and bulimia.

I began to recognize that while the obsessive behaviour of my friends and I was applauded and encouraged, similar behaviour of women with anorexia nervosa and bulimia was labelled a psychiatric disorder. This reality was frightening for me. Much of what we were doing was necessary to achieve and maintain the thin ideal. Nowhere is the fine line between mental illness and ultimate conformity to the cultural ideal so obvious as it is in the psychiatric labelling of anorexia nervosa and bulimia and in contemporary medical practice. Patients are weighed in, slimness advocated, diets promoted. Some physicians profit from stapling stomachs and sucking tissue from women's thighs. The price we pay to "measure up" is seen as mental illness in one realm and as new and exciting advances in science in another.

Women are the sex we look at, and to be a desirable woman is to be a thin woman. That is the way we are socialized. The message is everywhere: in magazines, on television and radio. And family members tend to actively reinforce the thinness message. Identity based on our individual worth is secondary. We leave our family homes and enter the adult world with a fragile sense of worth beyond our body's marketability.

The feminist approach to counselling women encourages us to consider weight preoccupation on a continuum. This perspective asserts that many women are at risk of becoming anorexic or bulimic. It removes the stigma to admitting that we have weight and food issues. Given that we live in a weight-and-body preoccupied society, it is not surprising that anorexia nervosa and bulimia have a place at the extreme high end of the continuum of "normally obsessive" behaviour. This "normally obsessive" behaviour is marketed by diet and fitness clubs that promise a more "desirable" body size and shape. All of us who respond to sales strategies in the hope that we can alter our bodies are engaging in this "normally obsessive" behaviour. When an obsessive preoccupation becomes a societal norm, it is very difficult for us to ignore the pressure to conform. We live in a thin-crazed society. Depending on our particular life stresses and our perception of our bodies at any given time, we move along the continuum of weight preoccupation from "normally obsessed" to "eating disorders."

To see how pervasive the thin ideal has become in our society takes only a few hours of casual observation of daily life in a city like Winnipeg. Walking through the downtown business district during lunch hour, I think about this ideal for women and how our bodies are the subject of constant scrutiny and observation. Reinforcement of the notion that the less space we take up in this world the more socially acceptable we are is evident everywhere.[1] Benches and concrete ledges are crowded with women and men sitting outside during their lunch breaks. Walking along the sidewalk means navigating a maze of food carts and groups of men feasting on hot dogs, fries and gourmet ice cream. Lunch for those women eating is typically a few carrot sticks, a leaf of lettuce and a spoonful of cottage cheese, a combination otherwise known as "dieter's delight." I wonder how many women are skipping lunch; how many feel a small triumph at their ability to sit in front of the food carts and deny their appetites; how many think of food in "good" and "bad" terms and how many have "fat" and "thin" clothes in their closets.

I suspect that the number of women who truly like what they see in the mirror each morning is far less than the number who feel they must improve some aspect of their body. Two women "power walking" during their lunch break stride briskly by the food carts. I am reminded of contemporary women's magazines advertising chocolate cake recipes on one page and "thin thighs in 30 days" on the next. The contradictory messages are evident everywhere. "Food will make you feel good/Food will make you fat and undesirable"; "Be a gourmet cook/Deny yourself that which you prepare for others." The old familiar saying, "You play, you pay," popular during the days of sexual freedom, now seems to be a motto for those who ease up on their diet and exercise regimes. To "cheat," to "indulge," to "sin," to be "decadent" was once the language describing an exciting one-night sexual rendez-vous. Today it is more apt to describe late-night coffee and dessert with a good friend.

Browsing through a women's fashion boutique, I watch a woman trying on clothes. As she critiques her reflection in the three-way mirror, I overhear the salesperson say how gorgeous the dress is on her. Poking the customer's hips, she says, "You can fix 'that' with some spot reduction exercises. They worked beautifully for my daughter who had the same figure 'flaw.'" The customer goes to the change room and returns with the matching jacket. It would solve "the problem." I think about the good intentions of the salesperson. We have been so effectively sold an unrealistic image that we can, with relative ease, voice our disapproval of the body shape of a total stranger.

Women's natural body shape is even further denied and distorted through the use of faceless oval metal pipes that are the mannequins of today, and the modelling of women's clothing in fashion magazines by young androgynous males. The fashion industry is promoting lingerie in more styles and colours than we have ever seen before. I note with interest that women's breasts are popular again. This poses a new dilemma for women. We are encouraged to reduce our natural body fat, but serious diet and exercise regimes eliminate body fat on the entire body – including the breasts. As breasts become fashionable once again, silicone breast implants are becoming more readily available. Silicone breast implants were once almost exclusively used by actresses and other women whose careers were dependent upon "the look." But today, breast implants are widely available and used by women throughout North America. Thin women who have put tremendous amounts of time, money and energy into dieting and exercising away their natural body fat are now encouraged to have it added on artificially in "the right places." The attainment of the cultural ideal is considered worth the risk of medical complications and unknown long-term effects.

Saleswomen in starched, white lab coats standing poised beside elaborate displays of cosmetic products promise me a seductive scent and eternal youth. The women promoting the products look scientific, stiff and artificial. I think about how much energy it must take to be on display throughout an entire work day. Most saleswomen seem to be very young. I wonder what it must be like to be 20, selling anti-aging creams. What must it be like for a customer twice that age to be boldly told that she is to fight against her body's natural changes?

At an aerobic studio I observe a group of adult women participating in an exercise session that is frenzied and chaotic. The yelling of the instructor amidst the din from the "blaster" encourages body punishment and disrespect. Orders such as, "Burn that fat," "Whip it into shape," and "No pain, no gain, girls," sound more like a military drill than a health-and-fitness class. The message that we should be "at war with our bodies," "fighting fat," and engaging in the "battle of the bulge" certainly suggest the kind of military propaganda that promotes hatred of the enemy so that it can be eliminated. The recent trend toward low-impact aerobics, walking and aqua-fit water exercises ironically began as a result of the casualties suffered from this adversarial approach to fitness.

Receiving negative messages about my body as a child, being preoccupied with my weight as an adolescent and exercizing compulsively as an adult has made me sensitive to, and frustrated with, the constant pressure on women to achieve and maintain a "desirable" body shape. The way we perceive our bodies stems from the interaction of two factors: first, how our body seems to us to compare with the cultural ideal promoted by the media; and second, how we relate to our body from our childhood experiences.[2] Unfortunately, the cultural ideals for women rarely, if ever, reflect reality. The "desirable" body shape is promoted as a possibility within our reach, but in fact it will remain unattainable for the vast majority of women. The diet, exercise, clothing and cosmetic industries thrive on and profit from feelings of insecurity in women, but they also create and perpetuate these feelings. The fact that cosmetic companies search the world over for the perfect face to advertise their products is testimony to the rarity of "the look" they are promoting.

Throughout history, the various ways to alter women's natural body shapes have included foot binding, lip and neck stretching, rib removal (to form the hour-glass figure), liposuction, cosmetic surgery and breast implants. All are expressions of the desire to control the shape and size of women's bodies and ultimately to control women. It is no coincidence that with the development of the feminist movement and women's increasing independence, the ideal female body has become a younger, more vulnerable, adolescent shape. We live in a society that rejects whatever is seen as powerful in women. The fashion industry's promotion of thinness as an ideal for women reflects rejection and fear of female power as does the sexualization of underdeveloped adolescent bodies.[3]

The messages we heard as children about our bodies have a powerful influence on our lives as adult women. Many women who are struggling with eating difficulties and weight preoccupation share with me the painful criticisms they heard as little girls. Some heard that they were fat, some that they were ugly or stupid, or that they ate too much. Many share with me their experiences as little girls, and how their bodies were invaded and violated. Many were the subject of sexual comments. Too many experienced sexual abuse. To grow up in this kind of environment is to grow up never learning how to accept and love our bodies as they are. The body shame of a little girl often becomes expressed as body punishment in the adult woman. Anorexia nervosa, bulimia, binge eating and fasting are desperate attempts to gain control in a life that feels chaotic and confused. Just as the weight, body and food issues of these women can be viewed on a continuum, so might the environments they grew up in. Many come from families "normally obsessed" with upward mobility, high achievement and an emphasis on attaining and maintaining the cultural ideals for female and male bodies. Others come from homes dominated by alcohol and other drug abuse, and a lack of love and compassion. If messages from our family environments parallel those of the cultural ideal for women, and if they further contribute to body insecurity through glorifying our bodies or punishing them, we leave that environment perplexed and confused. We will be uncomfortable with our bodies, yet we may believe that controlling our bodies is the only way to negotiate our place in the world. A feminist approach asserts that we must look beyond the individual to family and cultural environments to understand why women are dying to be thin. Given the rising incidence of eating disorders in affluent countries throughout the world, this is a positive and empowering step.[4]

Childhood messages about food can have as profound and lasting an effect on our adult lives as the childhood messages we heard about our bodies. The role of food in women's lives is complex and confusing and is wrought with ambivalence and contradictions. As female children, many of us observed our mothers prepare meals, serve the food to men and children, and then scrape the remainder onto their plates. In a society where there is an expectation that women deny their appetites, this ritual is seen as normal. Many of us grew up with the knowledge that since our mothers were so intimately connected to the food they prepared, our refusal to eat their own cooking was one of the most powerful protests available. Similarly, withholding food from children as a way to punish unacceptable behaviour can mean much more than going without dessert. In both instances, food takes on an emotional meaning. Food becomes more than just a substance that satisfies physical hunger. Most of us associate certain foods with particular people and events in our lives. Feelings of warmth and connectedness (as well as feelings of loss and deprivation) are invariably interwoven in the patterns of family relationships and food consumption.

Recently in a therapy session, a woman with bulimia identified rice as her binge food. All four elements on the stove could not cook the rice quickly enough to accommodate her urge to eat. Rapidly consuming the pots of rice, she stirred in sugar, cinnamon, raisins and milk. Immediately after eating the soft, warm mixture, she would purge by vomiting. An exhausted but rather peaceful sleep would follow.

In therapy, this woman recalled the violence in her family home. When her parents fought, she would leave the house and go down the street to her grandmother. Grandmother would comfort her with rice pudding. In my client's adult life, the rice pudding mixture had become a soothing calming surrogate for what she received as a child at her grandmother's house. Rice pudding was her comfort on a lonely evening, her stress reliever after a hectic work day, or her sedative when she felt agitated or restless.

Food for many women is both friend and foe, both stress reducer and tension producer. It is both comfort and discomfort. Many women experience the soothing nurturance of ice cream, cakes and puddings, and the guilt that follows. They also know the relief of angry feelings in crunching salted chips, peanuts and carrots. I remember baking pans of soft fudge and toffee for my brothers and sisters when we were home alone. It was my attempt to nurture them, filling their emotional hunger with a physical remedy because that is what calmed me and that was what I knew. Sweets were gathered and stored in a cache under my bed to comfort me and to calm my fears when the abusive language from my parent's bedroom could not be muffled by the pillow over my head. If we learned as children to respond to our emotional hunger through food, we can do the same in our adult lives. Comforting ourselves with food can be a creative survival technique for children and adults. It is important that we honour and respect the survival tools that we have developed, and also that we learn how to tell whether we are hungry emotionally or physically. Acknowledging our body's wisdom, we learn to know what it needs and to respond with caring.

Women with bulimia are generally uncomfortable expressing their feelings. Somewhere in their past experience, the expression of feelings was not allowed or accommodated. But, typically, their way of dealing with strong feelings was to stuff them down with food and then to eliminate them through vomiting or laxative-induced diarrhea. The feelings that are being covered up and then purged from the body do eventually need to find expression. Consuming take-out food while driving to and from dozens of hamburger joints, only to vomit it all up in a gas station washroom, is the experience of many bulimics. What they are really doing is stuffing down what they need to feel and say.

Women with anorexia nervosa starve, rather than feed, their emotional and physical hunger. They hope their emotional and physical needs might go away if they deny them long enough. Disciplining and controlling their emotional and physical being becomes the focus of their lives. Anorexics starve for days. In reality they have been hungry much longer, often for years.

Changing one's body image is a slow, often painful, process. The work is hard, because many of the messages we tell ourselves about our bodies have their origins in the voices of our parents and loved ones. As feminists, we need to continue to address society's obsession with weight, food and women's bodies. The weight-preoccupation continuum can help us be aware that we are not immune from being or becoming body-and-weight obsessed. We are creating and living through the changes when we work together to provide safe therapeutic places for women to heal negative body images and painful body experiences.

I feel hopeful when I reflect on a recent telephone call from a woman who was in hospital slated for stomach stapling that morning. The pain of living in her "undesirable" body had become overwhelming. She had waited for surgery for several months because the number of desperate people opting for this radical and dangerous procedure was growing daily. In the final moments before surgery, she changed her mind, realizing that decreasing her food capacity was not going to decrease her emotional hunger. The courage of this woman is an inspiration.

I am hopeful when I work with women who can live without bulimia because they have been encouraged to share the painful experiences that they had been stuffing down, vomiting up and flushing down the toilet. I am encouraged when an anorexic woman no longer needs to be invisible to protect herself from revealing the emptiness she feels inside. Healing our feelings of body shame and negative body experiences is crucial to our growth. I am encouraged by the positive steps of the women I work with and by my own development. We are living the changes when we begin to know what we hunger and thirst for. We must continue the struggle to know and respect our physical and emotional needs.

Everything Looks at Me Hungrily

Irene Heaman

When I
Open the kitchen door
cats and dogs run to me
with food, only food
in their minds.

Children
stand on my feet
hang on my legs
as I step back and
forth from the sink
Babies hold out their arms
saying Mama Mamma Mamma
Am I a hot crusty frank
mustard or cream?

Working for Access

April D'Aubin

Sexism and discrimination exclude disabled women from full and equal participation in Canadian society. Disabled women tend to occupy a lower socio-economic status than either disabled men or ethnic women. They are more likely to be unemployed, and if they are employed they earn less than their disabled male colleagues. Women who become disabled as adults are less likely to be employed after rehabilitation than are men. Disabled women in ethnic minority groups confront an even bleaker reality, bearing a triple burden of oppression. But now disabled women are speaking out about their problems, empowering themselves, and taking action. I am employed by the Coalition of Provincial Organizations of the Handicapped (COPOH), a national advocacy organization whose headquarters is in Winnipeg.

During the 1980s, a large civil rights movement of disabled people developed their own groups to speak for them and to lobby nationally and internationally. The major civil rights issue concerning disabled feminists now is that of reproductive rights. We are fighting for the right to have babies, the right to adopt, the right not to have children, the right to know about contraceptive methods and their side effects, the right of access to abortion clinics, the right not to be involuntarily sterilized, and the right to have access to the women's health care system. Disabled women encounter obstacles in all these areas.

REPRODUCTIVE RIGHTS

For mature non-disabled women the decision to have a child is usually supported warmly by family, friends and the medical profession. This is not the case for disabled women. We want the right to choose a partner (a male or female partner, depending upon our orientation), the right to have a home of our own with our chosen partner, and the right to have children. However, it is more usual for us to be advised to have an abortion or to be sterilized rather than to give birth to a baby.

Sterilization is a surgical procedure requiring informed consent. However, sterilization of a disabled woman is often performed without the woman's consent, but with the consent of a third party –

a parent, doctor or guardian. Both sterilization and the threat of it exist as a problem in the lives of women with disabilities. Prior to 1986 non-therapeutic sterilizations were routine in many Canadian institutions for mentally handicapped people. The sterilization issue can be divided into two separate but related categories: forced involuntary sterilization; and, what we refer to as environmentally coerced sterilization. Both can be viewed as a form of violence against women with disabilities.

The issue of non-therapeutic sterilization of mentally disabled women received considerable media attention in 1986 in the "Eve case." On October 23 the Supreme Court of Canada ruled that Canadian courts could not authorize the non-therapeutic sterilization of mentally disabled persons. The decision marked the end of an eight year battle by a Prince Edward Island woman to have her mentally disabled daughter sterilized. It also legally ended the involuntary non-therapeutic sterilization of disabled women in Canada. Mr. Justice Gerard La Forest, who wrote the decision, summarized the Court's position: "The grave intrusion on a person's rights and the certain physical damage that ensues from non-therapeutic sterilization without consent, when compared to the questionable advantages that can result from it, have persuaded me that it can never be safely determined that such a procedure is for the benefit of that person."[1]

However, some women with disabilities experience "environmentally coerced" sterilization. They might be quite capable of making their own informed decisions and may have agreed to the procedure, but their "informed" consent has been elicited in a negative and/or coercive environment. Anne's story illustrates this. Anne, who has cerebral palsy, and her husband, John, wanted to have a baby. But her gynecologist presented her with numerous arguments against motherhood and suggested sterilization. Three days later she was sterilized. Susan, Anne's non-disabled friend, who was married and had three children, had to wait two months, go through three counselling sessions and get her husband's written approval before she was considered to have made an informed decision.

Women disabled from birth often grow up in a social environment that leads them to believe that motherhood is not an option for them. Micheline Mason, who has osteogenesis imperfecta, an inherited disability that causes brittle bones, describes how her disability affected her thoughts about motherhood: "I always dreamed that one day I would have a baby, but never spoke of it. Whilst I was growing up, everyone assumed that because of my terrible condition I wouldn't have boyfriends, much less real sex and babies, and to some degree I believed this too. In my teens, I began to wonder, well . . . what if . . .

supposing I was able to get pregnant. . . . But still I never, never spoke of it. I was so afraid that I would be told it was impossible, I preferred to keep the dream guarded and safe inside my head.[2] Micheline now has a daughter, Lucy Rose.

Some of society's messages are direct, others more subtle. A survey of disabled Quebec women indicated that although they unanimously believed in a disabled woman's right to have children, parenthood was for others, not for them. Intellectually they believed in this right, but were unable to see themselves exercising it.[3]

Adoption is an option for women who want children. However, for a woman with a disability, adopting a child can be very difficult or impossible. Much often depends on the availablity of children for adoption and the attitude of adoption workers. Women with disabilities who are accepted as adoptive parents tend to be offered babies who are perceived by adoption agencies as difficult to place (a baby of mixed ancestry and/or with health problems). Disabled people in the helping professions who have experienced difficulty adopting children have searched for the reasons behind workers' hesitancy to place children in families where one of the partners is disabled. To their amazement, they have discovered that some of the literature available to the helping professions postulates that disabled parents have a negative effect on their children's social adjustment. Disabled professionals, through their own studies and articles, are working to dispel these myths.

Why do we confront discrimination when we want to have children? The answer to this seems to be related to society's deep-rooted belief in "normality." Society inculcates in all of us a belief that we should be striving for normality, even if that vision of normality is the unrealistic one created by Madison Avenue advertisers. A disability is viewed as abnormal. Taking the argument one step further, then, the child of a disabled mother would be deprived of a normal childhood. Therefore, disabled women are encouraged to forego motherhood. The prevailing ableist ideology is so strong that even friends and relatives of a disabled woman often discourage parenthood. It is impossible to say how many disabled women forego having children because remaining childless seems to be the only realistic choice in today's society. Even finding an obstetrician with an accessible office and a maternity ward that can deal with a particular disabled mother's needs can be insurmountable problems. Necessary support services, such as day care, health services, financial support, also must be in place.

Existing sex information and counselling for persons with disabilities tends to concentrate primarily on the male concerns of potency, performance, and penis-in-vagina intercourse, while neglecting the very real concerns of women with disabilities. Many publications tend to deal almost exclusively with spinal cord injuries and give little helpful information for women with other disabilities. Relatively nothing is available for those who are blind or deaf. Women who become disabled later in life often encounter difficulty in obtaining information about how their disability will affect their sexuality. For example, coronary research is conducted almost exclusively with male subjects, and women who have had heart attacks who ask about resumption of sexual activity are given male-derived standards or are left without answers. It is even more difficult to get practical "how to" information about sexual activity and satisfaction. The disabled women who attended Montreal's Échange Entre Femmes conference in May 1988 spoke out strongly on this point. Another area of difficulty defined at the conference is that of locating information on the effects of medication on sexuality. This paucity of information exists because disabled women are not viewed by society as sexual beings. As a consequence, their sexuality and reproductive rights are ignored or denied.

VIOLENCE AND ABUSE

Owing to their powerless position within society, women with disabilities are often victims of violence. Sometimes abuse is present in the home, and sometimes it is perpetrated upon disabled women by the very service delivery systems that have been created to help them. Pornography continues to promote the abhorrent idea that victimizing disabled and vulnerable women is an acceptable sexual practice.

Joan Meister, past-chair of the DisAbled Women's Network Canada (DAWN Canada), views violence against disabled women as part of a vicious circle in which disability leads to sexual assault or battering, and the assault results in further disability. Disabled women who remain at home with their parents often encounter emotional abuse and are made to feel that they are a burden upon their family. Incest is mentioned frequently at disabled women's conferences.

The silence that shrouded the topic of violence against disabled women is now being broken by expressions of concern and outrage. Organizations of women with disabilities, such as Winnipeg's Consulting Committee on the Status of Women with Disabilities, are beginning to do ground breaking research on the issue of violence against disabled women. The Winnipeg committee's *Research Project Report on Women with Disabilities* discovered that half of the 30 women interviewed stated that they knew of examples of, or had personally experienced, sexual assault.[4]

Winnipeg activist Elizabeth Semkiw, herself a survivor of violence, provides an analysis of why women with disabilities are so vulnerable to violence. Speaking from her own experience, she says that "there are some women even more vulnerable to violations on their person or premises, and these are: the psychiatrically disabled, the developmentally disabled, elderly women, and the physically disabled. They are not only more vulnerable, but, in addition, very dependent on care givers in hospitals, personal care homes, doctors' offices, and their own homes. Dependency situations offer high potential for assault."

After being assaulted by a care giver, Elizabeth reported the incident to the care giver's employer, a government agency. The result of the complaint was not disciplinary action against the perpetrator; rather, Elizabeth herself was threatened with loss of essential services. Without attendant care Elizabeth does not get out of bed in the morning. Women in such situations have very little negotiating power.

Lisa, a survivor of domestic violence too, shared her story with me in order that various service providers within the community would become aware of the needs of women with disabilities. Lisa tried marriage counselling before leaving her husband. She comments: "The counsellors would mostly look confused. They'd look at my able-bodied husband, then at my wheel chair, and seem to think that the best thing to do was to pretend that the wheel chair didn't exist. They'd treat us exactly like a couple of able-bodied people. In that situation, that was entirely inappropriate, but they couldn't see it was inappropriate." When Lisa finally did flee her husband, the police response also proved to be inadequate:

The police, too, were ignorant about the reality for disabled women. For example, take what happened one winter. My husband came home very drunk at two o'clock one morning. He beat me up and went off to bed, threatening to come out and shoot me if I made any noise. As soon as he fell asleep, I got out the front door. I couldn't get any aids or get dressed, so I crawled across the street to a friend's house. They said that they would take me, but not my kids, to a transition house. One of them said, "A man has a right to enjoy the company of his children in his own home." This was [said] despite the fact [that the children] were with a man who was drunk and abusive and had threatened to shoot someone for making a noise. Finally they said if I wished to "kidnap" my children, they would look the other way, but they wouldn't help me. However, I could not just cross the street, pick the kids up, and walk out.

The Toronto Rape Crisis Centre reports that it is not uncommon for women in psychiatric institutions to be sexually assaulted by hospital staff.[5] Violence exists as a constant threat within these institutions owing in part to overcrowding and lack of education and supervision of staff. But these are not the only places where the abuse of psychiatrically disabled women occurs. It also happens in community settings, particularly within psychiatric boarding houses, where many deinstitutionalized people live. Often security in these facilities is poor or nonexistent. (For example, a woman may not be able to lock the door of her room.) In addition to this, there are reports of landlords and boarding-house personnel abusing women residents. It is not surprising that female psychiatric patients are often sexually violated; these women are exceedingly vulnerable to all types of exploitation. After all, who is going to believe the word of a woman labelled mentally ill by society over the word of some upstanding man who has been looking after her for her own good? As one crisis worker commented, "Crazy ladies rarely have any credibility when testifying against those who assault them."

What resources exist for the Lisas and the Elizabeths of Canada? Unfortunately, the answer is: not many. Disabled women often cannot use community resources because accessibility features – such as wheel-chair ramps or telecommunication devices for the deaf – tend to be absent. In some shelters, blind women's guide dogs are unwelcome.

There are some transitional programs for women with children fleeing an abusive situation, but they are almost always inaccessible. Lisa describes one Christmas:

When we had to get out of our house fast, I phoned around trying to find a temporary room in one of my city's transition houses. We were refused because they said they were unequipped to meet my needs. One [shelter] finally did, but its bedrooms were up three flights of stairs. I had to ask people to help me with the stairs and carry my children up and down. It was exhausting. The support services were pretty well non-existent because all the services were geared to able-bodied women. The professionals had little comprehension of what I would do after I left. . . . All the places they suggested were inappropriate; either there were steps and no walkway to the entrance, or the doorways were too narrow to accommodate my wheel chair.

The inaccessibility of community resources forces women with disabilities to remain in or return to situations that are potentially life threatening. Lisa tried several times to manage in the accommodations offered to her: "I had two very young children. Every time I did leave (and I left many times), I would not be able to find an accessible place to take them to. . . . A lot of times I had to give up and go back to my husband." It is clear that a disabled woman's problems can be compounded by the solutions offered to her.

Whenever I tried to cope in an inaccessible place with the kids, I did a really terrible job. I would be afraid of being seen as an unfit mother. Once, a public health nurse came to see me. She looked around and started asking what kind of foster parents I wanted for the children. I said I wanted to keep my kids. She said, "Oh, I'll make a note of that in the margin." I was really scared of losing them, so the next day I called my husband and suggested a reconciliation.

The inadequate solutions provided by one service system caused another system to question Lisa's competency as a parent. Regaining custody of children apprehended by the child welfare system is difficult enough for any woman, but the difficulties are exacerbated if the mother is disabled.

Eventually Lisa was able to leave her husband and establish a new life for herself and her children. This was only possible, however, because she was able to secure a wheel-chair adapted family unit in a co-operative housing development. Lisa looks back on her experiences in shelters with sadness:

Every time I tried to leave, there were many obstacles I had to face on top of the ones an able-bodied woman has to face, which are formidable enough. After a month I'd [always] give up and have to go back home. The professionals couldn't see this as a reasonable response to the situation. They'd say that I must have an emotional problem, that [if I would always go back] I must "like" the abuse. That would hurt. Nobody seemed to understand what it is like for me to try to take care of two little kids in an inaccessible place.

A consumer movement of women with disabilities working together with other disabled people has called for the increased study of violence against disabled women and for the publication of findings. "The consumer movement" is the term that disabled Canadians use to refer to their movement for equality rights. Through it, disabled people work for empowerment. It advocates increased funding for programs so that special features such as ramps, telecommunication devices for the deaf, sign language interpreters are available. It recommends that workers in all violence oriented programs be educated by disabled women themselves so that they can be properly sensitized to the needs and abilities of disabled women. This need for special education also applies to staff in medical facilities that treat victims of violence. Also, it is essential that information about outreach programs be targeted at all women, including disabled women, because women with disabilities are often isolated and may be unaware of the existence of shelters and other community services for abused women.

LIVING IN THE COMMUNITY

Disabled people used to be shut away in institutions, or they lived out their lives in their parents' homes. Today we are living in the community, but we often experience great difficulty finding even something as basic as shelter that meets our needs. In Canada, women with disabilities are dying because appropriate accommodations are not readily available. Drina Joubert died of exposure in the back of a truck one December night in Toronto in 1985. Why? Drina died because the mental health and social-service system in Ontario, and society in general, failed her. They failed to provide her, and other women like her who have psychiatric disabilities, with decent housing. Outside of an institution, the only accommodation available to many women with psychiatric disabilities is a temporary shelter for the homeless. These shelters tend to be dirty, overcrowded and sometimes dangerous. Rules and regulations, such as developing contracts on behaviour change, attending weekly house meetings, avoiding street drugs and alcohol use, taking part in mandatory therapy programs, make them unacceptable options to many. Drina preferred the back of a truck to the accommodation offered her. The mental health and social service systems must begin to respond to the housing needs of women such as Drina Joubert.

Gertrude Wright also died because she was unable to obtain specially equipped housing. For some reason even the Ontario Housing Corporation, North America's biggest landlord, was unable to provide her with a unit that would meet her needs. She was a double-leg amputee who used a power wheel chair, and at the time of her death was living in an apartment without grab bars and low cupboards. She had had many serious falls. Perceiving herself a victim of injustice, she initiated a case against the Ontario Government under Section 15 of the Charter of Rights and Freedoms. When an inquest was held into Gertrude's death, the jury delivered six pages of recommendations. It suggested that five percent of Ontario Housing Corporation units be modified for disabled persons, and that there be a central registry of these units. Recommendations like this were not really new. Similar ones had been made in other settings. What we need now is not just recommendations, but action; we do not yet have even a minimum supply of adequate housing for disabled people in Canada.

HEALTH ISSUES

Many disabled women report inadequate medical treatment and indeed even maltreatment. Members of the medical profession tend not to take us seriously and refuse to give complete answers to our questions, focusing on our disabilities and excluding other aspects of our health, such as the medical problems associated with substance abuse and sexual exploitation. It is not uncommon for women who are experiencing the onset of a disability to be dismissed by their doctors as having emotional problems and be prescribed tranquillizers. Sometimes such mis-diagnosis occurs without thorough investigation of the woman's physical symptoms. This is quite common for women in the early stages of multiple sclerosis.

Sharon, a polio survivor, went to her doctor reporting breathing problems. The doctor dismissed her concern as just another aspect of her disability by saying, "It's just post-polio syndrome. You are just going to have to get used to this as you get older." Dissatisfied, Sharon visited another doctor, who did a thorough case history and discovered that her breathing problem was an allergic reaction to her new dog. Women with disabilities require a holistic approach to health care. The disability should not blind doctors to other factors.

The sexual exploitation of women within the mental health care system by male therapists remains a problem. Often, however, male doctors who are consulted about it fail to take the complaint seriously; in many cases reports of sexual exploitation are discounted as just symptomatic of the disability.

In Ontario, the Sexually Abused Patients' Defence Fund was established by women who had been abused by a male Toronto psychiatrist who continued to practise with impunity. The abuse went on for some 20 years. The scepticism with which the medical profession views women's complaints of sexual abuse by psychiatrists has caused the survivors to realize that they require legal counsel when they approach the College of Physicians and Surgeons. The problem must be legitimized, it seems, by the involvement of lawyers, before it will be taken seriously.

Women with mental disabilities have also been the victims of dehumanizing experimentation within the mental health system. One horrifying example is the series of experiments conducted by Dr. D. Ewen Cameron at the Montreal Allan Memorial Institute in the 1950s and '60s. The Ontario Coaltion to Stop Electroshock points out that over 76 percent of Cameron's research subjects were women. The women were subjected to regressive electroshock, psychic driving, massive drugging and sensory deprivation in a series of "brainwashing" experiments.[6] Bonnie Burstow and Don Weitz, in *Shrink Resistant,* report that "Velma Orlikow was forced to listen thousands of times to: 'You are a bad mother. You are a bad wife.'"[7] The sexist nature of the message cannot go unnoticed.

Many women with disabilities experience much frustration in finding good, accessible health care. The traditional health care system is not meeting our needs. Some of us look to practitioners of alternate medicine only to find them in inaccessible places. Others look to women's health care clinics. These too are often inaccessible. We must continue lobbying for better comprehensive health care for disabled persons.

MOVEMENTS FOR CHANGE

Working through the cross-disability consumer movement of disabled people, women with disabilities are rejecting such terms as "patient" and "client," renaming ourselves "consumers." We speak out as consumers about the systems and services that have been designed ostensibly to meet our needs. Typically however, these systems have been designed without our input. Now three organizations, all part of the consumer movement, are working on our concerns to resolve the issues affecting us. First, there is the disabled women's movement, DAWN, which was organized nationally in Canada in 1985. DAWN works co-operatively with, and as an associated member of, COHOP, which is Canada's largest cross-disability organization of both men and women with disabilities. At the international level, through Disabled Peoples' International (DPI), Canadian women are working to achieve greater equality for women with disabilities both in Canada and in other countries. Canadian Irene Feika sits on the Executive Committee of DPI.

The disabled women's movement works to ensure that the unique issues of women with disabilities are addressed. When asked, "Why does DAWN exist?" Joan Meister, DAWN's past-chair, answers: "Well, women with disabilities have special needs compared with men with disabilities, and we've felt for quite a long time now that those needs were not being addressed by either the women's movement or even the consumers' movement." DAWN keeps both these movements attuned to the concerns and issues of Canadian women with disabilities.

Meister highlights the following issues on the DAWN agenda:

We are working toward . . . providing women with disabilities with support, information and resources which are accessible. We want to make it easier for women to talk to and explain issues of concern to other women, to other persons with disabilities, and to the general public. We want to do consciousness raising in the area of the general public. We want to make sure we are inclusive rather than exclusive, and we want to reach out to all women with disabilities. We also want to provide role models for young disabled girls, because we, those of us who are working with DAWN, have acknowledged and have known all our lives that there has been a dearth of role models. Now young male paraplegics can look up to someone. . . . We all need role models in our lives, and disabled women especially need them.

DAWN has taken a leading stand on many important concerns, and one that immediately comes to mind is the one concerning Depo-Provera, a birth-control method considered unsafe by many experts. DAWN alerted the entire consumer movement to the negative effect the use of Depo-Provera was having on women with disabilities in Canada. COPOH has supported DAWN's efforts on this issue by encouraging its own members to advocate against the use of Depo-Provera as a contraceptive in Canada.

COPOH is a voluntary national umbrella organization that coordinates the views of its provincial member groups to enhance the status of disabled people in Canada. In recent years, COPOH has worked diligently to educate those within its network about the issues of women with disabilities. As a result, many within the COPOH network now define disabled women's issues as a priority.

In recent years COPOH has become involved in international development work, and in 1988 COPOH representatives were active participants in the Disabled Women's Leadership Training Seminar held in Dominica. Irene Feika, COPOH's past-chair, and Francine Arsenault, COPOH's representative on the DPI International American/Caribbean Regional Assembly, who also participated in the Asia/Pacific region's Disabled Women's Leadership Training Seminar in Korea (1985), assisted women with disabilities from the Caribbean in planning the seminar, and they also acted as speakers and resource people during the seminar. Joan Meister, who also attended this international event, led the session on leadership development. COPOH and DAWN collaborated to prepare resource materials on leadership development. Activist and development consultant Georgina Heselton was struck by how many similarities there are between the problems experienced by disabled women in Canada and those living in the Caribbean: "Actually many of the problems experienced by disabled women in the Caribbean are the same as the ones we have here: negative attitudes, inaccessibility, unemployment, lack of job training." Heselton is a member of the Saskatchewan Voice of the Handicapped, one of COPOH's member organizations.

The voice of Canadian women with disabilities has reverberated around the world owing to our participation in the international consumer movement. In the fall of 1985, DPI held its second world congress in the Bahamas. There were a large number of women with disabilities in the Canadian delegation, and, along with women from Australia and Britain, we took the lead in presenting a resolution calling for greater representation of disabled women in the decision-making structures of DPI.[8]

DPI's world council, taking its lead from the congress, passed a resolution stating that one woman from each of its five regions be appointed to the council. The resolution also called for the increased representation of women in DPI's regional and national levels, and an affirmative action program was proposed. The women also called for a series of leadership training seminars that would focus particularly on the concerns of women with disabilities. Following the congress, DPI implemented the leadership proposal in the Asia/Pacific region and the North American/Caribbean regions. Training sessions have also been conducted in Africa.

Some writers have described women with disabilities as an invisible population. But this statement now holds little truth. Canadian disabled women are working vigorously with our international sisters, in both the disabled women's movement and the international consumer movement, to reshape a world accessible to us. It is only through the continued active participation of disabled women in these movements that the dream of accessibility, justice and equality will become a reality.

In Search of the Right Prescription

Sari Lubitsch Tudiver

My mother, a creative and intelligent teacher, was also a prescription pill junkie. Suffering from migraines and gastro-intestinal problems for all of her adult life, she went from doctor to doctor in a quest to relieve her pain, and was prescribed a wide range of medications. As a child, I sat with her for hours in crowded doctors' offices. There were high hopes with each new medication and disappointments when they failed to help.

Our medicine cabinet held many of the new drug discoveries of the 1950s and 1960s – some of them experimental and potentially dangerous. When the thalidomide disasters were publicized in 1961, my mother realized that she had been prescribed Kevadon for headaches, a brand name under which thalidomide was sold in Canada. Many children of women who had taken the drug during pregnancy were born with shortened limbs, and while there was little chance my mother might have become pregnant at that time, she wondered what other effects the drug might have had. Her doctor had urged her to try something new and "experimental." There was an aura of scientific progress and positive results; the risks were hardly considered.

After gall-bladder surgery, my mother became dependent on Seconals, a class of barbiturates given as a pain killer and sedative in the hospital. Her dependency on the drugs scared me: I recall her hiding the pills behind a drawer so my father wouldn't know she was taking them. Access to the drugs was not difficult. One of her cousins was a pharmacist who provided additional pills on request. Following confrontations with my father, due in part to me revealing the secret of the hidden pills, she reduced and eventually stopped using those drugs.

But there were other drugs. In the early 1960s, pharmaceutical companies were aggressively promoting estrogen hormones to help "keep women young." Armed with articles from the *Ladies Home Journal* extolling the virtues of hormones, my mother asked her gynecologist to prescribe them, and for the next five years he did. My mother died of cancer in 1969 at the age of 55; a malignant brain tumour was discovered two years earlier, the primary source of malignancy in the fallopian tubes. I will always wonder whether the heavy doses of hormones in some way hastened her end.

Many of my mother's drug stories were told as "anecdotes" within our family, evidence of problems she experienced, a particular doctor's failings or an unusual set of circumstances. We were all swept along by the common belief that medical science, doctors and the pharmaceutical industry could be trusted. If luck was with her, somewhere there was a pill to cure my mother's ills.

In the 20-odd years since my mother's death, I have often wondered about the meaning of these stories. More recently I have come to see how much they have determined many of my personal interests, directions in my professional work and my commitments to social change. In the 1950s and '60s, my mother kept files about "wonder drugs" that might help her. My files document the disasters that some of those, and other wonder drugs and devices, became – thalidomide,[1] diethylstilbestrol (DES),[2] the Dalkon Shield IUD,[3] and Valium,[4] once thought to be non-addictive. I monitor current research, government actions and marketing on hormonal contraceptives and other medications targeted to women, and track the major pharmaceutical companies' global holdings, mergers, profits, losses and diverse product lines – from seeds and fertilizers to drugs and cosmetics. I find the book *Inside Ciba-Geigy* as riveting as the mysteries of P.D. James.[5] I have been actively involved in women's health and consumer advocacy groups and in professional associations working for the rational use of drugs for over a decade. I suppose I too could be considered something of a pharmaceutical junkie.

But unlike my mother, I tred warily when it comes to taking drugs, having the benefit of hindsight that she and those of her generation, including the mothers prescribed DES, did not have. Our privileged scepticism is rooted both in the painful, sometimes tragic, experiences of these women, and also in the actions that some people have taken to inform others, and to ensure that dangerous or irrational practices of drug use are changed.

My appreciation for the complexities of my mother's stories has deepened over the years. This has come about because I have taken two very different, but related, approaches to the stories, and because I have asked questions that did not occur to me 20 years ago. Both approaches are essential to understanding the meanings the stories hold.

First, I try to place my mother's stories in their social, economic and political contexts in the decades of the 1940s through the 1960s. I ask: How did her experiences reflect an expanding pharmaceutical industry in the post-war period? What do the stories tell about the role of governments in protecting consumers from potentially dangerous drugs and devices? What do they reveal about how male doctors related to female patients? What were the popular attitudes and deeper ideologies concerning the role of science and medicines in health care? How did this "outer world" of profits, politics and power weave its way into the personal, idiosyncratic happenings of our household?

Second, I explore the nature of an "inner world" that I can never fully know: the circumstances in which my mother grew to adulthood. I pose some difficult questions. Why did my mother suffer from migraines and gastro-intestinal problems, conditions in part associated with emotional stress? Were there other stories from her past that provide clues to her illnesses and that, if identified and explored, might have helped alleviate some of her pain? These questions raise complex issues about the links between biochemistry, heredity and the effects of family dynamics and different forms of stress on patterns of illness. They were not asked by the doctors my mother saw in the 1950s and '60s; but, due largely to insights from the women's movement, we are compelled to ask them today.

SEEKING THE OUTER WORLD: POWER, POLITICS AND PROFITS

Since the mid-1970s, a growing literature has analyzed the workings of the pharmaceutical industry in Canada and internationally. The sources of this material are varied and include major government inquiries into industry practices such as pricing, in both the United States and Canada; detailed documents on the structure of the global industry by United Nations (UN) agencies; critical overviews of the pharmaceutical industry and its relationship to governments in one or more countries; case studies of the role of specific companies and governments in drug disasters; and the occasional "insider" critiques written by former company employees.[6]

The practices of the industry in third world countries are particularly well researched by consumer and health organizations in Asia, Latin America, Africa, Europe and Australia and by those working with international aid and development agencies, particularly in areas of health. Through Health Action International (HAI), a co-ordinating network, such organizations monitor and share information about the practices of industry and governments, warn consumers about drug hazards and lobby the World Health Organization to promote rational drug policies among its member governments.[7] HAI has been instrumental in bringing together doctors, pharmacologists, social scientists, policy analysts and consumers from different countries into a formidable social movement, closely watched by the pharmaceutical industry.

The considerable research now available points to serious, world-wide problems in the use of pharmaceuticals. These problems include: very limited access by the majority of the world's poor to essential drugs (that is, the 200-odd medications determined by the World Health Organization to be necessary to meet most of a country's health needs); a proliferation of thousands of non-essential, therapeutically useless or potentially harmful drugs, in both the third world and in western countries; double standards in marketing practices, where a drug approved for the treatment of specific medical conditions in western countries is advertised for a much wider range of indications in the third world and may also list fewer adverse effects in the information provided by the manufacturer. Legislation concerning the safety of medicines is lax or absent in many countries, permitting drugs to come to market without adequate proof of safety and efficacy, including those banned or withdrawn from countries with more stringent standards. Generally, doctors have very limited knowledge about medications, possible adverse effects and drug interactions, leading to poor prescribing habits. Many communicate poorly to patients about drugs. In addition, major trans-national corporations exert extensive political influence over governments, allowing companies to secure policies favourable to their business interests and not always in the public interest. The push for market shares and higher profits has led to the development of unnecessary products, inadequate testing and a system of very aggressive advertising where, far too often, false or dubious claims are made and risks downplayed.[8] Yet the industry tries to maintain a public image as dedicated providers of health care, responsible for most major improvements in public health.[9]

Women are particular and lucrative targets for research and marketing by the pharmaceutical industry.[10] As care givers to children and other family members, they purchase and administer most over-the-counter medicines. Because of their potential to conceive children and because they bear the primary responsibility for birth control, they are consumers of contraceptive drugs and devices, and of drugs associated with pregnancy, menstruation and menopause. Women in western countries are prescribed minor tranquillizers more frequently than men, all too often as a way to cope with difficulties in family relationships and with frustrations of being female in a sexist world.[11]

Coming together, women share stories about their frustrations in not knowing what over-the-counter medications to trust; the difficulties of finding doctors who take their complaints seriously; the side effects of contraceptives and minor tranquillizers; and the difficulties women have in obtaining information about the effects of drugs on their bodies. Whether they live in Kenya, Canada or Bangladesh, women discover that there are striking similarities in their experiences, and that these similarities defy the boundaries of class, ethnic group and nationality. As in many other countries, Canadian women have organized victims' associations like DES Action to provide mutual support, to secure better medical care from doctors and to inform women in other countries about the dangers of particular drugs. Coalitions have been formed to research the injectable contraceptive Depo-Provera and to lobby the Canadian government not to approve such drugs without stringent review. Women have developed services geared to the special needs of women with addictions, and have used popular theatre such as the innovative play "Side Effects" to heighten public awareness of the issues. These initiatives have been part of broader goals to develop more women-centred models of health care.[12]

Through these actions, women are also learning that the science behind pharmaceutical research and development is rarely objective or gender free.[13] The interests of companies, governments, population planners, other institutions and individuals affect decisions at each stage of how pharmaceuticals are researched, tested, brought to market and used. Such decisions are made predominantly by men, and reflect a great deal about the subordinate position of women in society. For example, the heavy emphasis of research on high-technology hormonal contraception places greater importance on effectiveness than on safety. Despite the fact that millions of women use hormonal methods of birth control, not enough is known about the long-term effects of such drugs. Research reports tend to minimize the side effects experienced by many women, such as intermittent bleeding, reduction of libido, weight gain and depression. Questions concerning the possible impacts of such side effects on a woman's sense of self-worth and body image, on her relationships with others, and on her overall quality of life are not integrated into the research design. Instead, research is directed towards finding other medications to treat the side effects. Less invasive methods, such as barrier contraceptives, combined with the education of both men and women about the risks and benefits of particular forms of contraception, do not yield high profits and are given lower priority.[14]

Where and when drug testing is carried out, and on whom, reflect biases of both racism and class. Such testing has frequently been done on poor women from third world countries or on poor women of colour in the West, under conditions where access to research subjects is easier, less subject to public scrutiny, and where ethical guidelines of informed consent are frequently contravened without penalties. Much of the research on hormonal contraceptives and on sterilization falls into this category.[15]

Decisions about what lines of research to pursue and the length of animal and clinical testing are profoundly affected by market pressures. The health of women and their children has frequently suffered as a result of poor science. For example, a methodologically sound study published in 1953 determined that DES was not effective in preventing miscarriage.[16] Companies might have chosen to replicate such studies and determine the toxicity of DES on animals. Instead, the drug was aggressively marketed to doctors as safe and effective until the early 1970s, with disastrous results for many daughters and sons of women who took the drug.

Drug ads directed towards doctors reinforce stereotyped images of women as needing to be controlled or managed by drugs. Minor tranquillizers are promoted to help women cope with a wide range of life situations, including the "empty-nest" syndrome, the demands of small children and household tasks, job stress and aging. While very short-term use may help a woman get through a crisis, prolonged use of such drugs may be addictive. Drugs may prevent a woman from taking necessary action; for example, remaining with an abusive partner may put a woman's life and her children's lives at risk. Women's health organizations have pressed the industry to alter sexist ads, arguing that they have little place in discussions about the scientific merit of a drug. While some blatant examples, such as women in bondage or women as elder nuisances, have been retired from use, some very demeaning images remain.[17] Unfortunately, many doctors are influenced by these ads. If they were not, companies would not spend hundreds of millions of dollars a year on advertising.[18]

The workings of the pharmaceutical industry and governments, and the practices of science, provide essential clues to understanding my mother's experiences with drugs. For example, her dependency on Seconals was hardly unusual. It has long been known that these barbiturates were addictive; today, clear warnings are provided by the manufacturer to doctors and pharmacists to be passed on to patients. Whether my mother was warned by doctors, nurses or her pharmacist at the time I do not know. It was to her credit that she managed to reduce her dependency. Other less potent forms of pain killers and sedatives are available today – but the problems and potential for abuse remain. Large numbers of women are prescribed minor tranquillizers for long periods of time (five, ten, even fifteen years) despite the evidence that they are effective for relieving anxiety only for periods of several weeks of regular use.[19]

My mother's experience with thalidomide also becomes more intelligible when placed against a background of heavy industry promotion and lax government bureaucracy. Her doctor prescribed the drug to her *before* it was approved in Canada; it is likely that he gave her samples provided by the manufacturer for testing on patients. In the United States a watchful female doctor working for the United States Food and Drug Administration questioned the efficacy and safety of thalidomide and prevented its approval, while in 1961, the drug easily passed through the drug-approval process in Canada. Widely promoted as a sedative, thalidomide was advertised to be non-habit-forming and safe for pregnant women. Such claims were based on data now known to have been falsified. Thalidomide was also known to cause polyneuritis, an inflammation of the nervous system that could result in permanent damage, but warnings about this were down-played by the manufacturer. When the links to birth deformities were identified, Canadian authorities were slower than those in other countries to take action and to withdraw the drug from the market.[20]

The benefits and risks of estrogen replacement therapy (ERT), particularly its risks as a cancer-causing agent, are still widely debated, despite the presence of the drugs on the Canadian market for over 30 years. During the 1980s, the drugs were heavily advertised to doctors as effective in relieving symptoms of menopause. More recently, they have been promoted for prevention of osteoporosis, a condition affecting some older women, and characterized by loss of calcium and brittleness of bones. Such claims are now the focus of considerable debate in the medical literature.[21]

In the mid-1950s and into the 1960s, ads for ERT reflected little more than carefully calculated marketing strategies and a dubious science. Premarin was hailed as a way to keep women young. Manufacturers provided journalistic articles to women's magazines and newspapers; they were hardly the impartial sources that my mother believed them to be. Early advertisements also promoted these hormones as a treatment for headaches. By the 1970s, manufacturers warned that the drug could *cause* headaches and should be avoided by women suffering from migraines.[22] My mother was certainly a victim of the hard sell. Her headaches became worse in the years she was taking ERT, but no one considered estrogen as one possible cause, nor as a relevant factor in the malignancies that developed.

The decisions about drugs and treatments made by in this case male doctors also reflect a good deal about the pervasive sexism in the practices and ideology of medicine.[23] As medicine became professionalized in nineteenth-century Europe and North America, doctoring became a male domain from which women were actively excluded, a state of affairs that began to change only in the 1960s. Within a hierarchical health care system, women have been relegated to such subordinate positions as nurses, aides and domestics. Doctors exercise considerable social control and authority over female staff and patients. Women seeking medical help find themselves intimidated by mostly male doctors, who have information about how the body works, new technologies, drugs and diseases. But doctors do not readily share this information. Medical education has continued to reinforce stereotypical and demeaning views of women and their sexuality, assumptions about women's "natural" roles as mothers and wives and portraits of "normal women" having psychological inadequacies. As women repeatedly comment, many doctors trivialize their complaints – with two consequences: doctors do not always check for physical causes and sometimes miss serious symptoms; the highly technocratic approach to medicine has left doctors untrained to deal with social problems and the physical pains they may bring. A pill is offered to quell a revolution.

All too frequently, doctors make decisions *for* female patients, offering minimal explanations about their diagnosis and treatment. They provide little, if any, information about possible drug side effects and interactions. Such patronizing behaviour on the part of doctors is still common, but is being challenged by the women's health movement. During my mother's era, the authority of the doctor was near-absolute. My mother's relationship with her gynecologist was based on loyalty, gratitude and trust in his professional abilities and in his mastery of the "modern" technologies of obstetrical intervention. He had seen her through a difficult pregnancy and a breach birth. Critical and articulate in all other spheres of her life, she accepted his decisions without question. For example, in 1946 she was given a post-partum shot "to dry up that milk."[24] As she put it somewhat ironically years later: "After all, what did I know? He was the expert."

Over the years, my mother tried to be actively involved in her own health care. She searched out new specialists, read widely and tried to identify certain foods that seemed to trigger her headaches. No doctor seemed particularly interested in her observations, now recognized to have validity.

Her most frustrating encounter was with a headache specialist who told her: "I can see from how you dress and walk and shake my hand that you are a perfectionist. You will always have headaches. I can't help you." The doctor was quite right in calling my mother a perfectionist. She placed high demands on herself and others, was vibrant and talented. But he dismissed her plea for help. He would not bother with tests, nor would he probe for emotional causes. The message was clear: there is no hope for change.

SEEKING THE INNER WORLD:
THE ROOTS OF THE PAIN

My mother's stories have meaning when placed in the context of the workings of the pharmaceutical industry, the limitations and failings of the Canadian drug-approval process, the structures of sexism in the medical profession and in how science is practised. No longer anecdotes and fragments, they reflect how broad economic, political and social processes, specific to a period in history, affected our family and shaped some of the patterns of our daily lives.

But there are further dimensions to understanding the stories. For me, these only become clearer as women find their voices to speak about painful experiences and to identify their experiences as common to others. The women's movement gives these experiences a name and demands action. Until such issues are named, they are difficult to perceive and to articulate, especially when they are close to home. Battering is one such issue.

It is likely that some of the pain my mother experienced had deep roots in a profound and abiding rage towards her father, who physically and verbally abused his wife and children. My mother rejected any reconciliation with her father and even refused to attend his funeral. These "other" stories that my mother told me as I grew up showed my grandmother to be a battered woman, in those days a condition without a name.

No doubt these early experiences of abuse took a serious emotional toll on my grandmother and her children, including my mother. As the eldest, my mother also absorbed the responsibilities and grief – and, I have always felt, a good deal of guilt – associated with her mother's death from breast cancer at the age of 44. She had been the one to go with her mother to the doctor. "Go home, Sarah, the lump is nothing to worry about," he told my grandmother. By the time an accurate diagnosis was made, it was too late to attempt any treatment.

We know something today about the links between early childhood abuse and later emotional and physical scars, including addictions. I am led to ask: Was there a relationship between the early abuse my mother witnessed and experienced, her unrequited rage and grieving, her headaches and gastro-intestinal problems, and her quest for the right prescription?

There are no simple answers to that question. There was a family predisposition to migraines.[25] Some of her stomach problems were caused by gall stones, but other complaints persisted long after her surgery, and were often associated with her headaches. The many drugs she took may have had adverse effects and interactions. There are situations and factors that cannot be known, because she and others close to her have died.

The fragments of these stories will never be assembled into a whole, but they do offer tantalizing insights into what health care practices more finely tuned to women's experiences and needs might be like. In a woman-centred approach to health care, practitioners listen carefully and acknowledge what women say about their very real pain. If medications are to be used, there is discussion of what is known about their risks and benefits, drawn from impartial sources of information. Reactions to drugs are closely watched. The woman is encouraged to monitor herself, the conditions under which her feelings of illness occur, and to document these, if she is able, forming the basis for possible treatment strategies. The relationship between the health provider and the woman is ideally one of mutual trust and understanding, permitting an exploration of the deep emotional issues that may affect a woman's health and well-being. The the relationship between the health care practitioner and the patient relationship is based on respect for a woman's strengths and vulnerabilities.

Would my mother have benefited from such an approach? I believe so. A supportive medical system would have gone a long way to improving the quality of her life, validating her experiences. She should not have felt accused of being "overly dramatic" in her descriptions of illness. She might have experienced less isolation and despair.

In the past 20 years, women have organized a wide range of self-help groups, women's health clinics, shelters and other alternate health services to seek greater control over their lives and health. Women are struggling to be more democratic and participatory in these organizations. Others, including some nurses and doctors, are working to make traditional health institutions more responsive to women's needs. Many women and men are working in the consumer movement to develop rational drug policies and are lobbying to implement them. Most groups have few financial resources but considerable skill, resilience, nerve and commitment among their members.

At the same time, the medical establishment, pharmaceutical companies, research institutions and governments are committed to continuing the development of high-technology hormonal contraceptives and new reproductive technologies, reflecting approaches to health that further concentrate information and services in the hands of specialists. They consider body parts mechanistic fragments to be fixed. Increasingly, commercial interests turn fetuses and wombs into commodities that can be bought and sold. The social and ethical implications of this approach are vast. It is clear that such directions have the potential to undermine the control that women seek over their health and fertility in ways previously unimagined.[26]

In struggling for a feminist approach to health care, we are up against powerful interest groups and institutions. The stakes are high: the struggle is about control over women's bodies and minds, and the methods and practices of science itself. The struggle *is* the world of battered women, of government departments and industry research closed to public scrutiny. In a world of lobbying, motions, briefs and media campaigns, it is arduous work to ensure that women's opinions and experiences are heard. It is a struggle that is at root a popular movement and that women and many men recognize as just.

It is difficult to measure long term progress in these struggles. We know when a minor victory has occurred: a dangerous drug has been removed from the market, or a woman is helped because of the services she received. Part of the struggle takes place in that "outer world" of power, politics and profits. Ultimately, the struggle has meaning if it helps us better understand ourselves. The stories of my mother and millions of other women are a rich legacy in that quest. In order to go forward, we must also look back and listen carefully to the pain and the wisdom in our mothers' words.

Reflections

Mary Meigs

Four of us gather, all lesbians just below or just above senior status, two who have been married and divorced and have grown children, and two who have never married; our purpose is to discuss aging. I have sought out the others to enlarge or confirm my own experience and find that we have much in common, particularly a determination to make the changes of age work for us, to make new creative constellations of changes that are forced on us. All four of us are still actively thinking and working. Jane Gapen, Barbara Deming and I are painters or writers or both, and have always had a sense of vocation. Ruth, who has changed her married surname to Dreamdigger, did not feel herself to be an artist and did not suffer the frustration, as Jane did, of an artist-mother. Her children are a source of deep happiness to her. Her vocation has been non-violent action for peace and against nuclear weapons, and the study of human relations; she has worked with disturbed and economically deprived children, and, though nominally retired, now belongs to the Movement for a New Society, an organization that stresses personal growth, and she works in a general way in conflict resolution and peer counselling. She was moved to change her name to Dreamdigger because she used dreams to understand herself and in her work with others, not to discover neuroses as Freud did, but to discover the multiple layers of conscious and unconscious being, the creative complexity of every human being. Jane Gapen, who has written a fictional autobiography, *Something Not yet Ended*, and is also a poet and a painter, is now concentrating on painting. She says that as an aging woman, her creative life can be more fully expressed in painting than in words. As I look at her recent work, I feel that the poet and painter are still in equilibrium, and that she has found a visual poetic language for states of being beyond words. But at this point in the conversation, when Jane is suggesting that looking inward and outward is more in harmony with the physical truth of her aging, I say that I now have the impulse both to look and to push and prod my brain and force it to think.

"Writing is what makes me know my mind is alive," I say. Later, I feel this aliveness as I write, sitting on a platform built on the spreading branches of a big banyan tree, leaning against one of its thick trunks, as I think about our four-way conversation and watch two warblers hop along the branches above me and a turkey vulture sail overhead

Photograph of Mary Meigs, by Marik Boudreau

close enough that I can see its red hood. It seems to me that the integration of thinking and seeing and finding both words and images is as essential to me as the circulation of my blood.

We all agree about two things: that we have less energy than we used to have, and that we do things more slowly. We like to do things at our own pace and we hate to be hurried. We take longer to get started in the morning; we putter around; we forget what we are looking for in the refrigerator; we forget names. Forgetfulness and how to combat it is something we discuss with eager despair. We all make lists. I say I like to make lists of things to be done, then to check them off, one by one. Jane says that the making of a list tempts her to think that the things have been done. But lists do not prevent us from having the blanks that seem to accompany the effort to remember something. These blanks are like an impenetrable fog, interposed between the mind and what it seeks to remember. A certain amount of forcing will further thought, but memory is as uncertain as grace: no effort will summon it, only the paradox of forgetting what one wants to remember. Then the memory will suddenly appear, perhaps the next day, like a tropical fish swimming in front of one's mind. The patience to wait to remember has to be learned. Barbara thinks of these thought-blanks as times of unconscious growth; she loses herself in them and finds that, just as sleep solves problems, so blanks have their subconscious power to clarify thought that will only get muddled if it is forced. Age gives us leisure to turn what may seem like its negative aspects – absent-mindedness, forgetfulness – into states akin to trance. Barbara has always complained about her slow and painful struggle to think and write, but her work is evidence of the creative energy of meditation, and aging provides new forms of meditation.

Both Barbara and Jane seem to float with the current of age, almost to welcome the reasons it gives them to live in harmony with the physical process of aging. Ruth uses memory to coax dreams up from the subconscious, and her creative life consists of digging out the multiplicity of meaning in her own dreams and those of others, and using them as a path to understanding. Every day's harvest of dreams expands her cosmos of images and of clues to human behaviour. It is an endless source of nourishment, unaffected by age. I say that my forgetfulness has begun to prevent me from remembering dreams, that those I remember are fragments that have none of the old beauty and resonances. But she insists that I can train myself to remember.

When we talk about physical symptoms apart from forgetfulness, we all laugh. "My hands don't obey me as well," I say. "I drop things." Barbara says that her hands tremble so that she can no longer do speed writing, or rather that she can't read what she has written and has had to give it up – a real grief to her. And one realizes, reading her work, how important speed writing has been to her when she wanted to write accounts of conversations or meetings as immediate and true as life. Nor can she type as fast and surely as she used to. And I think of my own fear – that my hands, which have begun to draw quivering lines on occasion, will refuse my instructions to make a detailed drawing or to control the painting of the eyes or the mouth in a portrait. I remember hearing that Renoir, with a paint brush strapped to his arthritic right hand, was able, having looked intently at his portrait, to place a highlight precisely in an eye. If one has never tried to do this, one cannot know the difference a fraction of an inch can make in the direction the eye is looking or its intensity. Renoir was guided by a lifetime of accuracy like a Zen archer; perhaps my shakiness will move me in the direction of greater freedom and less fussiness. Our disabilities have to be turned to use in the sense of opening new ways.

Still, there are disabilities that cannot be transformed, and that take the form of annoyances and restrictions. All four of us get tired easily, and have to go to bed relatively early. I fall into what I call my stupors, days when nothing seems to work, body or mind, when the mind is like a leftover pudding and the body feels infinitely old and creaky. We laugh over our nights, punctuated by trips to the bathroom, by the fear sometimes of not getting there quickly enough, by having to get back to sleep again – as though we were wakened by an alarm clock two or three times a night.

We are all in agreement about the life-giving aspect of having come out as lesbians. I have found my life as a writer, I have shed my fears, am no longer secretive and defensive with my siblings, I have many new friends and a new sense of ease with them. All this happened after the age of 55 and is still true 10 years later. I have never found that age makes me invisible to other lesbians even when I am the only senior lesbian present in a group, as I often am in Quebec. There is more emphasis on looking young among lesbians in Quebec than there is in the United States. I know senior lesbians who dye their hair, have their faces lifted, and have the satisfaction of feeling younger when they do these things. I do not think that every effort to resist the visible effects of aging should be blamed on the patriarchy; it can be a way of saying, "I look younger to myself; therefore, I feel younger." I, too, feel younger when I am sunburnt, when the brown spots of old age on my hands seem to vanish.

As I think about aging, I realize that I have not yet begun to suffer from the general contempt for older women and from a sense of my invisibility. I have only felt it once, when in Italy in 1982 I saw myself as I was seen there – a white-haired old woman, wearing slacks and running shoes, without a wedding ring, without a husband – when the stereotype of the old-maid lesbian was clamped on me inescapably and prompted a quite unfamiliar kind of rudeness and impatience. Some people, both men and women, went out of their way to be helpful, but for the first time it came to me as a shock what it means in a macho country to be old and single. And, too, for the first time I felt literally invisible to the young. When I went to France, I encountered single women more or less like me, and in Quebec I was back in the land where lesbians, old or young, recognize each other and exchange smiles.

Quite recently, the problem of ageism has become a topic for discussion in feminist consciousness-raising sessions, and like many once-invisible minorities, aging women are becoming vocal and visible. Remarkable books have been written in the last decade, such as May Sarton's novel *As We Are Now*, in which the rest home where Caro, the aging heroine is confined, is a metaphor for the ugly psychological and physical suffocation that old age can bring. Like that other Caro in Margaret Laurence's novel *The Stone Angel*, this one preserves a precious remnant of dignity and dies with it. Another book written by an aging woman is *Look Me in the Eye* by Barbara Macdonald with Cynthia Rich, her younger lover, in which they look unsparingly at the patriarchy's imposed view of old women and its blueprint for integrating them into its machinery.[1]

We four who are talking are lucky to have each other and to be part of the wider conversation and sharing of experience of all women. In the course of our talk, I ask the two mothers what it has meant to them to be mothers, if it is comforting now as they enter old age. Jane says, "Well, motherhood is one of the sacraments." Another of the sacraments is art, she thinks; art, too, is a giving-birth, as necessary to the human spirit as biological birth. Jane has lived through difficult times with her children, but now they are there for her, they phone her, they worry about her, are friends. I ask her if her idea about the sacrament of motherhood doesn't give her a kind of absolution, a sense of having the right to be a lesbian because she has sacrificed to the patriarchal idea of women's role. I say that those of us who didn't want to be mothers have felt the obligation to work twice as hard to prove ourselves as artists, to overcome society's wish to diminish us, as women artists and as lesbians. Jane's life as an artist was slowed by years of child-care, but the children seem to have enriched the very life that was slowed down by them. Ruth was able to combine her children with her outside work and says that they have always given her, and still do give her, great joy. She describes Christmas in her old house in West Philadelphia when her biological family, together with her ex-husband and her "hodaka" family[2] were all gathered happily together. She has discovered the widest meaning of "family." She has lived the whole spectrum of women's experience: as lover (she had men lovers before her marriage), as wife and mother and grandmother, and now as lesbian. She has a feeling of completeness, and her work with dreams and tarot cards is completing her in a new way, in the unity of conscious and subconscious.

It is striking that none of us has a feeling of bitterness or defeat or of the horror of old age. I think this is true, for Jane and Barbara and me, at least, because the old woman artist, lesbian or not, is respected even by patriarchal society. She has survived and she is allowed her physical disabilities and eccentricities if she produces acceptable evidence of herself as artist. One thinks of Georgia O'Keeffe, of Sonya Delaunay, of Kathe Kollwitz and of Emily Carr. The older we get without falling into senility, the more we surprise people by the fact that we are still there, still working. Lesbian artists over 65 who have come out are likely to be snubbed or obliterated by the patriarchy, but that too is changing little by little, partly because of those who have come out posthumously, so to speak, through disclosures about their lives: Willa Cather, Ivy Compton-Burnett, Elizabeth Bishop, all of whom have such a secure place in literature that they cannot now be excommunicated because they were lesbians. These women who kept their secrets until they died give added power to aging lesbian artists and to aging women in general – the old-women power that is essential to all of us, old and young, engaged in the feminist revolution.[3]

There is no rule to determine at what point in her life a woman, lesbian or not, will begin to feel old, or at what point she is old, regardless of our society's ruthless emphasis on youth. Society views women with tri-focal lenses; we are seen as young, middle-aged or old, whereas my own lens is multi focal, and I've had no sense of any point at which I became either middle-aged or old, rather of accumulating evidence of change: greater slowness and lesser energy, eyes and ears that are less sharp, hands that are less obedient to my commands. This is being old, but feeling old can happen before any of the objective signs of age appear. I've heard young women groaning because a twenty-fifth birthday is imminent and saying (tactlessly, if I'm present), "I feel so old!"

In her essay "Simone de Beauvoir: Aging and Its Discontents," Kathleen Woodward says about *La Force des Choses,* published when de Beauvoir was 55: "The entire book is a chronicle of the crises of aging that she experienced between the ages of 35 and 45. She tells us that when she was 36, she calmly accepted the fact that she was old." Woodward continues: "For her the ideal body – that is the 'normal' body – is young and active. By contrast, the body of a person of advanced age, a decrepit body, is marked by imminent dissolution, by a lack of firmness, by frailty, by decay, and hence by a lack of identity."[4] De Beauvoir's obsession with the body's changes, her disgust for old age long before she is old, casts a shadow over the future and forces her to live her own dissolution and death (and Sartre's) long before they happen.

Woodward connects de Beauvoir's fear of aging not only with her fear that Sartre will die before she does, but also with her view of the past, and of autobiography as "the retrieval of the factual record" as opposed to what Woodward sees as "true autobiography – the achieved understanding of one's psychic past (and present) in the psychoanalytic mode." And she quotes Karl Weintraub in his definition of autobiography as "an interpreted past." With the exception of one book, de Beauvoir seems deliberately to avoid interpreting her past. "She rejects *la vie intérieure*" and refuses to find any meaning in her dreams. "For de Beauvoir, the appropriate or valuable form of memory is not personal memory, but rather social memory."[5]

As an autobiographer, I believe that my reliance on "personal memory" has prevented me from feeling old. Indeed, this kind of memory, which is not a factual recitation of the past, but an attempt to make creative use of it, can work like a draught from the fountain of youth for any woman of any age. And why should it not be put to use – the always extraordinary material of every life that piles up, full of trash and treasure, with its power, when it is sifted and scrutinized, to enlighten and heal? Each of my books has, without my having intended it, healed a damaged part of me. I think of this kind of therapy not as the purpose of writing about one's self, but as a by-product of creative work that forces memories to the surface and finds words for them. My first book, *Lily Briscoe: A Self-Portrait*, was about my becoming an artist and was also my first public appearance as a lesbian.[6] Until then my secret fears had twisted my life out of shape; with the book's publication, I had a sense of relief and of release, and of shared experience. Thus it healed, but it also set in motion the joy of searching for words to express the most elusive states of being and give them a dancing energy. I discovered that words can fuse with destructive anger, jealousy or hate; in the act of finding the right words for an ugly state, laughter begins to bubble up from my depths, and the exacerbation of the ugly state is dissolved. The right words must never express self-pity or they will fail both as art and as therapy. They have the power to awaken and enlighten, but only if full attention is given to the task of bringing them to life.

Every lesbian writer, by coming out, has taken a lonely political position that she will have to defend in subsequent books. She may have to invent a new language to express it, as Mary Daly, Monique Wittig and many French-speaking and English-speaking Canadian writers have done. Conventional patriarchal language is not adequate to describe the lesbian experience, and particularly the power contained in it. It is the power that comes from breaking our dependence on patriarchal society. Many lesbians have had a head start in independence; some of us have learned how to be alone and how to put loneliness to creative use. If lesbian lovers break up and pass through states of unforgiving rage, if they seem at times to forget the whole concept of sisterhood, they do not, like those women whose husbands or lovers have left them, desperately seek to hook themselves up again to the big patriarchal tank, full of a polluted substance that they somehow manage to breathe. Lesbians may find it frightening to be alone, but we never lose our footing (or our standing) in a society that decrees that women shall depend on men to exist as human beings.

A married woman's traditional ideal of loyalty to her husband is so strong that she will go through hell in the name of it. And if she loses one man, she will feel the commanding urge to find another to whom she can be loyal. Married women go through ordeals by alcohol, by beating, by the discovery that their husbands have sexually abused their daughters, before they cry, "No more!" They are forced by conditions of particular stress to open their eyes to the long non-existence of their true selves, and now they look at these new selves with wondering eyes. They are like young birds that sway and shuffle and teeter on the edge of the nest and shrink back in fear, and then leap into the water or the air and find that they already know how to swim or fly. Married women artists and scientists sometimes go through the ordeal of diminishment and put-down for years before they claim their freedom. Aba Wells, the American photographer, who moved to the mountains of New Mexico to find self-realization, said of her new life: "Never before have I felt the courage to just be, without excuses for my 'being' . . . without looking for some man for my reason/excuse for breathing. . . . Now the real beginning of the 'freedom' which we have discussed for many years . . . to finally discover all I had to do was reach inward, and it was waiting all the time for me."[7] Diane Arbus's younger daughter, Amy, said about her: "She never realized that as a woman she really could have her own style, do her own work. She had always thought that to help Pa do his thing was all there was to it."[8]

Every woman who has freed herself knows what it was like to have been a cog in the great machine that at first invites you to share its power and then squeezes you to death. Perhaps for the first time, lesbians and heterosexual women can look at each other with the understanding that we occupy the same space both of loneliness and freedom to be. Many of us have taken the same route, through sexual abuse, alcoholism and battering. Ironically, old age, which is popularly seen as a handicap, becomes a help in the freeing process. A friend my age said recently about her married life: "I just decided I wasn't going to be pushed around any more." She said it calmly, but there was a spark of defiance in her eye.

In old age a woman, whether she is married or not, discovers the power in herself not to be pushed around by anyone or anything, and she makes another discovery – that in old age the differences between women disappear and we begin to be bound together by our resemblances. These are not disabilities, but abilities peculiar to old age: detachment, the wish for harmony, and the creative sharing of memory, both to illuminate our personal pasts, and, if we are writers, to bring to life the great unrecorded history of women. Simone de Beauvoir, who in 1964 spoke of "the furious gallop to the tomb," said in 1982, in a conversation with Alice Schwartzer, that she believed that, "whereas love affairs between men and women often do not last, by contrast great friendships with women often endure." She asserts in complete confidence, in the same conversation, that "up to my death, I will never be alone."[9] She had lived her horror of old age prematurely, and emerged into the sunlight of friendship with women. Through bonds of friendship we can seek meanings to our puzzling memories and feel less fear before the enigma of death. As a lesbian writer, I am enjoying the prerogatives of old age as a unique time for questioning, and for paying attention to answers.

Farm Women Fight for Survival

Lilly Julia Schubert Walker

Women make life hard for other women because they do not think. And thinking comes hardest for the comfortable women.[1] *Nellie McClung*

As we journey away from the city into the countryside, we are struck by the change in scenery. Buildings and traffic are replaced by planted fields and the occasional farmer working the land. At first glance it seems a simple life. Mesmerized by the greens and golds of the peaceful fields basking in the warmth of the sun's rays, we may not suspect that there are troubled times here.

Farm families, like plants, struggle to survive. Who among us has not marvelled at the growth of plants whose roots have pierced rocks in sheer determination to grow – or the tenacity of vine tendrils to cling to rough edges as they reach out, or the flexibility of the trees when they are buffeted by strong winds. Each year seeds are sown; millions begin, many fail, but all struggle to survive. Farm families are no different. Establishing roots against difficult odds, they plant crops each year in anticipation of a bountiful harvest and of personal success. Their rootedness to the land, their determination to withstand the elements, their tenacious beliefs and optimistic outlooks, have provided them with a strategy for survival. But times are changing.

The role of farm women in the survival and success of the farm has often been overlooked or minimized. Hardworking traditionalists, they viewed themselves primarily as homemaker-helpers and partners to their producer husbands, responding to the demands made upon them. But as agriculture has evolved, women's work roles have also evolved. Some of the traditional responsibilities – like cream separating or egg handling – have become part of commercial food processing. And contemporary women are assuming responsibilities that have been considered men's work (for example, accounting and field work). Yet because farming is viewed as a male profession, any work women do tends to be labelled "homemaking." Women's contributions to agricultural productivity are often invisible, their work unappreciated and under-valued.

The proportion of women in all classes of agricultural worker (farmers, farm managers, farm labourers, nursery workers) has increased from nine percent in 1951 to 43 percent in 1981. In 1984 only 21 percent of women who work on family farms were paid for their hours of farm work.[2] Female farm operators work an average of 39 hours per week.

Female farm spouses work an average of 38 hours a week, yet 44 percent of their hours are unpaid. (These workloads do not include any of the hours spent on tasks that are considered to be "home-making" – such as food production, family accounting and child care – duties that if performed by someone else would be assessed as agricultural workload.) Studies of rural women indicate that they spend an average of 42 hours a week on household work in addition to their farm or off-farm employment. Household work remains an exclusively female responsibility in farm families.[3] Many factors (for example, type of farm operation, age, work involvements and respon-sibilities, number of children and age of children) influence women's work roles, so it is difficult to assess definitively the effect that farm women have on agricultural production. However, it is obvious that farm women's contributions to agriculture are largely undervalued by the women themselves, by their families, by their communities and by government.

DISCONNECTED AND DISILLUSIONED

Contemporary farm women, like their frontier grandmothers, value independence, industry, integrity and ingenuity. They tend to be individualists who patiently persevere. Without these qualities they could not cope with the isolated lifestyle of farm life. They have learned to adapt to physical isolation, but psychological isolation is more difficult to resolve. Farm women tend to feel disconnected from urban women and from each other. The farm crisis of the 1980s has exacerbated this tendency.

As farm women work for the political issues that are relevant for them, they often feel unsupported by their urban sisters. There is a tendency to criticize and complain about the other and to feel misunderstood. Sometimes our language or our definitions separate us; sometimes there are actual difference between us. For example, we each define "workplace" differently, and an issue like equal pay for equal work, important to urban women, might appear irrelevant and unimportant to farm women. At the same time farm women may be fighting for higher prices for their agricultural products. Because our viewpoints and values differ, we have difficulty hearing one another. We may be speaking in separate voices – voices that often seem like they are competing with each other. We are divided; we are separate; we feel alone.

If we pause for a moment, we see that there are many similarities between farm women and urban women. We all need child care services, health services, access to credit, training opportunities and protection against violence. Many of our needs are similar; our misunderstandings arise because we often seek different solutions.

Farm women, whether working full time on the farm or engaging in paid employment off the farm, have difficulty gaining access to child care services. Surveys indicate that farm women are dissatisfied with the availability of child care services for both pre-school and school-age children.[4] Because the work patterns of rural women are different from those of urban women, different factors affect the delivery of child care services. Rural women need child care arrangements that recognize their geographic and social isolation, the economic restraints of the family, and the seasonal variation in work hours. They need subsidized, flexible and diversified arrangements such as home-care services, temporary child care, and registries of home care workers. In order to provide quality child care, home-care providers need to be able to access training and resources through a system that recognizes rural realities.

Both farm and urban women need access to responsive health-care systems. However, due to the shortage of health-care providers in rural areas, farm families are under-served. Rural communities have difficulty attracting physicians. In 1988, 31 rural Manitoba communities reported doctor shortages.[5] Because rural physicians carry heavier case loads (rural Manitoba physicians carry an average load of 2,207 patients, while Winnipeg physicians have 676), doctors are overworked, and hence farm families get limited care. Furthermore, farm women suffer unique health problems such as impaired hearing, allergies and back pain. Some respiratory problems, such as rhinitis and farmers' lung, are unique to farmers, and can be fatal. Stress, which has been recognized as the root of many health problems, is significantly higher among farmers than among urban comparison groups.[6] As a consequence of the increasing use of chemicals in agriculture, farm women experience irregular menstrual cycles,[7] premature births, spontaneous abortions[8] and infertility because of their contact with brucellosis bacteria.[9] Farm safety is also a major health factor in rural areas. The incidence of fatal accidents is higher in agriculture even than in construction or mining.[10] As we as a society attempt to deal with the high costs of medical services, the needs of farm families are often lost in the name of cost effectiveness. Creative solutions to health care include: broadening the education of our health-care givers so that it includes substantive rural and northern experience; decentralizing services; and changing the roles of health providers. We should require medical practitioners to work in rural areas for a prescribed period of time after their training as repayment to society for the cost of that training, which includes significant rural tax dollars.

The technological changes facing farm families are similar to those facing urban workers. In both cases, the key to successful adaptation is training. Since education is a provincial responsibility in Canada, there are disparities among the provinces with regard to training and education. Some of the barriers that farm women experience are institutional (for example, complicated, urban-based admission regulations). Others are financial (for example, the high valuation of farm assets that adversely affects eligibility for student loans) or geographic (for example, the difficulty and cost farm women experience in travelling long distances to institutions offering relevant programs).

Rural women, like urban women, are too often victims of violence. The factors that lead to violence against women are similar in rural and urban areas. However, in rural communities there are greater taboos against open discussion of family violence, and consequently misunderstandings and prejudices prevail. The relatively small size of rural communities makes it difficult for victims to seek help; this factor, combined with the lack of services such as shelters and mental health centres, means that victims often feel isolated and alone. Victims on party lines may have difficulty using even toll-free numbers, fearing that their conversation may be overheard by their neighbours. All women need to have a place of safety available to them. Rural and urban communities must develop their own particular ways of providing solutions to the problem of violence against women, but co-operative endeavours and government funding are also required.

Farm women are not only disconnected from urban women; they are also disconnected from each other. Traditionalists clash with activists as their different value systems and viewpoints demand different solutions for farm family problems. And the prairie pattern of independence reinforces isolation just when people need to co-operate. Traditionalists believe that strength lies in togetherness as a family. They invest in the family enterprise and work harder and longer as times get tougher. Traditionalists live a life of sacrifice and restraint. Activists find strength in togetherness as women; they encourage an analysis of society by asserting not the power of the individual but the power of the collective. Activists question the old values and present solutions that threaten established ways. Traditionalists value personal solutions; activists strive for political solutions. Hence their differences divide them. Traditionalists and activists have difficulty talking together, much less working together.

THE PRICE OF POWERLESSNESS

During the past 17 years as a counsellor and consultant, I have listened to farm women talk about their lives, their families and their work. They feel disconnected, disillusioned and powerless. Historically, they have valued their ability to cope and take control. They have prided themselves on their ability to handle the daily demands, changes and challenges of farm life. They have responded to the multi-dimensional nature of their jobs and developed a wide range of abilities that have added to their feelings of personal effectiveness. Farm women have traditionally experienced power as a sense of inner strength.

However, power can be described more systematically as a hierarchy of three overlapping concepts: personal power, interpersonal power and organizational power.[11] Personal power is defined as the ability to feel in control of one's environment. Interpersonal power is the ability to influence the actions and views of others. Organizational power is the ability to mobilize resources in order to achieve results. Conversely, powerlessness is the lack of these abilities. Farm families express feelings of an increasing sense of powerlessness as they feverishly fight for the survival of the family farm. As their feelings of powerlessness increase, their stress levels and stress symptoms increase.[12]

To some extent, the values of independence, industry and sacrifice have permitted the development of feelings of pride and personal power in members of farm families. But as agriculture becomes increasingly controlled by factors beyond the farm family, these values are no longer effective. As a result, members of farm families feel personally powerless, and this powerlessness is manifested in depression and self-blame.

In a 1987 study my husband and I did in Manitoba, one-third of the farmers described themselves as depressed, one-half reported feeling discouraged about the future, and 30 percent admitted being disappointed with themselves.[13] Farm women expressed a greater loss of personal power than farm men, probably because historically they have been socialized to be more dependent and have even less control over their lives.

The much publicized Murdoch case and the recent changes to matrimonial property legislation have made farm women more aware of their rights as partners.[14] Farm women are now asserting their rights and are frustrated when they perceive barriers to gaining interpersonal power. In fact, farm women have identified lack of interpersonal power as their major source of stress. Farm women know that in farm family financial decisions, their input is often undervalued. Studies show that men generally make most of the decisions related to the farm enterprise. Although farm women may make decisions about daily farm tasks, they have minimal influence over their male partners with regard to the farm operation.[15] Whenever women are discriminated against by bankers and loan officers when applying for credit, their sense of interpersonal power decreases. Whenever they are excluded from family decisions, particularly in multi-generation family farm operations, their sense of interpersonal power decreases. For farm women to gain interpersonal power, they must challenge their own family systems. And this is often not a viable option for them, primarily because they know the fragility and vulnerability of their families and themselves as they struggle to survive financially. Instead, they engage in protecting their families from outside attacks and challenges, much as their mothers and grandmothers did.

The lack of interpersonal power that farm women experience as individuals is also experienced by other members of the farm family. As these families become more highly stressed, the degree of interpersonal power among the members decreases. Stress produces a negative circular effect: increased stress produces increased powerlessness, which in turn produces more stress. As these two factors increase, families withdraw into themselves, and when this happens the members are denied the social support that they need. Some families become interpersonally destructive, and the amount and intensity of family conflict, inter-generational disagreement and personal attack escalates.

The lack of organizational power of farmers is one of the reasons they are facing financial crisis.[16] Farmers feel powerless to change the world grain markets, public attitudes, government policies and other conditions that affect their financial survival. Current estimates reveal that one-third of family farms are in financial trouble.[17] If these families leave the land, the political voice of the farm population will be drastically reduced. Farm families currently experience difficulty being heard by the Canadian public, which values cheap food at the expense of farm viability, and by governments, which establishes agricultural policy based on international politics. Farmers tend to be competitive with one another, and their lack of unity adversely affects their ability to lobby effectively for public and political support. Farm women have almost no voice in agricultural policy or in the directions taken by farm organizations.[18] They possess even less organizational power than farm men. Their lack of organizational power is reinforced by the relatively low value placed on the workload that they carry. Farm families are experiencing a negative cycle: the decrease in power among its members produces greater vulnerability, which in turn adds to feelings of powerlessness.

The increasing loss of personal, interpersonal and organizational power among members of farm families is costly both financially and personally. Most family farms are struggling; many will not survive. Rural communities are slowly dying; as fewer farm families live in the area, businesses fail, schools consolidate, and the tax base erodes. Individuals are showing increasing signs of psychological distress (for example, one mental health centre reported a 200 to 300 percent increase in service utilization during a three-year period[19]). Some of the costs of powerlessness are recognizable, others are hidden. What is evident, however, is that the sense of powerlessness experienced by farm families appears to be increasing as the financial crises of the 1980s and 1990s continues.

The financial crisis has been divisive. The fabric of the rural community is breaking down. In contrast to the 1930s, when everyone was affected and no one survived unscathed, today there are divisions; there are victims and survivors. What produces a hardship for one family seems to help another family become successful. Some families can no longer fight, and they are forced to get go, leave their homes, their land and their heritage.

BUILDING BRIDGES

The demands of daily living on the farm has forced women to develop survival skills. They are required to be tough and tender, aggressive and submissive, resourceful and nurturing, rational and intuitive. Rural women are what many women aspire to be. Living their lives with many of the same values and needs as their grandmothers, rural women do the best they can so they and their families can live on the land. They fight for the financial survival of the family farm. The current economic crisis has highlighted the powerlessness of farm women and poignantly demonstrates that they must remember the lesson of their grandmothers: the key to survival is to take control." The difference today is that some different strategies are required in order to gain power and control. Some of the prairie patterns that served as guideposts for adaptation and survival are no longer effective in the current crisis. Today, farm women need to challenge myths, change perceptions and connect with others, for they are building bridges for survival.

Some of the myths about farming are: that farming is an idyllic lifestyle; that the old way of independent individualism is the only way to succeed; and that women's work is worth less than men's work. Farm women are challenging the myth of the idyllic lifestyle. As long as farming is perceived as romantic, the problems of living on the farm are discounted. As long as this myth is reinforced, the public remains unaware of the health hazards of farm life, unconcerned about the limited access rural people have to educational, commercial and health services, and blinded to the reality that life on the farm is highly stressful.

Farm women are also challenging the myth that independent individualism is necessary for survival. They argue that adherence to this value reinforces competition rather than co-operation between farm families. It makes it difficult for farm families to reach out to one another for support and assistance. Survival today depends on unification of farm communities.

Farm women are also calling for re-evaluation of their contribution to agriculture. As long as women's work responsibilities are underestimated, their financial worth is undervalued. They are not perceived as equal partners by society, or by governments.

Challenging these myths is the first step. The second step is to effect a real change in how farm women's work is perceived. And many farm women are already doing this; they are articulately demanding that definitions of work, work value, and productivity be reconsidered to reflect the reality of farm women's lives as co-operators, part-time workers, full-time workers and off-farm workers who support the farm. Loans officers, bankers, government workers, lawyers, business operators are being educated about women's contributions. And many farm women are directing their efforts toward creating legislative changes that more fully recognize farm women as co-workers and equal partners.

Farm women must work along with farm men to change the common perception that farm problems belong only to the farmer. Anyone who eats is part of the current financial crisis facing farmers. Yet because we live in a country of abundance, urban dwellers seem generally unconcerned about farmer's issues. The current farm crisis is an economic problem that belongs to all of us. The problems facing agriculture are not agricultural problems; they are global human problems.

Farm families must change their pattern of isolation. They must build bridges with one another and discover sources of support within farm organizations. Rural people and urban people need to learn more about each other, in particular how social, environmental and political issues are affecting all of us. We need to begin to talk together, plan together and work together. At a time when farm families feel disheartened, disillusioned and defeated, these beginning steps can provide an impetus towards overcoming the feelings of powerlessness that paralyze them. Farm families are accustomed to struggling and overcoming. Life on the farm has always been difficult; today is no different. The challenges may have changed, but the battle is the same: fighting to survive on the land and to feed the world.

Woman by Log Cabin

Irene Heaman

I see you
winging free
from your echoless past
a ghost form
by this skeletal house

Everything is gone

except the memories
planted
on this farm –
foundation
for prosperity

You weren't so poor
with chipped cups
holding bluebells
on rough plank
tables
rag rugs, quilts
and porridge
for breakfast

The green grass
stays beside
this house
where it always was
The sky is filled
with pleasure
in its size.

Knitting Empowering Configurations

Joan Pennell

Empowerment. Initially, this word expressed women's yearning to unite with other women in order to achieve individual and collective aspirations. In the late 1980s, through overuse and misuse, I found that the concept of empowerment had lost its appeal. Committed to the original ideal but searching for clearer and more invigorating terminology, I examined the theory and practice of democracy within the battered women's movement and found myself returning with renewed sensitivity to, and respect for, the meaning of empowerment. Democratization and empowerment both refer to gaining control over the conditions of our lives. The manner in which feminists employ the term "empowerment" best captures the duality of this process: the assertion of individuality within a united group.

The battered women's movement is dedicated to freeing women from violent oppression and to creating affirmative communities. To illustrate this point, I use the image of the traditionally feminine art of knitting. For me, this handcraft represents warmth, durability, suppleness and beauty; the loops are linked into flat rows, and are then wrapped to give volume and cover. Like knitting, empowering requires an even tension to balance the closeness and the separateness: if the links are too loose, the shape collapses; if they are too tight, the flexibility of the whole diminishes. Rich designs are created through the intermingling of varied strands.

Looking for alternatives to the authoritarian relationships prevalent within our society, I became first an activist within, and then a student of, the Canadian and American battered women's movements. I knew that the daily struggle against oppression of women through violence motivates women within these movements to translate principles of empowerment into organizational structures; that is, work is to be divided and co-ordinated in an egalitarian manner. In order to study whether and by what means the battered women's movement has realized democratic decision-making, I selected two associations that are nationally reputed to be cohesive and effective and are located in regions that have a historical commitment to collectivism. The Pennsylvania Coalition Against Domestic Violence (PCADV) is situated in an eastern American state founded by communal religious sects: the Society of Friends (Quakers), the Amish and the Mennonites. The Provincial Association of Transition Houses

Saskatchewan (PATHS) is located in a western Canadian province that has been shaped by agrarian socialism.[1] I also decided to focus on these two associations because I assumed that their contexts are sufficiently distant and dissimilar to foster the evolution of alternate structural designs, but also sufficiently close and similar to permit some generalizations about associations in the battered women's movement in Canada and the United States.

My optimistic hunches that PCADV and PATHS would have democratic structures were, on the whole, confirmed. I observed business meetings, participated in informal gatherings, and engaged a wide range of participants and allied resource persons in reflection on the associations' decision-making processes.[2] Measured against the minimal criteria of western national democracy, both associations are easily considered democratic. In each case, the member programs created the association and guaranteed that they are equally represented on a board of directors that elects its own officers, votes on resolutions, and oversees the association's staff. Besides instituting these mechanisms of representative democracy, the associations encourage participatory democracy: decisions are usually reached through consensus, and non-delegate program members are encouraged to contribute to discussions.

However, although democracy is reflected in membership participation and board representation in both associations, neither association meets the principles of inclusion advanced by the women's liberation movement.[3] In the associations' decision-making processes, there is no provision for involvement of currently battered women and their children; executive directors project stronger voices than program staff, volunteers and board members; white, heterosexual women overshadow other groups; and the associations' employees are particularly influential.

Such thinning of the democratic fibre is commonplace and is typically attributed to the requirements of organizational efficiency.[4] It is frequently, and I believe correctly, argued that, unlike the earlier consciousness-raising groups within the "collectivist strand" of the women's movement,[5] the battered women's associations have moved beyond helping their immediate participants to mobilizing resources for many other women. As a consequence, these women's organizations restrict participation in order to expedite decision-making. Such exigency, nevertheless, does not explain why the Pennsylvania and the Saskatchewan fibres vary in thickness.

The explanation lies in the two organizations' differences in size, age, environment, function and philosophy. All the voting members of the PATHS board of directors are appointed by the eight Saskatchewan member programs. Each program is a provincial shelter and/or advocacy service for battered women and their children. At the PCADV coalition, most, but not all, of the members are appointed by more than 50 Pennsylvania member programs. Four PCADV delegates represent non-geographical sub-units, the coalition's own staff and its three caucuses.

PCADV is and needs to be more inclusive of its own staff in board representation than PATHS for three reasons. First, PCADV has a larger staff than PATHS. PATHS has only one co-ordinator, while the PCADV director has a contingency to represent on the board. Second, PCADV, founded in 1976, is older than PATHS, which was founded in 1984. PCADV, has had more time to clarify in practice, and to acknowledge constitutionally, the role of its staff in uniting the coalition. Their differing founding ages has affected their philosophies about organizational collectivity. The early battered women's shelters were greatly influenced by the women's liberation movement, which emphasized the "sisterhood" of all women, and the sharing of power between managers and workers.[6] The philosophies of shelter supporters broadened over the 1970s and '80s as professional and community-based groups became more involved.[7] As a consequence, in the mid-1970s, the Pennsylvania programs called their new organization a "coalition," and asserted their radical feminism; in the mid-1980s PATHS adopted the more conventional term "association." And third, because of the broader mandate that PCADV has, its employees perform more functions and exert more power than do the employees of PATHS.

While both PCADV and PATHS were established to provide supportive networks and to mobilize resources, PCADV also serves as the conduit for federal and state funds. In each association, the staff co-ordinates the membership's activities and lobbies on behalf of battered women and their programs. In addition, PCADV employees exert a major influence over funding. Although staff members do not determine funding policies, they participate in the discussions (but do not have a vote) on the board's Contracts Committee. The staff's function in the implementation of funding policies is particularly significant. They screen the budgetary requests of the Pennsylvania domestic violence programs. Their careful recommendations are respected by the external review panel and usually authorized by the state Department of Public Welfare. As a consequence, the staff influences fiscal apportionments and program standards stipulated within grant contracts.

Despite the obvious potential for major conflict between coalition employees and programs over funding issues, PCADV has been markedly successful in maintaining a supportive working relationship in two ways. First, when addressing contract problems, the staff has adopted an educational approach, working with the programs to inform, to mediate and to resolve difficulties. Second, they have included the staff on the Board of Directors and the Contracts Committee, as well as at meetings and informal gatherings, thus ensuring that direct communication and a sense of mutual trust is maintained.

In terms of board representation of program employees, the Saskatchewan association is more democratic than the Pennsylvania coalition. Because of PCADV's contracting function, the program boards almost invariably fill their one delegate seat with an executive director. The Saskatchewan association encourages the inclusion of program workers by stipulating in its constitution that all programs have two voting representatives, one selected by the board of directors and one by the staff. While the executive director may be appointed as the staff representative, she often is not. PATHS's system of representation has been distinctive in Canada and reflects the higher level of labour unionization of shelter staff in Saskatchewan than elsewhere in Canada or the United States and, more fundamentally, the province's legacy of agrarian collectivism.[8] Because of PATHS's small membership size, dual program representation ensures a sufficient number of active participants. Conversely, since PCADV already has numerous voting delegates, it would become unwieldy to increase their number.

Neither PATHS nor PCADV allocate seats on their boards of directors to women receiving services from their member programs, primarily because they are program associations rather than coalitions of social movement participants. In Saskatchewan, moreover, a separate body, the Saskatchewan Battered Women's Advocacy Network, formally represents the interests of women who suffer or have suffered domestic violence, whether or not they avail themselves of shelter services. Nevertheless, from a democratic perspective, battered women (who constitute the majority of participants in the associations' programs) remain disenfranchised.

Generally, the battered women's movement has struggled with the issue of including women who are currently being victimized. On the one hand, it is recognized that, in order to maintain its mission and philosophy, the movement needs the participation of these women. The voices of battered women remind us of the vulnerability of all women in a sexist society and the necessity of the struggle against violence. On the other hand, it is recognized that these women may endanger their lives and those of their children through active participation, and may need to devote their energies to daily survival.[9] The survivors of battering, however, are at least informally represented in the two associations; many of the delegates have personally experienced domestic violence.

In addition, the Pennsylvania coalition allots formal representation to formerly battered women affiliated with its programs.[10] As one of the three subgroups commissioned by the coalition, formerly battered women form a caucus, and their chair sits as a voting member of the board of directors. Although their one official spokeswoman is numerically outvoted by the delegates appointed by more than 50 programs, the caucus representative can generally expect board members to have some comprehension of the needs of battered women.

In addition to the survivors of domestic violence, the Pennsylvania coalition formally recognizes two minority groups – women of colour and lesbians.[11] Unlike the chair of the formerly battered women's group, these caucus delegates cannot expect board members to have a prior understanding of their wants. As a consequence, their single voting delegates must spend time educating board members. In order to thread the voices of minorities more firmly throughout the coalition, PCADV is currently strengthening its affirmative action policies regarding participation on boards and committees of the coalition and its member programs; and in employment practices and expectations of allied coalitions and contracted firms. PCADV has formed task forces to study needs of and has initiated demonstration projects for rural and minority groups. PCADV includes under-serviced groups in its affirmative action plan. Generally, within this coalition, the commitment to represent minorities fairly has generated a "creative tension." The challenge is to increase sensitivity to minority perspectives without relying on minority women to educate the membership. At a more fundamental level, the issue is about sharing power.

Unlike PCADV, the Saskatchewan association does not have formal representation of minorities, but its membership is quite diverse. Saskatchewan has a varied population, and two of its member programs are predominately composed of aboriginal women. Differentiation of subgroups is difficult in any small organization, especially if its membership is spread across a vast land mass.[12] Saskatchewan has one-twelfth the population of Pennsylvania, but its land mass is five times as great.[13] Although the organization's size inhibits formation of internal subgroups, its members do not evince any smallness of spirit in serving minorities. For example, when government cutbacks threatened a northern town's predominately native shelter, Saskatchewan women drove long distances to the community to demonstrate.

For feminists, as is generally true of political activists from other grass-roots social movements, democracy is not a question of which groups are represented, but rather whether every member has a voice in making key decisions. The ideal, then, is that decision-making be decentralized. A decentralized, or bottom-up, approach typifies the decision-making process at the Saskatchewan association and, I believe, fundamentally reflects a prairie character. At first glance, a centralized, or top-down, approach appears to be characteristic of the Pennsylvania coalition, whose board dictates standards to the member programs. As I looked more closely at the decision-making process within this organization, instead of straight lines from the coalition board down to member programs, I found loops.

I believe that the Pennsylvania coalition's control over funding is the primary reason that its structure is more centralized than that of the Saskatchewan association, whose constitution forbids the association from distributing funds to its members. While sharing information and values through workshops, a newsletter and training materials, PATHS is hesitant to promote province-wide standards since they would infringe upon members' sovereignty. One long-term participant explained that PATHS has inherited a "prairie radicalism." Like the individualistic Saskatchewan farmers, PATHS members assert their differences and resist standardization. This non-conformist tradition may also be a product of geographical distance and isolation. Since the programs are widely separated, their local conditions are quite variable. Moreover, the driving costs and time between shelters prohibits members from meeting frequently.

The Pennsylvania coalition has divided its membership into three regions, a strategy not at present available to PATHS because of its small numbers. Decentralization of the Saskatchewan association encourages programs to develop their own service and management models, and each shelter's representatives confer with their constituents prior to voting on association policies. Since PATHS does not hold the purse strings, programs that disagree with PATHS's policies can choose to leave rather than struggle to change the association. True of prairie women historically, PATHS members are noted for their many close and warm ties across the provincial organization, but their main allegiance remains with their own shelter and its community.

While PATHS fosters program autonomy towards the association, PCADV promotes program autonomy towards the local community in order to link programs foremost to the coalition, and to bond them with a feminist community. PCADV seeks to preserve its historical commitments to the women's movement by setting and enforcing standards that promote participation of women and freedom from local control. For example, when applying for funds, programs are expected to provide evidence that the program meets certain criteria, such as: there must be a majority of women on the governing boards; programs must be autonomous from any sponsoring or parent organization; the board must appoint formerly battered women as employees, volunteers and board members; there must be affirmative personnel practices; and, there must be training that raises volunteer and staff consciousness on sexism, and that acknowledges the role of the women's movement in identifying wife abuse.

In addition, programs must demonstrate in proposals and records that, besides providing services, they foster social change by advocating institutional reforms and re-educating community groups. Concerned that the feminist activists who began the battered women's movement are being replaced by professional or community based service providers, PCADV has produced a series of training packages to sensitize its participants to homophobia and racism. In order to inform its membership of the movement's original approach, the Pennsylvania coalition has written a number of models that the membership are encouraged, but not obligated, to follow. Recently, the board of directors passed a motion approving a "shared power and responsibility" model. Member programs are to institute "decision-making structures which empower residents/clients, staff, volunteers and Board and assure distribution of authority and responsibility." Since PCADV models tend to become prescribed standards, the coalition appears to be moving toward mandating democratic practices. The coalition is deliberately using institutionalization to maintain what were, initially, radical goals.[14]

Centralization and decentralization each can reinforce and fray the democratic fabric. As participatory democrats and anarchists emphasize, centralization can abrade individual freedom and weaken the social bonds of mutual respect.[15] It can be argued that PCADV's imposition of standards, despite its democratic intent, is oppressive. Centralists could retort that the prime author of participatory theory, J.J. Rousseau, is notorious for his assertion that people should be "forced to be free" by inculcating democratic values and by compelling participation.[16] From this perspective, explicit standards are seen as less controlling than indoctrination. Furthermore, as battered women can testify, home rule does not guarantee egalitarian decision-making.

While the Saskatchewan association's autonomy model prevents the association from dominating its membership, it does not ensure democracy within each shelter. Member programs, however, are not solely linked to PATHS. The staff of half of PATHS programs – and these include nearly all of its long-term members – belong to a powerful provincial organization, the Saskatchewan Government Employees' Union. Through this progressive labour union,[17] the staff have achieved economic gains and have participated in union programs and policy formulation. Moreover, the collectivist traditions of

Saskatchewan's native and non-native populations encourage the participation of all members in program decision-making.

Because the founders of the Pennsylvania coalition were spun from the wheel of radical feminism, they cast separate program strands together as "sisters." Gradually, as more and diverse members joined, the coalition stretched in size, philosophy and function, and the tension among the loops became uneven, permitting various members to gather into regional groupings, caucuses and task forces. Through program development in under-serviced counties, affirmative action and service outreach, PCADV has sought to balance its design. And to maintain fundamental unity among its membership, PCADV has formulated standards and models, and has appointed a sizeable staff to instruct, monitor and inspire its membership to adhere to its principles. For the rapidly elongating Pennsylvania coalition, centralization is a means of tightening the links among its many subgroups.

Since the Saskatchewan programs wished to preserve their prairie individuality, their association resembles an Afghan of knitted shapes sewn together. Given their small numbers, the stitches between the programs are firm and reinforced by the co-ordinating efforts of their full-time and committed staff person. The friendly bonds and the system of dual representation provide a crosshatching pattern unifying the association's members into an overall design. For the Saskatchewan association, decentralization is a means of highlighting and supporting the separateness of its few components.

Looking for the appropriate tension between the independence and interdependence of their units, the two associations have moved beyond the conventional process of empowerment; that is, from granting power to the membership, to the feminist process of empowerment, where power originates within the membership. Discussing the meaning of empowerment, Susan Schechter, an activist-historian of the battered women's movement, states that "its premise is to turn individual defeats into victories through giving women tools to better control their lives and joining in collective struggles."[18]

On the one hand, individuals are to assert their autonomy and, on the other hand, they are to merge into a collectivity. In reality, these opposing relationships can co-exist if each individual's preferences are identical to those of the other group members. Both the Saskatchewan and the Pennsylvania associations were formed because they realized that alliance would empower. Over time, though, they have also increasingly recognized that, without affirming differences, merger disempowers. When views conflict, the membership may bunch into competing interest groups, eventually unravelling the organization, unless the associations re-adjust the tautness among their units. As animate and supple linkages, the Pennsylvania and Saskatchewan associations accentuate their memberships' diversity while maintaining sufficient tightness for support and sufficient looseness for mobility. Thus, they knit vibrant and full patterns that have the flexibility and unity to endure.

Removing our Blinders:
The Economic Participation of Women

Rosella Melanson

When the New Brunswick Advisory Council on the Status of Women researched the history of New Brunswick women for the book entitled *We, the Undersigned*, we found some fascinating accounts of debates on the issue of women's right to vote.[1] Some thought that women's participation in politics would change the world; some feared that women would be corrupted; some predicted that homes would be neglected, or divided. When, in 1919, after 50 years of struggle, New Brunswick women finally won the right to vote, a member of the Legislative Assembly suggested in a display of misplaced chivalry that elections would now have to take place in fine weather only.

Women's participation in politics has brought about neither the catastrophic nor the utopian changes predicted in 1919. Women have had to fight and work hard for all the changes realized in the last 70 years. Only now have we begun to see that, as women, we may have achieved a cumulative level of power sufficient to propel change internally. We have joined the labour market, we are in decision-making positions, and we are more politically aware. Women have launched the movement towards change – towards the most important social revolution that we will see. Although it is certain that women are not yet where we want to be, we will never again return to where we were. We move towards the integration of the public and private spheres of human activity.

This integration will not occur before the year 2000. It may happen in the twenty-first century. I think it is important to tell ourselves that the process of social change is long and difficult, but that change will happen. Men have benefited for thousands of years from an illegitimate affirmative action program. We are now entering a time when sexual equality will be created through legitimate action.

Sexual equality and the integration of women in political and economic activity involves more than admitting women to men's world. Rather, it is shifting the world towards the female sphere. It is integrating the values that women have represented, contesting the structures that were based on sexual division of roles, and eliminating the barriers to the full participation of women and men in all aspects of life. It is combining the female and male spheres of activity and broadening our concept of the economy to include all work, whether remunerated or not. The real goal of feminism is the abolition of false social divisions based on sex. It is the integration of the sexes.

DEFINING THE GOAL

The goal of sexual equality is often lost in the confusion around the definition of equality, a confusion sometimes present even at high levels of legislative and judicial functioning. Since 1985, the Canadian Constitution gives a guarantee of equality; equality before the law, equal benefit of the law and equal protection of the law against all forms of discrimination, including discrimination based on sex. Aware of the legal history of Canadian women's rights, feminist groups virtually wrote that clause (Section 15) of the Charter.

Canadian legal history includes a Supreme Court of Canada decision that women were not persons – at least not for the purposes of rights and privileges, although women could be said to be persons in matters of pains and penalties.[2] Another judge, in the 1970s, determined that equality exists if all women are treated equal – even if men receive different (that is, better) treatment.[3] Yet another judge – again of the Supreme Court of Canada – stated that discrimination against a pregnant person cannot be construed to be sexual discrimination.[4] By the 1980s, Canadian women had realized the importance of constitutional and legal protection of equality rights.

The equality we are seeking cannot be the absolute equality that imposes the male norm and that does not recognize women's needs and values. Rather, it must be equality that respects the specific needs of both sexes, does not tolerate arbitrary distinctions, and does allow for measures to compensate for disadvantages created by systemic sexism.

The Charter of Rights is only a promise of equality, a recognition of a debt. Women do not yet live in equality. Even if equality in the law and in the application of the law is respected, equality of results is not assured. Since men and women are not equal at the starting line, the race will not be fair without compensatory measures and a supple definition of equality.

The social forces that brought about constitutional protection of equality rights are also responsible for a change in the dominant legal ideology of Canadian jurisprudence. We have finally recognized that it is as a group that women are disadvantaged.

Some predict the beginning of a period in which the law will act as agent of social change: the constitutional clauses on equality may be the reform that opens the door to a more radical critique of society and the law.[5]

The equality clause seems destined to be used for activist purposes. Some groups have been created to instigate precedent-setting equality cases. Women's Legal Education and Action Fund (LEAF) is one such example. It seeks to develop and implement legal strategies to bring before Canadian courts those Charter cases that are most likely to be won and to establish strong positive interpretation of equality under the new Charter. LEAF is interested in creating equality of results.

WOMEN'S PARTICIPATION IN THE LABOUR FORCE

If the first phase of the feminist movement in Canada can be called the decade of legislative change, the next phase will, I think, be dedicated to progress in women's economic status. Our status in relation to the paid labour market has changed a great deal in the last 25 years. Our increased participation in the paid labour force is part of long-term social and demographic trends: lower birth rate, greater longevity, the industrialization of domestic work, the boom in the service sector, the increase in divorce rates and a heightened motivation for work and consumption.[6] The convergence of these social trends and the increasing dependency of the labour market on women renders female participation permanent and irreversible. The participation rate of New Brunswick women aged 15 to 64 has more than doubled in 30 years, from 20 percent of women in the 1950s to 52 percent of women today.[7] By the year 2000 the national female participation rate is expected to reach that of men.[8]

The greatest increase in the national participation rate has been among married women, rising from three percent in the 1930s, 11 percent in the 1950s, to 53 percent in 1986.[9] The right of married women to paid employment was one of the first struggles of the recent women's movement.

The increase in women's participation in the labour force has been significant for full-time employees, and it has been dramatic for part-time employees. Today, about one-quarter of working women work part time.[10] Several studies suggest that the number of part-time employees who would prefer working full-time is significant and increasing.[11]

In an effort to measure the female-male gap, we are continuing to monitor gender equality indicators. We are looking at such key areas as the number of female university graduates, the number of women participating in the labour force, the unemployment rate according to age, marital status and education, and the distribution of income by sex. Taken in isolation, the statistics on women's status seem to indicate that the situation for women is improving. However, we are finding that, in comparison to men's status, women are losing ground.[12] For example, the unemployment rate of female university graduates, which has decreased, is actually increasing in relation to the unemployment rate for men. The unemployment rate for women is now twice as high as men's. After receiving the *Gender Equality Indicator Report*, the Ontario Minister Responsible for Women's Issues concluded that the popular notion that women are closing the economic gap is false; actually the opposite is true. Women are losing ground in some important areas, and in other areas, progress is hardly noticeable. The dimensions, but not the characteristics, of women's economic profile have changed.

It is evident that, when compared to men, women continue to be economically disadvantaged. In absolute terms, women, especially those living without partners, are poor. The feminization of poverty in Canada is a long-term trend. The war on poverty in the 1960s seems to have helped mostly two-parent families and elderly persons, leaving behind a growing number of poor women, especially single-parent women.[13]

OCCUPATIONAL SEGREGATION

The segregation of women into a small number of traditionally female occupations remains the rule. The structural changes that expanded service-sector employment and part-time work, which made women's increased participation possible, have also served to limit the impact of women's massive entry into the labour force.

In 1975, clerical and service jobs accounted for 56 percent of women's jobs in New Brunswick; in 1986, these jobs accounted for 52 percent.[14] Only two percent of engineers in Canada are women, and the number of women in the sciences remains statistically insignificant. In several occupational fields, such as transportation, construction, processing, primary occupations and material handling, the proportion of female workers is the same as it was in 1975. The number of women in professional ranks has increased from 23 percent (1975) to 27 percent (1986), the major increases having been in law, medicine and management.[15]

THE PAY AND BENEFITS GAP

The pay gap between women and men is another example of economic inequality. However, the measure most often used – the average earnings of full-time, full-year workers – is, according to some, one of the greatest distortions of economic thinking. New Brunswick women earn approximately 64 percent of the average male salary; this gap is almost as wide as it ever was.[16] But this statistic only speaks of the situation of a minority of women; most women are either employed part time and/or as homemakers, or are unemployed. A more relevant measure of the female-male economic gap would be the average income from all sources. Women who have some income receive, on average, 55 percent of what men earn, the same proportion as occurred 25 years ago.[17]

The measure of the average salary is useful to show that women do not earn the male average salary in any occupation and that the gap exists at all educational levels. In the Atlantic provinces in 1986, female university graduates earned on average $26,000; male graduates earned an average of $38,400. Canadian women with a high-school education earn, on average, 57 percent of what male high-school graduates do.[18]

Jobs that are traditionally female have rarely offered benefits. Only 25 percent of women in the labour market in New Brunswick are covered by a pension plan, as compared to 40 percent of men.[19] Because of this, and because fewer women than men are members of unions, any gaps in the minimum employment standards legislation have a greater effect on women.

NON-MARKET WORK

Women and men differ not only in their labour market participation characteristics, but also in the non-labour market work that they do. In a recent United States study by Stanford University professor Victor Fuchs, the economic well-being of women and men was compared for 1959 and 1983 using computer data available from census and population surveys.[20] Fuchs studied the income, number of hours of paid work, domestic work and child care, the value of the non-paid work, and the household income and income sharing. The study concluded that despite structural, legal and behavioural changes over the past 25 years, in comparison with men, women's economic well-being has not improved. Women's monetary income had increased due to a rise in paid work, but this gain had been offset by fewer leisure hours, increased financial responsibility for children, and an increase in the number of women living on their own.

We are beginning to understand that we cannot achieve economic equality of women and men without taking family life into account. Economic measures must recognize domestic work. Unfortunately, some economists and politicians still assume that women must reach equality under the same conditions that men have had, and that women must act like men in career choice and commitment. The persistence of the income gap between women and men, and occupational segregation, should convince women otherwise. Social responsibility towards the family as a production and reproduction unit makes it necessary to end the division of public and private spheres. As long as parents are held responsible for children and most of the work is done by women, sex differences in the labour market are predictable.

TOWARDS INTEGRATION

The first step towards integration is to bridge the reality gap. Current economic and social programs and policies do not reflect reality. What is considered the traditional family – that is, the employed father and the mother at home with children – accounts for less than 20 percent of Canadian families.[21] Most females in the labour force have family responsibilities. Such issues as child-care services, parental leaves and flexible working hours became public issues when women joined the paid labour force. The work of parents at home needs to be recognized through pension credits and bridging programs.

Since women entered the labour force, the total amount of work we do (including what we do at home) has increased, and that of men has decreased. We often hear of the pay gap – but we seldom hear of the work gap, or the leisure gap. Women do two-thirds of the world's work and have almost no leisure time.[22] How much longer will women accept double work days?

The reality gap will certainly be at the heart of political agendas in the future. Women cannot close the gap by themselves. What was once personal has become political. Issues related to women will take up an increasing part of the public agenda. The political power of women is already being felt: electoral platforms – if not elected governments – are now beginning to integrate social and women's issues.

In order to achieve the full integration of women and men, we also need employment equity. In many jurisdictions outside New Brunswick, employment equity programs are being implemented.

Furthermore, economic analysis must be non-sexist. We can no longer afford economic theories and policies that ignore non-market production. Although the value of domestic work and child care is gaining recognition in law (such as in marital property legislation and pensions), the economic value of this work is still unrecognized. Only market exchange is studied as an economic activity. The domestic sphere seems to be considered a place of leisure and consumption, where women are invisible. Even when we are participants in the paid labour market, women seem to be of interest only because our behaviour varies from the norm, the norm being the prime-age male. To base labour-market analysis on the behaviour of men between 25 and 50 is unacceptable.

The Royal Commission on Economic Union and Development, commonly known as the Macdonald Commission, based some of its proposals on this kind of limited analysis. The Commission recommended the reduction of unemployment insurance and the creation of a fund to encourage workers to move to jobs in other parts of Canada. Men whose wives are at home may benefit from this program, but in most families today, both spouses are in the labour force. And since on average men are better paid than women, it is unlikely that families will move if the wife is the one who is unemployed. Furthermore, it is by no means certain that more than one person per family would be declared "employable" under such a program. Some economists recommended to the Commission that "secondary workers" – an economic term meaning "women" – be disqualified from the program. Single parents – another term to signify women – are not part of the program's target population. Such proposals reflect the bias of economic analysis in Canada. It also demonstrates how the impact of economic policies on women is often ignored.[23]

More evidence of sexism in economic policy is found in free trade and the Mulroney-Reagan Agreement. None of the hundreds of research studies done for the Macdonald Commission considered the effect of free trade on women, nor on the service sector, where 80 percent of them are employed, nor on social programs.[24] The fact that the sectors most affected are those where women are the majority escaped attention. No labour force retraining plan specific to women has been developed, although it is well-known that women are underrepresented in general training programs and that the women who will be most affected by free trade are older and have less education and skills than the average person.[25]

Economic analysis has shown little interest in the poverty of women, the effects of dependency, or the efficient use of domestic resources. Not only does this render women and our economic problems invisible, but the exclusion of domestic production from economic analysis calls into question the validity of these analyses. Neglect of an important area of economic activity has consequences for our ability to measure production and the efficient distribution of resources. Economist Marjorie Cohen has pointed out that if a productive activity is not counted, its cost of production will not be counted either.[26] Efficiency is an important concept in economics, and it can only be measured if all productive activity and all costs are known.

If economists are concerned with efficiency and the efficient use of rare resources, they cannot limit themselves to the study of market activity. As Cohen says, economic models are biased against certain solutions because these models do not take domestic production into account.[27] For example, some economists and politicians maintain that the cost of day care is too high and that society cannot afford such a service. Since domestic production is not valued, any alternative to domestic production, such as day care, will be considered only in terms of the cost and benefits of their effect on the market. Total use of resources must be considered.

Similarly, we can no longer accept circular explanations of women's economic position. We are told that women have a relatively lower economic status because we have more domestic responsibilities than men and, therefore, supposedly do not invest as much in the marketplace. We are also told that division of labour in the home is based on the relative income levels of women and men. This circular argument only explains how the system is perpetuated, not why things are as they are.[28]

The fact that women are at an economic disadvantage is an economic problem. If we can say that women do two-thirds of all work and receive one-quarter of all revenue,[29] it should be evident that it is not by working harder that women will "reach equality." Rather, it is by removing our blinders and recognizing the full economic participation of women. This is the challenge of the 1990s.

An International Feminist Book Fair

Lise Weil and Linda Nelson

The Third International Feminist Book Fair, held in Montreal, Quebec, in 1988 between June 14 and 22, was to us, the United States editors of *Trivia: A Journal of Ideas,* an event of historic importance. Attended by over 6,000 women from around the globe, and genuinely multi-lingual (the program itself was printed in three languages and simultaneous translation of all panels was available in French, English and sometimes Spanish), the Fair established a space where crucial questions about women's relationship to language could be raised – and exhibited both the enormous diversity and the subversive power of women's writing.

The Fair offered two trade days designed for the international community of publishers and writers, featuring panels such as "Publishers and Authors: Expectations, Attitudes and Ethics," "How to Promote Lesbian Writing" and "Writing by and for Women of Color," and four days of public panels and workshops organized around the themes of memory, power and strategies of feminist thought. In its structural commitment to exploring broad themes from many angles of vision, and in the diversity of its participants, this fair exemplified a process of questioning and expansion grounded in language, writing and thought.

In the panel entitled "Lesbian Memory and Creation," Judy Grahn, quoting from her book *The Highest Apple,* urged women to "be at the center of your lives," while at the same time "acknowledging that more than one island of centrality exists, more than one 'House of Women' is operating." The atmosphere of the Fair was one in which all participants seemed to be trying to live up to these words. It was clear that the organizers had built on successes and learned from the mistakes of previous fairs – held in London in 1984 and Oslo in 1986. While there were obvious failings (the most glaring one being inadequate promotion), it was thrilling – especially to one who attended the Oslo Fair, where for the most part lesbian and third-world concerns were treated as peripheral – to be part of an event that reflected the absolute centrality of lesbian writing and publishing to the women-in-print movement, and where the myriad of cultural voices represented on panels, and in the choices of topics and themes made it impossible for any one voice to prevail. The dominant mood here was one of *respect*, and clashes of style and opinion tended to take the form of questions: for example, "What is the meaning of writing to women in countries with high illiteracy rates?" "What do we mean by 'revolutionary writing'?" Among those of us in the publishing world, there was both respect and pride: for having kept on all this time doing whatever it takes to put women's words out there in the public realm; and for continuing to keep on, against all kinds of odds.

The Fair itself was grounded in a passion for women's words – and for writing itself. That this was so was in large part due to its setting: Montreal, where the Quebecois population has had to fight for the right to speak in its native voice. An understanding of language as irreducibly political, and of work on language as itself a form of political action, is at the heart of feminist writing throughout Quebec, and in much of English Canada as well. The movement of women writing in Quebec has produced a major body of work – fiction, poetry, theory, translations, essays – which has, in Canada, pushed writing to the forefront of feminism, and feminism to the forefront of post-structuralist thought. The innovative energy and vision of this movement provided much of the impetus for the Fair itself.

The effects of colonization – on women's languages, on women's bodies – have given rise to a new consciousness in and about writing not only in Quebec but also worldwide. Native American, Afro-American, Latina, Asian, African and East Indian women, for example, are actively discovering the many ways in which writing from their own centre constitutes an extreme rupture with existing social fabrics. The visibility of such writing was one of the great joys of this fair. To incorporate elements from oral traditions, to practice "code-switching" (the confluence of two languages within a text), these writers are showing us, is both to be true to one's own cultural experiences; it is also to challenge Eurocentric definitions of theory, fiction, and writing itself.

Since the Montreal Fair, friends who attended – both from here and abroad – have sounded the same theme: "It changed our lives." The Third International Feminist Book Fair generated immense excitement. We hope that the crucial and extraordinary conversations begun there will be extended and elaborated.[1]

L'Immigrant/e

Jacqueline Barral

Hybride
Aux racines mythiques
Colle à tes semelles la glèbe de ta matrie

Une greffe est toujours un corps étranger
Qui porte en soi les stigmates d'origine

Entrée sur une nouvelle terre
Hybride tu seras
Etrangère nourrie de la sève étrangère
Tu seras pénétrée, imprégnée de ce monde nouveau
Par la glaise étrangère survivras

Tu es ce qui te nourrit
Tu es ce que fais de ta vie
Tu es ce que tu partages
Tu es ce que tu reçois

Hybride
Venue d'un univers hors du temps
Un monde qui n'est plus et qui ne fut jamais
Tue es pétrie de la matrie perdue
Tue es nourrie de la terre élue
Greffe d'une vie apatride
Hybride

The Immigrant

Jacqueline Barral, translated by Jane Brierley

Hybrid
Of mythical roots
The soil of your motherland sticks to your soles

A graft is forever a foreign body
That bears within it the stigmata of origin

Spliced onto a new land
Hybrid you will be
A stranger nourished on foreign sap
Penetrated, impregnated by this new world
Surviving in the alien clay

You are what feeds you
You are what you make of your life
You are what you share
You are what you receive

Hybrid
Voyager from a universe out of time
A world that is no more and never was
You are moulded from the lost motherland
You are nourished by the chosen soil
Graft of a stateless life
Hybrid

Mangoes to Maples

Uma Parameswaran

1

Chorus:

Under a sky more vast than any I've seen.
On snow more cold than ever I dreamed,
I stand alone
Amid masks that speak an alien tongue.
Far far are those I loved and love
And far the fragrance of my native flowers
O'er which bees murmur homeland tunes.

Small comfort I find in these needle pines
That stand bleak against the white.
Where's the fire that can sustain us
In this alien land of endless skies?
Where the friend who'll lend a hand
So we stand tall in our own eyes?

Some day we shall surely sing:
Under a sky bluer than any I've seen
On snow whiter than ever I dreamed
I stand beside the Golden Boy
Holding golden sheafs of corn
Against a dawn heralding the joy
Of years to come.

2

Amma, I like school.
It is such fun.
We play most of the time.
And sing songs in French.
Amma, fingerpainting is such fun
So many bright colours
And we can use all we want.

Photograph of Matriarch, by Joan Turner

Amma, if a crayon breaks
You can just throw it away
And take a new one!
Ma, you think you could change my name
To Jim or David or something?

Photograph of Matriarch, by Joan Turner
Amma, I love recess time.
Did you see the tyres?
The tyres tied together?
I can climb up
And sit inside and swing!
Such fun.

3

Namaste! Savitri behn*, come in.
So good you are, behn,
Looking me up so often
to see if all is well.
Seat your good self, behn,
Yes, we got vacuum cleaner,
It is so convenient, no?
You phoned yesterday? O I am sorry
I was not being here.
It happened this way.
That good lady in next flat, no?
She was going to food store,
The Italian one on big street yes?
And our Indian store so close
So I am also going.
What pleasure it is to buy vegetables!
Bhindi, and fresh brinjai, and even karela **
No seasons here, behn, all through year
One gets whatever one wants,
Great place, no?

* sister, used for all female friends of same age group; older women would be
called "aunt" or "mother"
**okra, eggplant and bitter melon

4

What kind of place you've brought me to, son?
Where the windows are always closed
And the front door it is always locked?
And no *rangoli* design on porch
To say, Please come in?

Son, son it gives me great joy
to see you so well-settled,
children and all,
Though my hairs do stand on end
when your wife holds hands with men
and you with other men's wives.
But I am glad, son, I really am
that you are settled so good good
and thought to bring me all the way
to see this lovely house and car and all.

But I cannot breathe this stale air
with yesterday's cooking smells
going round and round.
Son, cooking is an everyday thing
not a Sunday work alone.

Open the windows, son.
I am too used to the sounds of living things;
Of birds in the morning
of rain and wind at night,
Not the drone of furnace fan
and hiss of hot blasts
and whoosh whoosh of washing machine.

Open the windows, son,
And let me go back to sun and air,
even sweat and flies and all,
But not this, not this.

5

Eightnineten years ago we'd walk from Stradbrook,
Father and I, to see the floes float by
and watch the migrant gulls far above
the stronger lead the way, he'd say,

explaining the U. And in the winter
He'd walk on water, my father.

Now the Red flows by our backyard
And Father, two weekends early May
and late August, trails the Evinrude III
to the cottage so it can be all summer
at the dock to others' envy.

6

Chorus:

We are new Canadians
Come from faraway places,
The Alps and the Andes
Essequibo and the Ganges,
Our memories, our faces
Chiselled by ancient cultures
hose course had been half run
Long ere Cartier's had begun.

We are New Canadians
Come from many races,
Black, white, olive, brown,
All alike, for all the many places
High-tech, mid-tech or no-tech
Are one.

We are New Canadians
Same as the old, we grew
Ten moons in our mother's womb,
Learnt to love, play and pray
On parents' knees.
Tasted youth's sadsweet greenness
And love's silver dreams.

Canada's field are sown with gold,
Some said, and so it is.
It will not be easy, some said,
And it has not, as we well know
Who have worked hard, or worse still
Have no work at all, though willing
And waiting for the break
That would set us on our own.

What we were not told, never guessed,
Is written on our children's faces
Furrowed with tears because of our race
Or colour, or tongue that stumbles
Over words so alien to the many places
From which we've come.
Will doors shut on them as on us?
Landlords', employers', neighbours'?
Have we come from the Niger and Luzon
From the Antilles and Hongkong
To these vast empty spaces
Only to see our young ones' faces
Slapped by unthinking scorn,
Unfeeling barbs
From closed fists and closed hearts?

7

Twenty hours a week, I thought,
was surely something I should give
my people
now that the children
were at school all day.

It was satisfying at first
To drive them back and forth,
Shop for apartment, furniture,
kitchen things, winter clothes;
a wooden stake and stocking bands
to withstand the first winter's winds.

Lovely the clematis
Against our trellised wall.

And then I found people
who needed more
than apartments, winter clothes.

They are with me all the time
twice twenty hours each day
My people.
But there is so little I can do
that anyone can do
alone.

They are with me everywhere.
As I shampoo my Sita's tresses
I see Harjit
pinned to locker floor
by four of his school mates
while the fifth lopped off his hair.

As my Mohan
whacks mosquitoes off his bronzed back
I see the welts on Pritam's
bruised by a drunken father.
Was drink the cause
or the result
of his joblessness?

Hasina, new bride from India
of one who lives common law
with Maria mother of three
two his.

Bihari, driven to suicide
in his basement bachelor suite
of six years.

Lata, caught between love
for her halfwit daughter
secreted away at an Ontario school,
And her husband's steel egotism
that wants no sign of his genetic flaw.

Tara's mother homesick for open windows
encaged until the baby grows up
or Tara quits work.

My heart can hold them everyone
but not my head, which clamours
at the futility of it all.

And nearer home,
Usha's daughter now blind
wasting away like the moon
of an incurable and many-tentacled disease.

8

The green-gold of prairie fields was mine
Till Spring.
And mine the brilliant blue of my mother's lakes.
I delighted in the lady-bug's black wing
And the turquoise hidden in the down of birds.
Bright orange was the factory's spurting flame
And auburn the roof of my brother's barns.
Till Spring.

A sudden thaw broke all resisting banks
And burst the floodway of my sight.

But the murmur of wind amid cedar and pine was mine
In early Spring,
And mine the music of books and rain and splashing cars.
Freely my vision raced across the prairie blue
With meadow larks, sailboats, skateboards skidding through.

Lysol, I.V.s and intercoms,
Pneumatic wheels gliding along narrow halls.
Needles, distant whispers of pain shushed to sleep,
And then my dreams lay in prairie grass.

My eternal summer shall not fade
In the halls of my father's home
Where my fancies shall freely race
Across fields of prairie gold.

Something to Think About

Emily Elizabeth Warne

<u>Something to think about</u>

War is nothing. It contains niether beauty nor hapiness. All it is is a cruel, horrible way of expressing anger. Sometimes the war is for a good reason. For instance: Yeah, sure, I'll Kill 500,000 people brutily because I want their land. Or, Well, they wouldn't trade weapons with us so I'll rape and Kill off their population. What I'm trying to say is war is Stupind. Do you know what will happen if there's a nuclear war? Well, I do. For one thing, we would all get cancer. The instane you stepped out your door, you would see people with there arms and legs lying a few feet away from them, yet they'd still be alive. Think of the adam bomb that was dropped on Hero-shima. It would be much worse than that. If the human race is stupid enough to start a nu-clear war, the living will envy the dead. But Killing isn't the only type of war. There are many others. Some of them are: Rape, pourity, child abuse, Wife abuse, slavery, ra sisem, starvation, crime and many, many others. Why would any one want to beat some one? Anyway? Either ser-ually, Phisicly or mentely? Why? I am a child. I will grow up. children are your future. Yet I <u>still</u> have to make up my own world to play in! And do you know why? Because this world stinks! Who says children should be seen and not heard? Well, I'm a voice, a tiny, tiny voice, but I will grow stronger! There are millions of people in this world who want to stop war! All types of war. War against blacks, war against women, war against children, All war. What is wrong with you people? If we don't stop every single type of war, our race will die out. Think about the holocaust. What right did Hitler have to kill so many people just because of their religion?

Please! Help me stop war. help all of the people in our world. All of the people whos' voices have been drained out. Help their voices grow strong! Help the women who have been raped, help the women who can't walk the streets at night because they might be raped. Help the ~~People~~ who are starving and living in pourity out in the streets. Help the people who are not even free to live their own lives, who are <u>owned</u> by someone, help the children who have been bout. They say in the commercials, "Fight in the **war**, do it for your country." Well, fight against war, do it for your race! Join your voice with mine! Help stop war! do it so your children can grow up in peace! Please, I'm begging you, stop war!

- Emily Elizabeth Warne,
Age 9

14 femmes sont mortes, Joss Maclennan

Swimming Upstream:
Reflections of a Feminist at 66

Helen Levine

Dear Joan:

You will know that writing seems almost impossible for me these days. It feels like swimming upstream against tough currents moving in opposite directions.

You phone once more, telling me your new anthology is in the hands of the publisher. You say there is a bit more time for me. You quietly encourage and make a few suggestions. The message is that you would welcome a short, modest piece, that writing a few words is, after all, not brain surgery. Thank you for believing in me, for reminding me that I might just be able to write again.

My random reflections wander in different directions. Thoughts don't follow in predictable sequence. No footnotes, no detailed references – only the noting of sources. No computer – just pen and paper. I did not retire from academia for naught. Yet I think there are threads and connections in these reflections that, in some strange way, help weave personal, political, private and public together.

I have warm memories of reading *Sisterhood is Powerful*, by Robin Morgan, in 1970. It was one of the first feminist anthologies I encountered. It did not follow the rules. It was informal, personal, provocative, readable, jumbled, unapologetic, disorganized and inspiring. Women were using the forbidden "I" as they told their stories, explored ideas, experiences and possibilities. That book gave me permission to imagine reading and writing in new ways, much as you have given me permission 20 years later. It was probably where I first began to develop the cardinal principle of always, in some way, including the personal in my writing and my politics. *Sisterhood is Powerful* defied pompous, conventional, masculine norms of writing and thinking. It burst forth with woman-centred prose that spoke to me and my reality in ways I never before had seen or heard. Strange, recalling this book. It was no literary masterpiece, no classic. But it gave me, and I suspect many other awakening women, permission. It broke a kind of log jam, it allowed new possibilities.

I think of Aritha van Herk's short story "Planning a Future," recently published in *Canadian Forum*. It resonates, in a very different way, with some of the elements I found years ago in *Sisterhood is Powerful*. The tale is of the complexity of one woman's hopes and plans, memories and fears, of the interconnections between inner and outer worlds. Van Herk writes:

"He left me because I was smarter than he was," she says aloud to the crashing breakers. "He couldn't handle it.". . . She looks at the green, green, ocean, its eternal pull. "Well, at least he didn't kill me," she thinks, and then, recklessly, shouts it into the liquid plow of sound. "AT LEAST HE DIDN'T KILL ME."

The Montreal massacre has taken its toll of many more than 14 women. The male terrorism it represents stalks all of our lives. It is a nightmare that too many women live. It is a nightmare that most of us fear. Not generally deemed "political," such violence against women and feminists is translated over and over again into pathology, into the bizarre and sick behaviour of one individual man. Thus is such terrorism depoliticized and reality turned on its head.

Mary Daly taught me the importance of "naming" many years ago. It sounded so easy. It proved to be so difficult. I thought of Daly when I saw the poster dedicated to the Montreal victims in particular, and to the victims of domestic violence in general. I felt the sorrow and consciousness that spoke from this poster. I was grateful that a woman artist thought to commemorate the unspeakable, to highlight the context.

And yet the poster says that 14 women "died" in Montreal, that 97 women in 1988 "died in domestic violence" in Canada. In my heart of hearts, I know "those women were killed, murdered, and in the case of the 97, likely battered, raped, tortured over time." By men. Yes, Mary Daly reminds me, we must name the actors, the agents of these barbaric acts, of this continuum of violence against women that has reached epidemic proportions.

How did Marc Lepine learn his hatred of feminists, learn to assume he had rights and privileges that women do not? Were Lepine's assumptions and behaviours exceptional? Pauline Bart warns us that violence against women is unexceptional, ordinary, and predictable in a woman-hating society. I wonder about the poisoned, dangerous environment in which we women play out our lives. Why do we not name this form of pollution?

My heartfelt gratitude goes out to some Canadian feminists who helped us grasp the underlying questions spawned by the Montreal massacre. In the February 1990 edition of *Canadian Forum*, Joan Baril of Thunder Bay wrote: "One also sees the constant attempt to differentiate between women and feminists. According to definition, feminists are extremists while women are not extremists because 'they don't make an issue of things' (that is, they remain silent)." Stevie Cameron wrote, in the *Globe and Mail* on December 9, 1990: "That we lost them has broken our hearts; what is worse is that we are not surprised." Lee Lakeman wrote, in *This Magazine* in March 1990: "These murders are not just expressions of the same misogyny women experience every day; they are the product of a vicious new strain aimed at women who fight for women's rights – at feminists." In the December 8, 1989, *Toronto Star*, Michelle Landsberg wrote a column entitled "Killer's Rage All Too Familiar," in which she said: "In your town and mine. . . violent women hating is a daily truth."

Earlier, in *Women and Children First*, Michelle Landsberg helped redefine reality with her wisdom about the centuries old affirmative action program set in place for men. I understand that men own power and privilege, not by virtue of competence or genius, but by excluding most women from significant places in the public sphere. Patriarchy has thus ensured that half the world – women – generally remain on the margins, at the service of men and children and those in need. Violence and the threat of violence helps keep us "in our place."

In the hierarchy of crime and punishment, terrorism against girls and women really does not rate. It is disheartening, to say the least, to monitor the minor sentences – if any – doled out by the "criminal justice" system. Embedded herein is a political view of families as private institutions where men's crimes – battering, incest, rape – are deemed less heinous than elsewhere. Here is one of countless examples:

A Val-des-Monts man sentenced to two years in jail for incest tried to shift the blame to his victims. His daughters told police they were sexually abused almost daily for five years, since they were eight and nine years old.
The attacks left the girls with nightmares, hallucinations and feelings of fear, guilt and responsibility; . . . they are now afraid of adults. The assaults were discovered after a complaint from a 13-year-old neighbour who was assaulted after watching pornographic videos with the man in his bedroom.
When the man found out he was under investigation, he beat one of his daughters and threatened to shoot both children and his wife if he were jailed" (*Ottawa Citizen*, April 10, 1990).

Two years in jail! One more in a series of male judges minimizing the secret brutality and torture inflicted upon girls and women held hostage in their own homes. As a society we condone these horrors even as we pretend to care. Mental hospitals are crammed with women, large numbers of whom were raped and/or battered repeatedly in childhood by fathers, grandfathers, uncles and brothers.

Recent events in eastern Europe are momentous. A system that held much promise but kept its people silenced whilst men grew corrupt with power is breaking down and breaking up. Now we hear of the pro-democracy movement bringing fresh winds of freedom. And I ask, "Where are the women?" Interesting how the word "democracy" seems to apply almost exclusively to one sex – still. I think about Dale Spender's *Women's Ideas and What Men Have Done with Them*, of how women's work and contributions and genius have been rendered invisible throughout recorded history.

Listening to "The Gorbachev Era" by Gwyn Dyer on CBC's "Sunday Morning," I notice that in this one hour glimpse of developments in the Soviet Union, Hungary, Poland, Czechoslovakia and other Eastern European countries, there is no mention of women. All the speakers and interviewees, with one exception, are men. The key words – "freedom," "liberty," "dissent," "democracy" – are there, but women are clearly absent at the centre. Their absence appears not even worthy of comment. Yes, I do know the president of Lithuania is a woman, but one position is really not the point.

Whether it be communism, capitalism or social-change movements, what does it matter if mainly men remain in charge? What is freedom or democracy, without us? Of what significance is revolution without women as a collectivity sharing the helm and contributing our immeasurable talents?

Closer to home, I pick up a memo at the Carleton University School of Social Work, a school that has struggled courageously and continuously with feminist issues. The memo dealt with a suggested list of current social and political questions that deserve attention. It reflected the input of a few faculty members. What struck me was that *women* and *feminism* were nowhere on the list. It was years ago that we began unmasking such general categories as poverty, work, family, age, health and violence in order to render visible the specific oppression of women. My fear is that the general categories, male-defined, are gradually beginning to reassert their primacy. Adrienne Rich wrote in 1981:

There is an enormous pressure, a pressure I think on everybody, but certainly specifically on feminists, to yet once again shelve feminist issues or what are seen as "merely" women's issues rather than . . . human issues and save the planet from nuclear holocaust.

It is clearly critical for us to continue to confront the tough personal and political challenges embedded in the struggle for women's liberation. Yet I also want so desperately for feminists to see ourselves in historical context – to celebrate how far we have come and how much we have done. Lately, I end workshops with a few songs, easy ones, where women quickly join in. Enjoying a bit of music, a bit of fun, is another way of being together, making our voices heard, touching one another in some realm beyond the obvious. It's a way of celebrating our solidarity, of grasping how wonderful we can be. We often join hands, and that joining sometimes sparks tears and hopes and smiles in women's eyes and hearts.

I dread the possibility of fatal divisions among us, tearing us and the autonomous women's movement apart. I want us to hang together, not separately. We need one another if we are to survive. Yet risk-taking is a must, and the cutting edge of gender, race and class squarely confronts our theory and practice as feminists, as human beings.

Recently I attended a conference on race and gender in New York. The conference was a living mix of women of colour, of varied ethnicity, of white women. A rare experience, a tough, uncompromising look at racism, a wealth of woman power and talent and presence, an unflinching exploration of theory and practice. No ponderous, obscure, mystifying papers designed to impress. Plain words, honest appraisals, clear differences, practical strategies.

I recall lunch most vividly: six women, three black and three white. We gradually begin to talk, sharing bits and pieces of our stories, connecting, learning politics and life in the remarkable way that feminists have evolved. We came together in New York in all our diversity and all our contradictions, tensions and different worlds. Momentarily, we find common and not-so-common ground. A young black woman lets us know that pro-choice for her and many other women means the freedom to have children as well as to abort. She talks quietly and pointedly of how women of colour are frequent victims of medical sterilization at an early age. She describes her own experience of a uterine fibroid and subsequent hysterectomy to illustrate. Another black women tells a similar story plus the demeaning requirement that she get her husband's permission. One of the white women shares her painful experience of male medical abuse linked to hysterectomy and additional surgery designed to tighten her vagina to preserve her husband's sexual pleasure. The facts are not new to me. The sharing brings a new level of understanding via the lived experience of the women at a conference lunch table. We listen to and learn from one another.

No special ending to this episode. Just a sense that this small group of women could break the silence and find the wisdom to explore real life together for a moment in time. A very political and very personal moment, made possible by a feminist context rife with struggle and difference and paradox. In some not-so-mysterious way, we were plumbing the depths of our connections, the fundamental and yet differing ways in which our bodies and our minds and our lives are interwoven.

I often wonder about my own stubborn refusal to displace gender and patriarchy as the core of my politics. What about the critical questions of race and anti-Semitism, sexual orientation, peace, poverty, age, pollution? Do I comprehend how intricately all these socio-political questions are interwoven and interconnected with gender and human survival?

The world does not transform in one fell swoop. Change – individual or social – does not emerge as some overall totality. Yet women – half the world – both cross-cut and constitute half the population or constituency of almost every other oppressed or vulnerable group. Within every race, economy, culture, religion, hierarchy, women have been rendered subordinate to men and kept consistently at their service. Thus, it seems so apt that when we attempt social change in any vital arena, we do so via women, via gender, via the largest oppressed constituency.

Repeatedly there emerges among women and men a sense of urgency focused on critical social and political issues of the day. Individuals, organizations, social change movements come together in a valiant attempt to mount serious opposition to disturbing societal trends and developments. My question is: What happens to women, to feminism, to autonomous women's movements and groups midst such moments in history? Dale Spender, Sheila Rowbotham and other feminist writers have reminded us of the ever-present danger that the changes wrought by the contemporary women's movement will go the way of feminist accomplishments in other eras. Our work and our achievements, our courage and our struggles, could be forgotten, rendered invisible, unknown to future generations. That has been our fate for centuries. Historically, we have been forced to collude in yielding the primacy of our own issues and oppression to priorities selected by a male-defined society. Will we learn at this juncture in history to remain woman-centred and woman-defined?

I often wonder whether we're still trying terribly hard to be "good girls" in men's eyes. Are most women – feminists and non-feminists alike – still fearful, consciously and/or unconsciously, of provoking men's anger and disapproval when we diverge seriously from their political territory? Certainly, heterosexual women like myself are frequently reminded by the men in our lives that we are vitally needed to work with the brothers on many other fronts. Unless and until we are on-side with men, we certainly are in danger of being viewed as reactionary, man-hating, unworthy, unlovable. With guilt and self-doubt sewn into the very fabric of our colonized minds, women worry endlessly about "not doing right" by others. We worry about being deemed undesirable by men and the culture they own and control. The critical question is: Who decides what "doing right" is, from the standpoint of whose experience, values and interests? Women? Men? And who gets to define political logic? Adrienne Rich reminds us that logic is a term men use to describe their own subjectivity.

In the late 1960s, North American women exploded into feminist action on our own behalf. We formed new women-only groups, organizations, collectives, feminist services. We kept the men out, knowing how paralyzing it would be to have to continue deferring to them. There was a turning away from men's priorities and politics, a turning towards women that forged an outpouring of female talent, energy and drive. We were amazed at our own growing strengths, individually and collectively. We felt like an unstoppable force committed to the liberation of all women. We stopped apologizing for spending time and energy among women. We revelled in it, and midst all the inevitable contradictions and disappointments, began to understand the potential of a woman-centred perspective and context. Politics was being redefined, concepts of knowledge and truth were being revised, ways of seeing ourselves and others and the world were being transformed. At some basic level we grasped the centrality of feminism and of women, for ourselves, our children – and yes, for men.

Recently, midst one of our endless fencing duels, my husband said he prefers that women and men all work together for "good causes." It's fine, he opined, for women to maintain their own autonomous groups so long as they form active coalitions with other good people and organizations at the same time. I could not quite believe that he was making such fatherhood statements in 1990. Could he be unaware of all the continuing oppression, the overwork and endless strains most women live with on a daily basis? In addition, feminists try valiantly to keep the women's movement and its offshoots alive and breathing, even existing. Does he know how many of us are stretched about as far as we can go and still survive?

I know coalitions and alliances are politically invaluable at certain junctures. But it is critical to not forget why so many women left progressive movements in the late 1960s to build a women's liberation movement. We had tried for years to be in solidarity with men, to work shoulder-to-shoulder (not foot-on-back) for good causes. We wanted desperately to like and to love men, to have them in our lives and in our politics, as equals, as partners. It did not happen. It is not happening. The patterns of male dominance still permeate our personal, political and occupational lives.

Did the men learn very much from our exodus in the late 1960s? Did they, together with one another, study and explore our politics, our ideas, our pain, our suffering, our history, our courage, our strengths? Did they individually and/or collectively engage in serious self-criticism, personally and politically? Did they seriously listen to and learn from the women? Twenty or more years later, with a handful of fine exceptions, I would say they did not. Most men refused the rich opportunity to transform their political theory and practice to be centrally inclusive and respectful of women, to redefine the very meaning of politics, knowledge, justice and oppression. In the face of escalating male terrorism against women, uncovered and made visible by the contemporary women's movement, most found neither the political courage nor the humility to tackle the power and privilege and violence of men, their own and their brothers.

Yes, some men said their *mea culpas* and did housework and child care. Yes, some women, often on men's terms, moved into the men's "clubs" – governments, universities, the trade unions, industry, the professions. But not much has changed for masses of women. Men have indulged in the mild reformism they label co-optation in their own spheres of influence.

My central theme at age 66 is "daring to keep women at the centre." Unless and until the question of women's oppression is ongoingly recognized and dealt with, nothing will fundamentally shift for women, children or men. We cannot leave men in a position to dominate and violate half the world's population and at the same time naively hope that these same men will take the courageous new directions required to dismantle patriarchy, racism and other forms of violence. There can be no global peace, no democracy, or justice for oppressed groups without this central component of social change.

It is by placing gender at the core – with women and men as subjects, as equals, as decision-makers – in both public and private spheres, that we can truly begin to address other massive social and political agendas that connect with human survival and human well-being. It is sobering to remind ourselves that "women constitute half the world's population, perform nearly two-thirds of its work hours, receive one-tenth of the world's income and own less than one-hundredth of the world's property" (1980 United Nations Report).

In sisterhood,
Helen

Olympic Ovulation Blues

Dorothy O'Connell

Our womens' teams are on the Pill –
Each day, while practising their drill
One will with water firmly swill
In order to forego a thrill
Which might Olympian hopes kill.

But now, they cry with voices shrill,
Authorities have said they will
Alter their medication 'till
No trace of steroids do they spill
When sample bottles they do fill.

It well may tamper with their skill,
Reduce their chances next to nil,
Make womens' sports again a frill,
Or, possibly, their ova grill
So reproductive systems still;

Or babes appear with fin and gill,
Fur, feather, scale and even quill;
And bark, or yap, or quack, or trill;
Their bodies forced to pay the bill
Conceits of umpires to fulfill.

Oh, would we could those bozos chill,
And douse them all with oil of squill,
Or tie them stoutly to a thill
And let the cart roll down the hill
Through valley, lake and little rill

Careen breathtakingly, until
They treat Jack equally with Jill
Or promise ne'er to cross the sill
Of that aristocratic mill
Which dares to make our athletes ill.

Of Desperation Born:
The Struggle for Children at Any Cost

Margrit Eichler

Until quite recently, infertility was a condition that some people suffered, and with no other alternative available to them, had accepted. Today, these same people are not likely to accept their condition as something that is unalterable, but to try a large array of new reproductive technologies. They will try to produce their own children – with the help of doctors, nurses, sometimes lawyers, surrogacy agencies in the United States, sperm banks, perhaps also egg banks and embryo banks.

For a few people, the often heroic efforts result in the child or children that are desired. For many others – how many, no one knows – similarly heroic efforts result in incredible time, emotional and financial expenditures, and uncertain health risks, with no child at the end that allows them to say, "It was all worth it."

Together, the new reproductive technologies have revolutionized how we, as a society, reproduce ourselves biologically. We are just beginning to realize the impact on women, individually and collectively, and to be justifiably concerned.

In this paper, I briefly consider some of the current new reproductive technologies, look at some of the effects that already exist, and identify some of the problems that have already emerged.

New Reproductive Technologies – NRTs for short – is a summary label for a complex of both new and old techniques and social arrangements to produce children. In other words, not all NRTs are new, nor are they all technologies. Nevertheless, the term serves as a convenient label to designate a complex or syndrome that in its totality is not only highly technical but also revolutionary in its impact. The various techniques and arrangements include: artificial insemination, in vitro fertilization (IVF), embryo transfers, sex preselection, preconception contracts for the production of children and prenatal diagnostic techniques, and many others.

These techniques are themselves based on other new developments, such as drugs to superovulate women, and freezing of sperm, ova and embryos. The technologies can be used in sequence or together.

ARTIFICIAL INSEMINATION

Artificial insemination is the oldest of the reproductive techniques. It involves the insemination of a woman by means other than sexual intercourse. It can be (and usually is) performed by medical personnel, but a woman may self-inseminate herself very simply, and that, too, is being done.

In spite of its simplicity, artificial insemination has an instructive history. The first recorded instance occurred in 1884 – over 100 years ago – when a Philadelphia physician inseminated an anesthetized woman with the sperm of the "best looking member of the class" of medical students. When the woman became pregnant, her husband was informed of the insemination by the physician, and he, fortunately for the physician, was pleased. His wife was never informed. The incident was not reported until 1909, when Addison David Hard, presumably the "best looking member of the class," wrote an article for *Medical World*, publicizing the event and triggering a debate about the ethics of the incidence.[1]

Some issues that arise with even such a simple technique as artificial insemination include:

– Who should select the donor? What are appropriate characteristics to look for in a donor?

– Should donors be paid?

– Should there be a central registry of donors? If not, how can one be sure that a man does not donate too frequently? One recent Toronto study by Rona Achilles found a man who stated that he had donated sperm approximately 240 times![2]

– Should donors be kept anonymous? What if the child develops a genetically transmitted illness where knowledge of the genetic forebears is crucial for treatment? How can a donor be traced if no records are kept?

– Does a child have the right to know her or his genetic parents? Is it ethical to set up a situation deliberately in such a manner that a child will never be able to identify her or his biological father?

IN VITRO FERTILIZATION

In vitro fertilization involves the removal of one or more eggs from a woman, usually after she has been induced to superovulate, and the fertilization of the egg(s) in a petri dish with sperm obtained by masturbation. Once one or more embryos are formed, they are implanted in the womb.

In vitro fertilization presents quite a different set of issues from those of artificial insemination. The procedure is extremely lengthy, painful, expensive in every sense of the word (financially, emotionally and physically), and highly likely to be unsuccessful. About 90 percent of the women who undergo the procedure eventually walk away without a child.[3]

There are many different stages in in vitro fertilization, each with its own set of stresses and problems. Linda Williams interviewed 20 IVF couples and documented some of these stresses.[4] Here is how Frances, one of Williams's respondents, describes her experience with ultrasound:

You have to have a full bladder through the whole thing, for the ultrasound to work. That's very, very uncomfortable, too. You're supposed to drink four glasses of water before you leave the house. I'd leave at 6:00 to be there at 7:30 [a.m.]. The first few times I'd drink four glasses of water here and by the time I got off the train at Union Station, I'm just about dead. And then you get there and they've got to do your blood and then you wait around and the . . . doctor comes waltzing in about 8:30 and there are 15 of you sitting there with your legs crossed. Like it's awful. . . . I still have problems with my bladder right now and I swear it's because it was stretched to oblivion going through that. There has to be a better way, I think.

Debra reports on the side effects of some of the drugs she was taking:

I had unbelievable, unbelievable headaches. Like nothing I'd ever, ever had in my life. I could not work. I could barely keep my head up.

One of the husbands tells of the effects of the drugs on his wife:

Amy literally becomes someone else. There are radical personality changes. There are tears regarding the contents of the mailbox, for heaven's sake. It just becomes outrageous.

EMBRYO TRANSFER

Embryo transfer designates a method of inserting an embryo into a woman's womb. This may be an embryo formed through IVF or flushed from a woman's womb before implantation. The woman who receives it might be the same woman whose egg is used for IVF, or it might be another woman who is not genetically related to the embryo.

Embryo transfer is an aspect of in vitro fertilization. It is important to realize that, technically, it makes no difference whether the embryo is implanted into the woman from whom the eggs were originally removed or into some other woman. As a consequence we now have women who have given birth to children to whom they are not genetically related, or to whom they are related in a previously impossible manner, such as in the case of the South African woman who gave birth to her own grandchildren. These children are the uterine siblings of their genetic mother, and the uterine siblings-in-law of their genetic father. Another consequence of this technique is that some women are genetic mothers but not uterine mothers.

SEX PRESELECTION

Sex preselection involves the determination of the sex of an embryo before implantation, or refers to a method of separating sperm into male and female sperm before artificial insemination.

Sex preselection may be a sub-aspect of one of the other techniques, such as IVF, or it may be done independently. Since IVF involves the creation, screening and implantation of embryos, the doctor who implants the embryos will always know whether they are female or male. The doctor, therefore, has to make a decision whether to implant the embryos of both sexes (if they are of both sexes) or of only one sex. Should the parent(s) have a right to choose the sex of the embryos?

Another form of sex preselection takes place when sperm are separated into male and female sperm, and the woman is impregnated with sperm of a particular sex. There is a profit-oriented sex selection clinic currently operating in Toronto. This clinic is based on a franchise system. The doctor buys the United States franchise, which involves the right to use the Erickson technique, treats the sperm, and artificially inseminates the woman.

PRECONCEPTION CONTRACTS FOR THE PRODUCTION OF CHILDREN

Preconception contracts for the production of children are commonly referred to as surrogate motherhood contracts. This is a misleading term, since the woman who gives birth is not a surrogate mother, but simply a mother. Preconception contracts come in a variety of forms, but they always involve a formal or informal contract between a woman and a second party – usually a man, sometimes a couple, possibly another woman – to produce a child for the sole purpose of handing it over to the second party. As stated, such contracts may be formal and involve lawyers, or they may be informal. They may involve money or not. They may be an arrangement between strangers who remain anonymous to each other or strangers who meet for the purpose of arranging a deal. It may even be an arrangement between friends or relatives.

I recently completed a study for the Law Reform Commission of Canada, looking at the incidence of these contracts. We found over 100 well-substantiated cases involving Canadians.[5] Forty-two of them involved the use of a United States agency. One of these agencies – Noel Keane's – allowed us access to the data about the Canadian cases in his files. Several interesting facts emerged from this analysis. When one hears about a preconception contract for the production of children, one tends to assume that there is one contractual mother for each social couple. However, the records reveal that often more than one woman serves as a contractual mother for the same couple, and in one instance, six women served as contractual mothers. Sometimes the artificial insemination is not successful, and the couple may sign a new contract with another woman. Sometimes a pregnancy ends in a miscarriage.

We also found that half the couples for whom this information existed and who contracted for a child already had at least one child who was the biological child of one of the marital partners, or was adopted; or, in one case, was the biological child of both the marital partners. With one exception, all of the other contractual mothers had at least one child before contracting to bear a child within a commercial contract. One wonders what the effect is on the children who see their half-sibling sold to another couple. And what is the effect on the social couple's other children when they acquire a half-sibling in this manner?

PRENATAL DIAGNOSTIC TECHNIQUES

Some of these techniques are new and some are well-established. Amniocentesis, chorionic villi sampling and other methods are part of this complex of techniques, as is ultrasound monitoring of the fetus. These techniques may be employed in *any* pregnancy – whether there is a fertility problem or not. Counter to other techniques so far discussed, prenatal diagnostic techniques potentially involve every pregnant woman. These techniques have generated a tendency among medical personnel to treat the fetus and the pregnant woman not as one patient, but as two patients. The interests of the woman and the fetus are thus seen as being potentially opposed. Now we confront questions such as:

– Who has the right to speak for the fetus? The woman or the doctor?

– Can the doctor prescribe treatment for the fetus that may be harmful to the woman?

– Does the woman have the right to refuse treatment for the fetus that is not beneficial to her?

– If the woman refused treatment, can she be charged? This has, in fact, happened in the United States. In Canada, there were two cases recently, one in Ontario and one in British Columbia, in which a fetus was declared a child in need of protection and apprehended. How do you apprehend a fetus without apprehending the woman who carries the fetus?

All the techniques mentioned so far already exist; they are not just in the process of being developed. Some effects are already visible; others will undoubtedly become apparent in the near future. One effect of the new reproductive technologies that is already apparent is that motherhood has been irrevocably re-defined.[6] There have always been three types of fathers: (1) a social and biological father (the traditional father); (2) a social but *not* biological father (a stepfather or adoptive father); (3) a biological but *not* social father (a natural father who is not involved in raising his child). Until recently there were also three types of mothers, which corresponded to the three types of fathers. With the advent of the new technologies, being a mother has been subdivided into seven, rather than three, types: (1) a uterine, genetic and social mother (traditional mother); (2) a social but neither uterine nor genetic mother (adoptive mother, stepmother); (3) a uterine and genetic but not social mother (birth mother who has given up her child or whose child has been taken from her, surrogate mothers; (4) a genetic but not uterine nor social mother (egg donor)[7]; (5) a uterine and social but not genetic mother (recipient of a donated fertilized egg); (6) a uterine but not genetic and social mother (embryo carrier); (7) a genetic and social but not uterine mother (user of an embryo carrier).

While the first three types of mothers have always existed, the fourth, fifth, sixth and seventh types of mothers represent new forms of motherhood that previously were not possible. The egg donor is in an equivalent situation to the sperm donor, except for the fact that egg donation and sperm donation are in no way comparable. Sperm donation is a simple, quick, painless and non-hazardous matter, while egg donation is neither simple, nor quick, nor painless, nor non-hazardous for the woman involved.

The phenomenon of a uterine and social but non-genetic mother already exists. That is, we now have instances in which a woman has given birth to a child to whom she is genetically unrelated. This was previously not possible.

Types six and seven represent two aspects of only one relationship.

Technically, there is no difference between types five and six – both involve gestating a donated fertilized egg. The only difference is that in type five the woman carries the child for herself, and in type six she carries it on behalf of somebody else, in a contractual arrangement.

Overall, then, some very dramatic changes have taken place in what constitutes motherhood: First, we must now cope with the separation of gestational and genetic motherhood – an issue that simply did not exist a few years ago, since it was technically impossible for women to be genetic mothers without being gestational mothers and vice versa.

Second, children are increasingly the products of highly sophisticated techniques. No longer is childbearing primarily an activity that results from sexual intercourse between a man and a woman and in which the woman becomes pregnant and gives birth. It has, to an astonishing degree, moved into the public domain. This means that it must be regulated by rules (for example about who can be a sperm donor or an egg donor). Possibilities of human error enter where none were possible before. If you remove, label, store and freeze sperm, eggs and embryos, the possibility of mislabelling, for instance, exists. It must, therefore, be guarded against.

Third, we are moving into an area where at least a part of childbearing has become commercialized, and in which the child itself has become a commodity to be bought and sold. This is the case in commercial preconception contracts for the production of children. The commercial tendency is also present in the sex preselection clinic, which operates on a franchise basis. Consider the implications: Medical students will not be taught the technique, since its learning must be purchased. New (non-human) life forms have been patented. Will we also patent cures for humans? Or even "improved" forms of humans themselves? Eggs, sperm and embryos are available for purchase on the market. Human childbearing thus turns into a production process, where quality of the product (the child), and the logic of production processes become a part of how we reproduce ourselves.

Fourth, we have already encountered judicial interference in the process of child production, and we can expect more of it. When the fetus is defined as a patient in its own right, the woman loses her autonomy, since the fetus is in her, not separate from her. We are confronted here with a potentially adversarial situation, where a woman may not have the right to decide what is best for her pregnant body.

Fifth, with all these new technologies, we find that it is harder and harder for a person or a couple to accept their infertility. Rather than dealing with a very painful issue and getting on with their lives, people may be on a psychological treadmill. As long as there is yet another technique that can be tried they may explore that avenue as well. What happens to them if all of these efforts are unsuccessful? In the media, we learn about only the few successful cases, not the many unsuccessful ones.

Sixth, heroic interventions are becoming accepted as "normal." A recent case, which was heard in Toronto in the fall of 1988, involved a Jamaican woman who was sterilized by her doctor without her written consent. The issue at stake was: Had she or had she not consented to the tubal ligation before it was performed? If she was found to be sterilized against her wishes, she would be able to claim damages. How highly do we value the capacity to give birth? The defence counsel asked her if she had explored the possibility of either reversing the tubal ligation or of in vitro fertilization. She "admitted" that she had not done so. Presumably this will count as evidence that she is not serious about wishing to have more children.

Seventh, social problems are often misrepresented as medical problems. This is a common feature of the relevant literature. For instance, certain techniques are often reserved for people who have a "medical need" for them. However, what constitutes medical need? If a man is infertile because of a previous vasectomy or a woman because of a previous tubal ligation, they are sterile all right, but the sterility is usually the result of a voluntarily chosen operation, based on a lifestyle decision. Is this strictly a medical problem? Or is it a social problem?

Even more obviously, when artificial insemination is performed, it is the healthy, fertile woman (who does not need any treatment to be fertile) who is treated, while the sterile man is not treated at all. The medical profession is therefore responding to a social need, not to a medical problem! The same applies in preconception contracts for the production of children. If the contracting father had intercourse with the contracting mother, the result would be the same as in the case of artificial insemination. In the case of sex preselection, with the exception of cases in which the parents preselect the sex because they are carriers of a sex-related genetic illness, they simply have a preference for a child of a particular sex. Is this a medical or a social problem?

To conclude, there are many problems associated with the new reproductive technologies, which raise a host of questions including the following:

– What are the reasons for infertility that induce a person or couple to seek out any of these techniques? Is it due to previous medical intervention? Voluntarily chosen or not? Is it due to preventable environmental factors? One of my nightmares involves a scenario, by no means far-fetched, in which factories that deal with hazardous substances will require their employees to deposit sperm or eggs in a bank before being permitted to work there. Rather than removing the hazard through appropriate safety procedures, firms might argue that they took appropriate precautions to safeguard the reproductive capacity of their employees by storing sperm and eggs.

– What are the socio-economic characteristics of the clients of these techniques? Are they the rich, the poor, white, or visible minorities? How many of them already have children when they seek out the new reproductive technologies?

– Who should pay for the use of these highly expensive techniques? The individual? This would mean that the rich can buy their children, the poor cannot. The public? This may mean that other social programs, even those that could prevent some of the infertility, may not get funded.

– We need to follow up on the people who have been involved in these techniques and arrangements to judge the long-term consequences for them. Chlomid, the drug that is commonly used in Canada to superovulate the women, is structurally similar to diethylstilbestrol (DES). A systematic long-term compulsory follow up of all women and children who have been exposed to this drug is indicated. Also, what are the effects of preconception contracts for the production of children on all participants? On the children who were bought? On the half-siblings (other children of the contractual mother) who saw their brother or sister sold? On the contractual mother's husband and parents (grandparents to the child that was given away)? On the contractual mothers who did not give birth? What are the effects on the women and their husbands who went through the excruciating experience of IVF and walked away *without* a child, which is what happens to the vast majority of them? What happens to the children of couples who selected their sex but received a baby of the "wrong" sex?

– We need to scrutinize whether the clients of these techniques are informed that they are, in fact, taking part in a large-scale human experiment.

– We need to examine critically the effects on women if the pregnant woman is seen as a potential adversary to the fetus she is carrying. If doctors can prescribe treatment with legal consequences for women if they fail to follow orders, what does this mean for the individual autonomy of the woman? What if the doctor is wrong? What if the choice is such that the woman will prefer to chance a miscarriage over following a prescribed regime – for example, if the doctor prescribes bed rest to a woman with other children who are dependent on her income?

– Are we dealing with medical responses to medical problems, or is medicine being used to address social problems?

– Should we really proceed with further developments, especially any type of human genetic engineering, without a widespread public debate on the issues? (We are already doing it with plants and animals – creating new life forms that are capable of propagating themselves.)

Is it worth having children at *any* cost? What limits should be defined for society and for individual people? Women must be thoroughly involved in the discourse and decision-making about the use of the new reproductive technologies. It is not true that everything that can be done should be done.

The Infertility Journey: Destination Unknown

Linda Trigg

As an infertile woman, I came to some uneasy conclusions about reproductive technology through my six-year journey to have a biological child. Moving full circle, I no longer asked myself, "When will I have a baby?" but "When will the pursuit to have a baby stop?" I eventually abandoned the fertility journey, stopping short of the turn in the road leading to in vitro fertilization (or IVF).

There is no snappy, sure-fire way of alleviating the pain of infertility. The pain is as real as are the feelings of shock, sadness and betrayal by one's own body. Coming to terms with a new self-image and with the fact that you will not be like everyone else is exceedingly difficult.

My journey began in an innocuous manner; well-intentioned medical personnel did their level best to help my partner and I have a child. It all seemed to make sense – the post-coital tests, the blood tests, the semen analysis, the hysterosalpingogram, the laparoscopy, the endometrial biopsy, insufflation, having sex by the calendar, sex by the thermometer and sex by the ovulation-predictor kits. Even after 18 months, the fertility drugs seemed to make sense, until I learned that my blurry vision was not a symptom of impending middle age but a nasty little side effect of clomiphene citrate. At least corrective lenses were not required! I was shocked to learn that "a tumour the size of an orange" growing near my ovary was also a side effect of clomiphene citrate. It took two months before they pronounced it non-cancerous and I was released from agonizing worry.

Ironically, a second opinion, which I had meekly requested, showed that the fertility drugs were irrelevant to my as-yet-undetermined problem. The second opinion brought into focus all my nagging doubts. The investigations were sloppy. We endured much re-scheduling, multiple reviews of my history by unprepared examiners, and repeated tests because results were lost. And there were contradictory results. I am sure that in someone's mind the process was not random, but it seemed that way to me. I began to feel as if I had stepped on a moving sidewalk – destination unknown. Was I to roll with this sidewalk, rapidly running out of control all the way to my menopause? Or, at some point was I going to get off? Perhaps I just gave up, not having the stamina to forbear. But I know that I have an abundance of stamina. Frankly, I gave up because I lost confidence in what was being done to me and in what was likely to result. I know now that reproductive technology is mainly disappointing and has fewer answers than we are led to believe.

Not being able to have a child is tragic, but is it the end of the world? I believe that the new "medical miracles" in reproductive technology are dehumanizing women. I certainly felt dehumanized. Having undergone the process, I wonder: "Am I entitled to have a child?" "Am I less of a woman for not having a child?" "Am I suffering from a disability or an illness?" I have concluded that childlessness is natural and normal for some people.

The feminist positions on the issues surrounding reproductive technology have been well articulated and I have no desire to restate them here. As a woman, and as a consumer of reproductive technology, I have experienced a gamut of emotions – from the agony of infertility to the rage of being considered an incubator from whence the product comes. It is terrifying to think about women as reproductive "handmaidens" whose fate is in the hands of a male-controlled scientific elite. It is indeed sad for a woman not to experience the joy of pregnancy and of giving birth. My sadness will never truly disappear. In spite of that, I am extremely cautious about the scientific approach to infertility. If a new remedy for infertility were offered I would certainly *not* be the first in line to take advantage of it. Nor would I deny other women the right to do so. Each woman should make her own informed decision about her reproductive life.

The Whore

"Candy"

She stands in the shadow peeking out of the door.
Innocence corrupted, a 14-year old whore.
Innocence rejected, purity defiled.
Who will come forward with love for this child?

She's scared and alone, her needs will not wait.
Oh where are the people who all congregate?
And when she seeks God and walks through the door
Will a finger be pointed? Will she be damned as a whore?
Her fear and her pain are all quite real.
Is there no one around with compassion to feel?
She was born in a time that does not understand.
Her parents were nice folk, but no one lent her a hand.

She met a man she felt she could trust.
She started a victim of a gentleman's lust.
This hurt child of innocence, who stands by the door
Is one of God's children, not a 14-year old whore!

The Junkie
"Candy"

You walk like a zombie in a world of your own.
Your eyes are on fire, you're perpetually stoned.
With pills in your pocket, and coke in your nose
You float like an angel. You can suppose.
That it goes on forever, feeling this way,
Light as a feather, your brain floats away.
You try to remember just where you were last
But your brain doesn't function, your mind a blur.
Then come nights spent with someone you don't even know
And your arms scarred with hole marks, they just seemed to grow
You can't even function without your white pills.
They fill you with passion, hatred and chills.
Cocaine, grass and uppers lie stashed away
Just waiting for someone who's willing to pay.
You tell kids it's candy, you make them like you
With a head that is clouded and a nose full of glue.
Then you wake up one morning, in a bed you don't own
With no one beside you, you feel alone.
But this pot you've been smoking has been treating you good
Helping you do things you didn't think you could.
But it isn't the drugs that helped you along,
It's your lack of emotion that's making you strong.
For you see:
These drugs you've been smoking, toking, sniffing
Cannot replace the times you've been missing.
They haven't been helping, or making you strong
Because they've been smoking you all along.

(Signed by an ex-junkie)

Miss Heroin

"Candy"

So now, little woman, you've grown tired of grass,
LSD, Goof balls, Cocaine and Hash.
And someone pretending to be a friend
Said, "I'll introduce you to Miss Heroin."
Well, Honey, before you start fooling around with me
Just let me inform you of how it is.
For I will seduce you and make you my slave.
I've sent much stronger women than you to their graves.
You think you could never become a disgrace
And end up addicted to poppyseed waste
So you'll start taking me into your arms very soon
And once I have entered deep down inside your veins
The crawling will really drive you insane.
You'll need lots of money (as you've been told)
For Darling, I'm more expensive than gold.
You'll swindle your mother just for a buck
You'll turn into something vile and corrupt.
You'll mug and you'll steal for my narcotic charm
And you'll feel contentment when I'm in your arms.
The day that you realize the monster you've grown
You'll solemnly swear to leave me alone.
Then Sweetie just try getting me off your back
The vomit, the cramps, your gut twisting in knots.
The jangling nerves screaming for just one more shot,
The hot chills and cold sweats, the withdrawal pains
Can only be saved by my little white grains.
There's no other way and there's no need to look
For deep down inside you will know you are hooked.
You'll desperately run to the pushers and then
You'll welcome me back into your arms once again!
And you will return (just as I foretold).
You'll give up your morals, your conscience, your heart.
And you will be mine till death us do part.

Your Ending or Mine

Evelyn Lau

in a certain light, with you
bent over so, the sky from behind snarling your hair
the lines on your face slide into position
the in/out dimpling of that nervous muscle
locked between chin and earlobe
depresses beneath my fingertip, sleepy and hollow
the smell of Polo rims the blankets like salt
crusting a margarita
I dream you grow three unhappy faces
and extract wedding rings that swim up
to the leakage of dawn
your eggshell eyelids open, the sun
squints your pupils shrewd and small

once you came up my stairs like a good thing
with a teeth-showing smile
your suit and tie and the slenderness of your legs
contrived to spell safety
the hand that took mine on the threshold
had reassuring knuckles
that was the beginning, you told about wife and teenage children
two hours later your mouth was on my pillow

now you arrive with money and books and on a good day,
drugs
to put me to sleep through supper
launch me clear through til grey evening, the drapes open
upon a parking lot and an alley
the only lights way off beyond touching
after waking I begin the experimental first step
stagger in scarves of dizziness
disrobe the fairy tale into non-fiction

the cruelty of the affair is kaleidoscopic
a turning wheel of coloured sand and broken glass
triangular windows of possibility
hours spent nursing the stomach-dropping illness of love
not knowing what to do with this new thing
except swallow it down where you can't extract it
hold it up twisting in your hands like some premature
ghostly/ghastly baby
slimy with eyes that see too far inward

you remain safe inside the skin of your house and marriage
I turn back the sheets in many hotel rooms
captured by the flat afternoon light
your tongue lashes the inside of my mouth
into the messy bleeding beginning of us
ending

Closing the Curtain

Joan Turner

The wind blows icy cold from Echo Lake, a clean, refreshing cold. I watch a gull as she tries to fly into the blustery wind. She makes no progress; flying forcefully into the face of the wind is impossible. Suddenly, with inspiration, she changes directions, angles across the gusting prairie wind, and flies away with ease. I think of feminism and T'ai Chi philosophy, both having to do with changing directions, with empowerment and the activating of latent energy, or *ch'i*. My reference book, *T'ai Chi Ch'uan*, says: "The proper application and functioning of T'ai Chi depends entirely on the player's consciousness: [it is] the capacity to take advantage of your opponent's defects and to use your superior position: to deflect the momentum of a thousand pounds with a trigger force of four ounces. It is only from the greatest pliability ... that you can attain power and ascendancy." These sayings from the Classics emphasize mental activity rather than the use of external muscular force."[1] T'ai Chi and feminism influence what I do and how I am in the world.

I am conscious of our power to create change without force. It may seem to some, as was recently reported in a uninformed article in *Chatelaine,* that feminism is at an "impasse . . . no longer relevant."[2] Rather, feminism is a powerful contemporary women's movement. The effects of feminism and personal and political change are almost everywhere – in universities, churches, bookstores, in disabled people's movements, in art and film, on the streets and in the community. We have placed the evidence before you in this book. And local feminists have been elected to the Manitoba Legislature, enough of them to take a collective stand on important issues, including violence. With our ideas, our consciousness, our political convictions and our actions, we are making a difference against mainstream strong winds.

As I write this chapter, I am at a retreat structured with personal space and time to watch the gulls, to climb the hills, to read and write. We are a small group of prairie women all interested in feminism and spirituality. We define God as female. When we're together, Godde or Goddess in the feminine is not radical. She is. Mother Earth is. We sing songs like "Standing before Us," which acknowledges the contributions of other women to our lives.[3] Together, we critique a video of the National Film Board film, *Goddess Remembered,* and marvel about the films created by Kathleen Shannon and her colleagues.[4] I am acutely aware how much my world has changed since my childhood summers by this same lake. Tomorrow we will all be back in our own communities, with feminine energy and images strengthened.

The snow has ended and the sun is shining. Saskatchewan, province of my childhood, you really do challenge one's flexibility and survival skills. Before the snow, there was a shroud of grey fog enveloping my childhood playground there below, on the south side of the lake. For a while I could not see more than a few feet in front of me. Sometimes we cannot see, nor can we describe what we are looking at.

As the fog clears, I am aware of the pride and prejudice that were a part of my growing up. It was *best* to come from the town of Cupar, to be of Grandmother Margaret Turner's clan, to spend summers on the south side of the lake. Pride and prejudice – my fog. Now I see where and who I was was not best; it just was, and is. A beginning – like Emma LaRocque, Irene Heaman and a number of other authors in this anthology who share rural prairie roots that have coloured our perception of the world. Each person's herstory is different from the other's. Some authors in this anthology have been influenced by childhoods lived outside Canada – the Caribbean (Rosemary Brown), Europe (Linda Trigg, Jacqueline Barral), or India (Uma Parameswaran). Some, like Jacqueline and Uma, bring other languages into their writing. What a rich and varied tapestry we create as we weave languages and images, and similar and different perspectives, into this book.

I am appreciative of my life and the contributions that all the authors in this book have made to it. I am no longer the little girl who lived on a farm and whose world was nine miles in radius. The circumference of the circle of my world did not include a library or a bookstore of any kind. Now I walk and talk among writers, arrange author readings and book launches, can use my computor, and am beginning to feel, for brief moments at least, like I belong in this exciting world of books (which like all of society is dominated by educated white men.) I am no longer so intimidated, although it doesn't take much for me to feel that old nervousness in the pit of my stomach and to feel like an under-educated impostor struggling with language to express what I feel and "know."

I know now that with "seeing" comes the possibility of "letting go." Letting go of the myths and the ways, even the places, of my youth, letting go of working on this book. Letting go brings me into a process of grieving, which, like many people in similar life situations, I try to stall, tightening my jaw and my shoulders, closing down. Grieving and letting go provoke tears and sadness. I'd rather feel happy, of course, and in time I will. How can one feel entirely happy letting go of a five-year project, this book and my connections with outstanding Canadian women? And yet, how I long for more time to be outdoors, to walk or ride my bicycle, to be free of the burden of this responsibility. Endings. I continue to ponder the meaning and the implications of endings, like death, a part of life. We'll grieve and celebrate. Endings allow for new beginnings, provide opportunities for change and transition.

I am changing internally and externally and am in another transition. My daughters have moved away, my marital status has recently changed to "just married." Erroneously, I learned, in my studies (and used to actually believe), that there was only one major transition, and that it occurred at mid-life and was called menopause for women. While I have no difficulty accepting the reality of menopause (although the hot flushes can be disconcerting), part of me is angry that there is more emotional work, inner processing, reading, writing, crying and "k'vetching" to do. I know this means I am alive, changing and growing. Sometimes I would like to grow up and that be that! All done! But life means growing and changing over and over again, or we go crazy, stagnate or die. I recall a few years ago conversing with my aunt, Ona (who will soon be 100 years old), who said that even at 95 she could not disregard her body's need for movement, for stimulation, for change, or she would stiffen and be in pain. "Didn't seem fair," we agreed. "Should be able to sit still like a rock more than living seems to allow."

For a while critics were saying that the women's movement was still or stagnating. Perhaps that was partly true, but I think we rested and re-grouped and did our personal/political and small-group work, the evidence of which is in this book. Now, the challenges are coming particularly from disabled women, women of colour and Aboriginal women, sometimes from rural women, sometimes from street workers. We are challenged to move over and give them space and recognition, to open our hearts and minds to encompass their realities and to recognize diversity as power and strength. Many different women's stories in this anthology show that there has been movement and change, some of it rather quiet and internal, some of it within small groups or organizations, some of it on more obvious political, even international fronts.

Feminism is making a difference in our lives and in the lives of my daughters, who are both physicians. For that, I am grateful. It seems, alas, to be making very little difference in the lives of my nieces who are growing up in the same rural community that I did, and leaving or preparing to leave, just as I did. There are very few educational or employment opportunities available for young people, particularly for women, in rural and northern Canada. I am concerned that many young women accept the romantic myths that include finding or being found by a young prince or a middle-aged squire who will sweep them away, give them his name, and take care of them forever.

In the rural areas, more women and girls seem to be smoking – it probably is a way to cope with stress, including the stress to be slim, and to dull hard realities – and there is concern about increasing alcohol consumption, particularly among youth. The young men at a recent graduation I attended are choosing computer science and commerce (not one said he wanted a career as a farmer); the women, with one exception (she wants to be a criminal lawyer!) are choosing traditional women's career paths, child care work, for example. "Must all rural youth leave for the big cities?" I ask. The viability of rural Canada seems (once again) to be at risk. I worry that feminism seems to have an urban bias and, as Lilly Walker describes, we have trouble communicating, and appreciating each other.

American feminists seem to wear blinders, which makes it hard for them to hear or see us or our third world sisters. At a conference I attended in the spring of 1989 in Banff, some American therapists treated Canadians like poor country bumpkins who did not know how to do anything right. It was a hard lesson and a painful experience as aggressive university-educated white American feminists dominated and took control, hurling verbal daggers until every Canadian was in tears. The leader of the organization called it an example of American colonialism at its worst. We Canadian women must therefore find our own voice, not rely on U.S. Americans to speak for and about North American women's issues. This anthology is a step in that direction. We claim not a better voice, but a different voice, one that reflects our particular experiences and the context of our lives.

But there are threats to the continuation of the Canadian women's movement. In early 1990, the federal government announced that federal funding for 79 women's centres in Newfoundland, Labrador, Nova Scotia, Quebec, Manitoba, Alberta, British Columbia and the Yukon would be cut 100 percent, while ironically the national defence budget would be increased. Other national women's organizations had their funding reduced 20 percent for the second consecutive year. In the attack against our communications, research and advocacy capacities, three feminist journals – *Canadian Resources for Feminist Research, Healthsharing* and *Canadian Woman Studies* – lost all their operating grants from the Secretary of State Women's Program.[5] Their fate is still uncertain. When women lobbied against the cuts, funding was reinstated to women's centres, but by that time five women's centres, including the Winnipeg organization called Prostitutes and Other Women for Equal Rights (POWER), had closed. Women of POWER were just beginning to make their presence known in this community, to be trusted by young women on the streets, to be considered credible by the police and social agencies, and to speak out at conferences. Will funding cuts silence people working particularly with and on behalf of prostitutes? Hopefully, women like "Candy" and Evelyn Lau, whose poetry is included in this anthology, will have developed the confidence and connections to be able to speak out to a world biased against prostitutes (sex-trade workers).

Sex trade workers are right when they say that feminists have formulated their analyses about pornography and prostitution knowing nothing about the actual lives of sex trade workers. We don't know each other. . . . We have perceived each other's struggles to be different and separate. Sex trade workers, like most women, have been kept silent, but they feel isolated from not only society at large but also from a women's movement that has, they feel, ignored or disassociated itself from women who work as strippers, hookers or porn artists. Indeed, feminists have been accused of not wanting to know and support sex trade workers. Now, sex trade workers are asking feminists to re-evaluate their relationship with sex trade workers, hoping that this will prompt some changes in feminist analyses and strategies regarding pornography and prostitution.[6]

Evelyn Lau, author of *Runaway: Diary of a Street Kid*, is sleeping in our guest room upstairs, the room that was my eldest daughter's. It's a May morning in Winnipeg. I sit in my pleasant but messy back porch feeling reflective. I want to tell Evelyn that it's possible to create your own beautiful space in this sometimes rotten world. It is spring, trees are in bloom. The begonia has flowered a brilliant fuschia. Birds are singing, their collective voice like ringing bells this Sunday morning.

Last night, I felt a kinship between Evelyn and me, enjoying her tender piano playing, talking into the night. When she joins me this morning she asks if I dream, and I say, "Yes, I dream. I believe we all dream. Sometimes I have very significant dreams through which I know and then take action." We talk of nightmares too, recurring nightmares like the ones I had when I was about 5. Night after night, everyone died. From my experience with wartime (two young uncles died, dead), life on a farm (animals died, dead), and the death of my grandmother, I knew dead is dead. And I was sad and brave, and didn't cry. Good girls didn't cry. I wonder about dreams and nightmares, the light and dark of life, about good and bad, about good girls and bad girls.

Evelyn Lau and I are sharing space and time. She's an 18-year-old author, still officially a foster child of the province of British Columbia, whirled around Winnipeg, old before her time, more experienced than I am about the cravings of men for women's flesh. I am angry at a society that supposedly offers young woman a "choice" between the insanity of crazy-making, abusive family life; or, the risks of life on the streets with drugs and violence, prostitution, sleepless, homeless nights. Whether you see *Donut City* in the theatre, or read *Runaway* by Lau, or *Never Let Go*, about Kitty who died at 17, or *Dead End*, about homeless Canadian teens, or study the report by the Social Planning Council of Winnipeg (1990), the picture is distressing.[7]

Ms. X., who prepped Evelyn for a television film while I watched, told us emphatically that she hates the preaching of social workers. It makes her sick, she says. I am silent as she dumps on social workers. Words stick in my throat. Then, I think of how she goes home to her middle-class home and her middle-class friends and pretends she doesn't know about the homeless kids, even the bright ones like Evelyn, who try to live on Winnipeg's cold streets. And sometimes I do that too, I try to pretend. At other times kids like Evelyn touch us at the core, and go home with us at night. But what to do? Can't make much of a difference all on our own can we? Lilly Walker began her paper with a quote by Nellie McClung about comfortable women. Yes, we do like our comfort, and the truth is hard to know.

Dining with Evelyn in Winnipeg, I see the way professional men are attracted to her. She's articulate and can be flattering. She keeps the focus on him: "I like your accent, it's beautiful." She means it. He loves the flattery and moves closer. He's hooked. It happened, all so swiftly. Aware of my age, for the moment feeling old and unattractive, I move away, giving them space, the mother in me saddened by the way the game is played.

She's beginning to wonder whether finding the right man is really the answer. Her mother said it was. The little girl keeps looking and believing, wanting love. We talk about love. What is it really? We exchange personal stories about our "love" experiences. I tell her that what I have now is genuinely, deeply, what I was looking for. I tell her there are some caring, strong and gentle, good men out there. She tells me about the ones that are "fucked up" and, she's right, they are. They have all the right trappings – three-piece business suits, the house, the car, the travel. "He was abused as a child," she says, as if to excuse him – the professional people-helper who fucks young women like Evelyn and young men he finds on the streets, then goes home to be husband and father to his family in the suburbs. Later she writes a poem about him, and she sends it to me. The experience of sexual abuse of girls and boys runs like a black, twisted thread through all this. His life, her life, my life. Will it never stop, never end? And now with AIDS we have even more reason to be concerned, for, as Carol McMillan, former staff person of POWER, said: "Kids are the least likely to protect themselves from AIDS – 10-year-olds (and prostitutes are as young as 10) don't go to walk-in clinics to ask for condoms. And while nobody is absolutely safe on the streets, kids are most likely to meet with violence."[8]

"Street kids say they really want to go home," says a Winnipeg youth worker. Evelyn and I are skeptical. If they could go home, wouldn't they? When you feel you have to go away, you often have to go. Even the street may be better than abuse at home. There you're trapped behind walls of secrecy and pride and pain. Twice in my life I have known that I had to leave home. My situation was rather different from Evelyn's, but I remember the pain and the fear – cold, cold fear. Yet, I had to go. She had to go. One day we'll tell our truths.

Yes, the conversations with Evelyn are gifts to me. I want to understand contemporary runaway kids – street workers – without working the streets. I don't want to be a front-line social worker again. It's too stressful. Thanks, Evelyn. I'm a bit clearer now, and I'm angry.

She's an incredible kid, a woman, trying to make it as a writer. I wish her lots of luck, I arrange readings for her and we write letters to each other sometimes. Writers in this country tend to starve, especially women writers, so I worry about her. Poets hardly have a chance unless they have regular paying jobs. Evelyn, protect yourself, care for yourself. The media and the critics can hurt you just as men did on the streets. They'll use you now, and disregard you next week when the next talent presents him/herself, or when runaway kids are no longer topical. May you live on – have a full and happy life like the little girl did before the age of three, when Daddy loved her. We both giggle, remembering how that was.

A woman was brutally raped and murdered six blocks away, in my safe neighbourhood. Her husband has been charged with murder, I'm told. Her kids attended the local high school. And I say I'm not afraid, . . . but this is too close. I want to prod and encourage men, including Evelyn's psychiatrist, Dr. Hightowers, and Dr. B., my client's psychiatrist, to get involved, to hear street kids and the voices of survivors of violence, abused women, men and kids, and get to work. Don't leave all the responsibility to women; the task is too big. Yes, be political; don't hide behind your walls of affluence, or apathy, or confidentiality.

I take Evelyn to the airport. Miles will separate us. It's a beautiful day. Scent of blossoms fills the air. I'll dig in mother earth, then wash the grime away, replenishing my spirit. The darkness was, and will be again. For now, I revel in the light, the sun, the warmth.

hope

Irene Heaman

elusive and frail
hung on its gossamer shreds
tendered by sun
lifted in light feathered songs
and frightened away in
tree swaying shadows of fear

rising, falling,
falling faster than the rise

there is nothing to hope
but someone's imagining,
inventing, a word.

Joy Tides

Irene Heaman

Like the rush of gulls that swoop
and dive, joy tides
over me, lingering
suspended over my waiting

       (pebbles from the beach fling
       their coils toward tomorrow)

Tomorrows are this night
sweet crystalline of now
mother of pearl shelled
circles of prayer, galaxies
swirled to the pivot of waiting
within me, fragile
as the break of fingered
waves that shore my dream.

The sea swells to the rising
rush of day.

Notes

SETTING THE STAGE

1 Lillian Allen, "Nellie Belly Swelly," and "Revolutionary Tea Party" (Toronto: Verse to Vinyl Records, 1984 [Oakland: Redwood Records, 1989]).
2 Joan Turner and Lois Emery, eds., *Perspectives on Women* (Winnipeg: University of Manitoba Press, 1983; reprinted 1989); and, Joan Turner and Shirley Kitchen, *Perspectives on Women in the 1980s,* video documentary, colour, 60 mins. (University of Manitoba, Faculty of Social Work, 1982).
3 For a thorough discussion of the relationship between meat-eating and patriarchy and, on the other hand, feminism and vegetarianism, see Carol J. Adams, *The Sexual Politics of Meat* (New York: Continuum Publishing Co., 1990).
4 Di Brandt, Carol Rose and Joan Turner wrote about their therapeutic journeys in "Let My Soul Soar: Touch Therapy," in *Healing Voices: Feminist Approaches to Therapy with Women,* ed. Toni Laidlaw and Cheryl Malmo (San Francisco: Jossey-Bass, 1990), pp. 221-239.
5 Mary Crnkovich, ed., *Gossip: A Spoken History of Women of the North* (Ottawa: Canadian Arctic Resources Committee, 1990).
6 Lesbophobia, or fear of lesbians, is thoroughly discussed in Sharon Dale Stone, ed., *Lesbians in Canada* (Toronto: between the lines, 1990).
7 See, for example, Sandra Burt, Lorraine Code and Lindsay Dorney, eds., *Changing Patterns: Women in Canada* (Toronto: McClelland and Stewart Ltd., 1988).
8 Adrienne Rich, *On Lies, Secrets and Silence: Selected Prose, 1966–1978* (New York: W.W. Norton and Co. Inc., 1979), p. 258.
9 "Programme Report," MATCH *International Annual Report, 1988-1989* (Ottawa: MATCH, 1989), p. 4.
10 Lee Maracle, *I am woman* (Vancouver: Write-on Press, 1988).
11 Dionne Brand, interviewed by Sadie Kuehn, "Dionne Brand: What People Can't Use They Will Throw Away," *Kinesis* (June 1988): 12.
12 Di Brandt, "letting the silence speak," in *Language in Her Eye: Views on Writing and Gender by English Canadian Writers,* ed. Libby Scheier, Sarah Sheard and Eleanor Wachtel (Toronto: Coach House Press, 1990).
13 Marilyn Burgess and Janice Andreae, "Introduction," *Canadian Woman Studies/les cahiers de la femme,* vol. 11, no. 1 (Spring 1990): 5.
14 Ibid.
15 Catherine MacKinnon, *Toward a Feminist Theory of the State* (Cambridge: Harvard University Press, 1989), p. 244.

WORRY ABOUT "CULTURE" AT A TIME LIKE THIS?

1 My favorite source concerning language and communication is Dale Spender, *Man Made Language* (London: Routledge, Chapman and Hall, 1985).

2 Carol Gilligan, *In a Different Voice* (Cambridge: Harvard University Press, 1982).
3 Several sources. See, for example, Nancy M. Henley, *Body Politics: Power, Sex and Non-verbal Communication* (New York: Simon and Schuster Inc., 1986).
4 Bonnie Klein heard Atwood make this observation on the radio. I later heard it quoted in a paper at the Status of Women Conference in New Brunswick called "Images" in 1987.
5 I cannot find the academic article that originally endowed my opinion with "authority." But anyone can try the simple exercise of reading six new novels by women, and the same number by men, and forming their own considered opinion.
6 Margaret Atwood, *The Handmaid's Tale* (Toronto: McClelland and Stewart, 1985).
7 Adrienne Rich, in "Canadian Women Artists: A Study," unpublished article by Sasha Mc-Innes.
8 *Branching Out* was published in Edmonton in the late 1970s, *Makara* in Vancouver in the late '70s, *Herizons* in Winnipeg in the 1980s and *Broadside* until very recently in Toronto. None of these Canadian women's magazines is published any longer.
9 The Canadian Broadcasting Corporation is the publicly funded national radio and television network. Studio D, which I founded in 1974 (and headed for 13 years) is a film-production unit at the National Film Board of Canada that makes films by women, from the perspective of women. I refer to it as an example many times – not to imply that all women's films are made there, by any means, but because it is the example I know best, and it is therefore the example I can generalize from.
10 Gail Singer (director and producer), Signe Johansson (producer), Kathleen Shannon (executive producer), *Abortion: Stories from North and South,* 16 mm, colour, 54 mins. 50 secs. (Studio D, National Film Board of Canada, 1984); Gloria Demers (writer), Margaret Wescott (director), Signe Johansson (producer), Kathleen Shannon (executive producer), *Behind the Veil – Nuns,* 16 mm, colour, part 1: 64 mins, part 2: 66 mins. (Studio D, National Film Board of Canada, 1984).
11 Bonnie Sherr Klein (director), Dorothy Todd Hénaut (producer), Kathleen Shannon (executive producer), *Not a Love Story – A Film about Pornography,* 16 mm, colour, 68 mins. 40 secs. (Studio D, National Film Board of Canada, 1981).
12 Suze Randall, photographer for *Hustler Magazine* when interviewed for *Not a Love Story.*
13 The Canadian Radio-television Telecommunications Commission, Public Notice CRTC 1986-351, "Policy on Sex-Role Stereotyping in the Broadcast Media," p. 43 (and elsewhere in this document and the documents it cites – notably those from Erin Research and Mediawatch).
14 Tillie Olsen, *Silences* (New York: Dell Publishing Co. Inc., 1989); Dale Spender, *Women of Ideas* (London: Ark Paperbacks, Routledge and Kegan Paul Inc., 1983); and, Dale Spender, *Feminist Theorists* (London: The Women's Press Ltd., 1983). The latter two now appear in *Books in Print* as "out of print" and "out of stock indefinitely," vividly illustrating what Spender was writing about.
15 Marilyn French, *Beyond Power: On Women, Men and Morals* (New York: Ballantine Books, 1986); Elizabeth Dowdson Gray, *Green Paradise Lost* (Boston: Roundtable Press, 1979); Elizabeth Dowdson Gray *Patriarchy as a Conceptual Trap* (Boston: Roundtable Press, 1982); Riane Eisler, *The Chalice and the Blade: Our History, Our Future* (New York: Harper and Row Publishers Inc., 1988).
16 Fritjof Capra, *The Turning Point: Science, Society and the Rising of Culture* (New York: Bantam Books Inc., 1987).
17 Rosalie Bertell, *No Immediate Danger* (Summertown, Tennessee: Book Publishing Co., 1986). See also films: Terri Nash (director), Bonnie Sherr Klein and Margaret Pettigrew (producers), Kathleen Shannon (executive producer), *Nuclear Addiction: Dr. Rosalie Bertell on the Cost of Deterrence,* 16 mm, colour, 18 mins. 47 secs. (Studio D, National Film Board of Canada, 1986); and, Bonnie Sherr Klein and Terri Nash (directors), Bonnie Sherr Klein and Margaret Pettigrew (producers), Kathleen Shannon (executive producer), *Speaking our Peace,* 16 mm, colour, 55 mins. 19 secs. (Studio D, National Film Board of Canada, 1985).

18 Penny Kome, *Women of Influence: Canadian Women and Politics* (Toronto: Doubleday Canada Ltd., 1985), p. 17.

WOMEN'S MUSIC AND THE MOTHERS OF INVENTION

This article is adapted from Connie Kuhns, "Rise Up! A History of Women's Music in Canada," to be published in 1991.

1 Meg Christian, "I Know You Know" (Olivia Records, 1974), from the album jacket.

I BLACK WOMAN

Reprinted with permission of Faith Nolan. Recorded on *Freedom to Love,* Aural Traditionn Records, Vancouver Folk Music Festival, Vancouver, 1989.

TESTIMONY

Reprinted with the permission of Nemesis Publishing.

BEYOND THE BARRIER: WOMEN IN THE MEDIA

1 Susan Crean, *Newsworthy: The Lives of Media Women* (Toronto: Stoddart Publishing Co. Ltd., 1985), p. 327.
2 Ibid., p. 61.
3 Ibid., p. 224.
4 Ibid., p. 326.

CHANGING TERMS OF ENDEARMENT: WOMEN AND FAMILIES

1 Canadian Advisory Council on the Status of Women, *Fine Balances: Equal Status for Women in the 1990s* (Ottawa: CACSW, 1987), p. 4.
2 Helen Levine, "The Power Politics of Motherhood," in *Perspectives on Women*, ed. Joan Turner and Lois Emery (Winnipeg: University of Manitoba Press, 1983; reprinted 1989), p. 35.
3 Gloria Steinem, *Outrageous Acts and Everyday Rebellions* (New York: Hart, Reinhart and Winston, 1983), p. 149.
4 Letty Cottin Pogrebin, *Family Politics: Home and Power on an Intimate Frontier* (New York: McGraw-Hill Inc., 1983), p. 5.
5 Pogrebin, *Family Politics*.
6 Kahlil Gibran, *The Prophet* (New York: Alfred A. Knopf Inc., 1923), p. 15.
7 Linda Cantelon, presentation at Western Regional Unified Family Courts and Conciliation Services Conference, Winnipeg, Manitoba, 1986.
8 Pogrebin, *Family Politics*.

9 Steinem, *Outrageous Acts*, p. 157.

10 Levine, "The Power Politics of Motherhood," p. 29.

11 S. Brandick, "Separation, Loss and Healing: Application of Feminist Counselling Principles with Women who Experience a Loss of Sexual Functioning," paper presented at the Annual Conference of the Canadian Association of Schools of Social Work, University of Manitoba, Winnipeg, June 1986.

12 Julie Brickman, "Feminist, Non-Sexist and Traditional Models of Therapy: Implications for Working with Incest," *Women and Therapy*, vol. 3, no. 1 (1984): 55.

13 Sheila Gostick, performance at Canadian Women's Music Festival Winnipeg, Manitoba, September, 1985.

14 Statistics Canada, *Women in Canada: A Statistical Report* (Ottawa: Ministry of Supply and Services, 1985).

15 Canadian Advisory Council on the Status of Women, *Fine Balances*, p. 15.

16 Susannah Jane Wilson, *Women, the Family and the Economy* (Toronto: McGraw-Hill Ryerson Ltd., 1982).

17 Ibid.

18 Maureen Baker, *The Family: Changing Trends in Canada* (Toronto: McGraw-Hill Ryerson Ltd., 1984).

19 Statistics Canada, *Population and Dwelling Characteristics, Families. Part 1: The Nation* (Ottawa: Ministry of Supply and Services, 1987).

20 Statistics Canada, *Women in Canada: A Statistical Report* (Ottawa: Ministry of Supply and Services, 1985).

21 Margrit Eichler, *Families in Canada Today: Recent Changes and their Policy Consequences* (Toronto: Gage Publishing Ltd., 1983).

22 Baker, *The Family*.

23 Zillah Eisenstein, *Feminism and Sexual Equality: Crisis in Liberal America* (New York: Monthly Review Press, 1984).

24 P.J. Conover and V. Gray, *Feminism and the New Right: Conflict over the American Family* (New York: Praeger Publishers, 1983), pp. 3, 4.

25 Canadian Advisory Council on the Status of Women, *Fine Balances*, p. 15.

26 This resolution, paragraph 120 of a United Nations Report entitled "Forward Looking Strategies," was quoted in a pamphlet entitled *Housewives in Training and Research*. The South Vancouver Family Plan has produced a report entitled "It's Time Women Speak Out: For Wages, for Housework and Pensions for Homemakers" (1987). Available from South Vancouver Family Place, 7595 Victoria Drive, Vancouver, B.C., V5P 3Z6.

27 Canadian Advisory Council on the Status of Women, *Home, Marriage and Money* (Ottawa: CACSW, 1984).

28 J. Dunaway, *Wife Assault/Victim Support Worker Handbook* (Vancouver: Justice Institute of British Columbia, 1987); and, Committee on Sexual Offences Against Children and Youths, *Sexual Offences Against Children: Report of the Committee on Sexual Offences Against Children* (Ottawa: Supply and Services Canada, 1984) [also known as *The Badgely Report*].

29 Harriet Rosenberg, "Motherwork, Stress and Depression," in *Family Bonds and Gender Divisions*, ed. Bonnie Fox (Toronto: Canadian Scholars Press, 1988), p. 390.

30 Pogrebin, *Family Politics*, p. 193.

31 Peggy Seeger, "I'm Going to Be an Engineer," recorded on *Different Therefore Equal* (London: Folkways 8563, 1972).

32 Meg Luxton, *More than a Labour of Love: Three Generations of Women's Work in the Home* (Toronto: The Women's Press, 1980).

33 Kathryn McCannell, "Family Politics, Family Policy and Family Practice: A Feminist Perspective," *Women and Mental Health*, ed. Kathryn McCannell [special issue of the *Canadian Journal of Community Mental Health*], vol. 5, no. 2 (1986): 67.

34 *Killing Us Softly*, colour, 28 mins. (Cambridge Documenary Films, 1979), distributed by the National Film Board of Canada.

35 Sheila Kitzinger, "Women's Experience of Sexuality," lecture sponsored by Planned Parenthood, Winnipeg, Manitoba, February, 1986.

36 Sonia Johnson, *Going Out of Our Minds: The Metaphysics of Liberation* (Freedom, California: The Crossing Press, 1987), p. 99.

37 Mary Daly and Jane Caputi, *Webster's First New Intergalactic Wickedary of the English Language* (Boston: Beacon Press, 1987), p. 167.

38 Eichler, *Families in Canada Today.*

39 We are keenly aware that very small steps toward "choice not circumstance" actually exist. The current wage disparity between women and men and the inequities in availability of abortion for Canadian women are two graphic examples of how state enforcement affects women's lives, and why the ongoing struggles for choice continue.

40 Eichler, *Families in Canada Today,*.

41 Adrienne Rich, *On Lies, Secrets and Silence: Selected Prose, 1966–1978* (New York: W.W. Norton and Co. Inc., 1979), p. 197.

TIDES, TOWNS AND TRAINS

1 Gail Sheehy, *Passages: Predictable Crises of Adult Life* (New York: Bantam Books Inc., 1977).

2 Chief Dan George, "My Very Good Dear Friends," in *The Only Good Indian,* ed. Waubageshig (Don Mills: New Press, 1970), p. 184.

3 *Town* is spelled with an initial capital letter throughout when used metaphorically. My birthplace was only six miles from Lac La Biche, which my family referred to as "town." Town, for me, came to have a metaphorical meaning, a point of uneasy contact between our land-based life and the Town's urban, industrial and profit-based culture, with its condescending attitudes towards Aborignal ways.

4 *Native* is an umbrella term for the Indian, Inuit and Metis of Canada. (The Metis of the 1950s to the 1970s were often subsumed under the term *non-status Indian.*) See my fuller discussion of the Native's dialectical relationship to the English language in my preface to Jeanne Perreault and Sylvia Vance, eds., *Native Women of Western Canada: Writing the Circle – An Anthology* (Edmonton: NeWest Publishers Ltd., 1990).

5 Howard Adams, *Prison of Grass* (Toronto: General Publishing Co. Ltd., 1975).

6 The Northern Alberta Railroad was a line that ran from Edmonton through Lac La Biche, Big Bay, Chard and Anzac to Fort McMurray.

7 The role of women changed somewhat, depending on the type of work men did. When the men trapped, the division of labour along gender lines was minimal, with women enjoying greater flexibility; when men were wage-earners, women played traditional roles with respect to housekeeping.

8 As a rule, Metis children did not go to residential schools, which were federally operated for Treaty Indians. Treaty Indians are defined by the Indian Act. Many Canadians of Native ancestry have been excluded by this act and do not have the same rights to education and health services. The Anzac Dorm was not a "residential school," as the term is traditionally used with reference to Treaty Indians. It was a dormitory centrally located to accommodate Metis children who lived along the NAR rail line. Most of these hamlets had no schools. Anzac Dorm was provincially funded by the Northland School Division and it was operated by a group of Mennonites through their Voluntary Services Program. The dormitory was not a school – it was a place where Metis children lived while they attended a public school nearby.

9 A comparable story is to be found in Anastasia M. Shkilnyk, *A Poison Stronger than Love: The Destruction of an Ojibwa Community* (New Haven and London: Yale University Press, 1985).

10 See Patrick Johnston, *Native Children and the Child Welfare System* (Toronto: James Lorimer and Co. Publishers, in association with Canadian Council on Social Development, 1983).

11 They cared not whether we were Metis or Indian – we were all tar-feathered in the same way. There are profound cultural, linguistic, historical, legislative and regional differences among Native peoples, yet the pattern of generalizing them persists.

12 See Emma LaRocque, *Three Conventional Approaches to Native People in Society and in Literature* (Saskatoon: Saskatchewan Library Association, 1984).

13 I use the word *apologist* in the literary sense – of explaining, speaking and writing in defence of. I do not mean it in the sense of apologizing.

14 Harold Cardinal, *The Unjust Society* (Edmonton: Hurtig Publishers Ltd., 1969).

15 Joy Harjo, "I Give You Back," in *She Had Some Horses* (New York: Thunder's Mouth Press Inc., 1983), p. 73.

16 John Steinbeck, *Travels with Charley in Search of America* (New York: The Viking Press, 1962).

17 Emma LaRocque, *Defeathering the Indian* (Agincourt: Book Society of Canada, 1975).

18 David G. Mandelbaum, *The Plains Cree* (Regina: The Canadian Plains Research Centre, 1978, revised edition).

19 Emma LaRocque, "On the Ethics of Publishing Historical Materials," in *"The Orders of the Dreamed" : George Nelson on Cree and Northern Ojibwa Religion and Myth, 1823*, ed. Jennifer S.H. Brown and Robert Brightman (Winnipeg: University of Manitoba Press, 1988).

20 The term *settler,* associated with Europeans, is often juxtaposed with the term *nomadic,* which is associated with Indians. In fact, Indians had settlements and were certainly rooted to their lands. Was it not nomadic Europeans who tried to unsettle aboriginal peoples from their lands?

21 The story of Betty Helen Osborne of The Pas, Manitoba, can be found in Lisa Priest, *The Conspiracy of Silence* (Toronto: McClelland and Stewart Ltd., 1989).

22 The phrase is from George Ryga, *The Ecstasy of Rita Joe,* recorded by Ann Mortifee and Chief Dan George (Vancouver: Jabula Records, n.d.).

23 See, for example, *Winnipeg Free Press,* April 26, 1988. Details on the Osborne and Harper deaths and police investigations may be published in a forthcoming report by the Aboriginal Justice Inquiry of Manitoba.

24 This is a horrible story of an Indian child who was initially "scooped" from a hospital by social service agents when she was a baby. Then when she was 14, she was forced to come back to her place of origin, where she was violated. See, for example: *Winnipeg Free Press*, October 13, 1988; January 12, 1989; February 17, 1989; February 25, 1989.

25 Emma LaRocque, "Racism Runs throughout Canadian Society," *Winnipeg Free Press*, April 26, 1989.

26 This is in reference to a Cree legend where Wisakehcha, the central "trickster," invites ducks to a dance, but the ducks had to have their eyes closed so that Wisakehcha could pounce on them for his dinner!

27 From my poem entitled "The Uniform of the Dispossessed," in *Native Women of Western Canada,* ed. Perreault and Vance.

THROUGH THE FOG: LOOKING AT ACADEMIA

1 *Canadian Association of University Teachers Bulletin,* prepared for the National Forum on Post Secondary Education, Saskatoon, Saskatchewan, 1987.

2 William Ryan, *Equality* (New York: Pantheon Books Inc., 1981).

3 My notes attribute these ideas to Catherine A. MacKinnon, "Making Sex Equality Real," in *Feminism Unmodified: Discourses on Life and Law* (Cambridge: Harvard University Press, 1987).
4 Catherine MacKinnon, *Toward a Feminist Theory of the State* (Cambridge: Harvard University Press, 1989), p. 234.

SEXUAL HARASSMENT: JUST THE BEGINNING

1 Gloria Steinem, "Perspectives on Women: The Baird Poskanzer Memorial Lecture," in *Perspectives on Women,* ed. Joan Turner and Lois Emery (Winnipeg: University of Manitoba Press, 1983; reprinted 1989), p. 16.
2 Sexual Harassment Policy, University of Manitoba, 1985. Revised 1989.
3 Marilyn MacKenzie and Thelma G. Lussier, *Sexual Harassment: Report on the Results of a Survey of the University of Manitoba Community* (September 1988), p. 6.
4 Pamela H. Hey and Lea P. Stewart, "The Extent and Effects of Sexual Harassment of Working Women," *Sociological Focus* 1 (January 1984): 17.
5 Canadian Human Rights Commission, *Unwanted Sexual Attention and Sexual Harassment: Results of a Survey of Canadians* (Ottawa: 1983).
6 The complainant is referred to as "she" since 95 percent of all complaints to date have been female.
7 Out of over 100 situations handled in the first five years, only three have actually gone to arbitration.
8 Arbitration between the University of Manitoba for the complainant, and the University of Manitoba Faculty Association and Dr. C. Award, October 12, 1988. John M. Scurfield, chair.
9 Author wishes to remain anonymous. Printed with her permission.

WALKING THE MOTHERPATH

1 Dr. J.H. Hertz, *Pentateuch and Haftorahs,* 2nd ed. (London: Soncino Press, 1971), p. 45.
2 Hallie Austen Inglehart, *Woman Spirit: A Guide to Women's Wisdom,* 1st ed. (San Francisco: Harper and Row Publishers Inc., 1983), p. 14.
3 Ibid., p. 84.
4 Hebrew for the *Five Books of Moses,* or the *Pentateuch.*
5 Marion Zimmer Bradley, *Mists of Avalon* (New York: Ballantine Books, 1982).
6 Diane Mariechild, *Mother Wit: A Feminist Guide to Psychic Development* (Trumansburg, N.Y.: The Crossing Press Feminist Series, 1981), p. 145.
6 Inglehart, *Woman Spirit,* p. 9
7 Ibid., p. 11.

TOUCHING THE WORLD GENTLY – THROUGH FEMINIST THEOLOGY

1 Shirley Kitchen, "Invocation to Worship," 1988. For an overview of writing on feminist theology see Carol Christ and Judith Plaskow, eds., *Womanspirit Rising: A Feminist Reader in Religion* (New York: Harper and Row Publishers Inc., 1979).

2 Helen Levine, "Feminist Counselling: Approach or Technique?" in *Perspectives on Women,* ed. Joan Turner and Lois Emery (Winnipeg: University of Manitoba Press, 1983; reprinted 1989), p. 75.
3 Mary Daly, "The Spiritual Dimension of Women's Liberation," in "Notes from the Third Year: An Anthology of Women's Liberation Writing," 1972), p. 28, available from P.O. Box AA, Old Chelsea Station, N.Y., 10011. See also Mary Daly, *Church and the Second Sex* (New York: Harper and Row Publishers Inc., 1968).
4 Unitarian Universalist Association, "Principles and Purposes," 1984 and 1985 general assemblies.
5 Christ and Plaskow, *Womanspirit Rising,* p. 1.

GIVING BIRTH

1 Barbara Ehrenreich and Deirdre English, *For Her Own Good: 150 Years of the Experts' Advice to Women* (New York: Anchor Books, 1979), p. 276.
2 Barbara Katz Rothman, *In Labor: Women and Power in the Birthplace,* 1st ed. (New York: W.W. Norton and Co. Inc., 1982), p. 284.
3 Michel Odent, *Birth Reborn* (New York: Pantheon Books Inc., 1984), p. 4.
4 Mike Samuels and Nancy Samuels, *The Well Pregnancy Book* (New York: Summit Books, 1986), p. 200.
5 Ibid., p. 276.
6 Suzanne Arms, *Immaculate Deception: A New Look at Women and Childbirth in America* (Boston: Houghton Mifflin Co., 1975), foreword.
7 Elizabeth Noble, *Childbirth with Insight* (Boston: Houghton Mifflin, 1983), p. 61.
8 Ibid. See outside back cover.
9 Eleanor Barrington, *Midwifery is Catching* (Toronto: NC Press Ltd., 1985), p. 9.

TEARS

Originally published as "you take the tears" in Di Brandt, *Agnes in the sky* (Winnipeg: Turnstone Press, 1990). Reprinted with permission.

ALREADY THERE IS NO GOING BACK

Originally published in Di Brandt, *Agnes in the sky* (Winnipeg: Turnstone Press, 1990). Reprinted with permission.

THE LOOK: WOMEN AND BODY IMAGE

1 Nancy Henley, *Body Politics, Power, Sex and Nonverbal Communication* (New York: Simon and Schuster Inc., 1977), p. 38.
2 Susie Orbach, *Hunger Strike* (New York: W.W. Norton and Co. Inc., 1986), p. 36.
3 Kim Chernin, *The Obsession: Reflections on the Tyranny of Slenderness* (New York: Harper and Row Publishers Inc., 1981), p. 99.
4 H. Bruch, "Four Decades of Eating Disorders," in *Handbook of Psychotherapy for Anorexia Nervosa and Bulimia,* ed. David Garner and Paul Garfinkel (New York: The Guilford Press, 1985), p. 9.

WORKING FOR ACCESS

1 Shari Stein, "The Supreme Court Requires Consent for Sterilization," *Archtype*, vol. 6, no. 3 (1987): 4.

2 Micheline Mason, "Welcome Lucy Rose," *From the Cold: A Liberation Magazine for People with Disabilities* (Spring 1985): 3-4.

3 Agathe Allaire et al., *Femme et Handicap: Rapport de la Recherche sur la Condition des Femmes Handicappes* (Quebec: Office des Personnes Handicappées du Quebec, 1985), p. 59.

4 Monique Raimbault, *Research Project Report on Women with Disabilities* (Winnipeg: Consulting Committee on the Status of Women with Disabilities, 1986), p. 14. This point is also supported by DAWN-Canada's more recent research by Jillian Ridington, *Beating the "Odds" : Violence and Women with Disbilities* (Vancouver: DAWN-Canada, 1989), p. 1.

5 "Do Crazy Ladies Get Raped," *Phoenix Rising: The Voice of the Psychiatrized*, vol. 1, no. 4 (Winter 1981): 15.

6 Val Werier, "Victims of Experiments Must Get Compensation," *Winnipeg Free Press*, May 1, 1986; Don Weitz, "A Psychiatric Holocaust," *Phoenix Rising*, vol. 6, no. 1 (Spring/Summer 1986)1: 8-14.

7 Bonnie Burstow and Don Weitz, eds. *Shrink Resistant: The Struggle against Psychiatry in Canada* (Vancouver: New Star Books Ltd., 1988), p. 28.

8 For a full account of DPI's history, see Diane Driedger, *The Last Civil Rights Movement: Disabled People's International* (London: Hurst and Company, 1989).

IN SEARCH OF THE RIGHT PRESCRIPTION

Talks with my cousin Anna Pellatt provided some important insights into our common family history that are developed in this paper; Ruth Corobow helped me think more deeply about headaches; Neil Tudiver and Simon Tudiver gave me the nurturing support and love necessary to write; and Joan Turner and Darlene Henderson offered patience and enthusiasm for my work. I am grateful to them all. This article is written in loving memory of my mother, Lillian Novick Lubitsch.

1 Thalidomide, promoted as a "sleep-inducing agent," was on the Canadian market between April 1961 and March 1962. See H. Sjostrom and R. Nilsson, *Thalidomide and the Power of the Drug Companies* (Middlesex, England: Penguin Books, 1972). Information on the drug is summarized in Joel Lexchin, *The Real Pushers: A Critical Analysis of the Canadian Drug Industry* (Vancouver: New Star Books Ltd., 1984), pp. 191-193.

2 DES, a synthetic estrogen, was aggressively promoted and widely prescribed in North America, Europe and Australia between 1941 and 1971 to prevent miscarriage. In the late 1960s, cases of a rare vaginal cancer began to appear in some of the daughters of women who had taken the drug during pregnancy; other daughters and sons have reproductive abnormalities. DES is still administered in pregnancy in many third-world countries and is used as a growth hormone for cattle. See Anita Direcks and Ellen 't Hoen, "DES: The Crime Continues," in *Adverse Effects: Women and the Pharmaceutical Industry*, ed. Kathleen McDonnell (Toronto: Women's Education Press, 1986).

3 The Dalkon Shield intra-uterine device was marketed in North America between 1971 and 1974, despite the fact that A.H. Robins, the manufacturer, knew the device was defective in design and dangerous to women. After deaths and injury led to the withdrawal of the device from North American markets, it was made available in numerous third-world countries. Thousands of liability suits have been filed against the manufacturer, totalling close to $3 billion U.S. The device is under international recall. For an excellent review of the history of this case, including early U.S. court proceedings, see Morton Mintz, *At Any*

Cost: Corporate Greed, Women and the Dalkon Shield (New York: Pantheon Books Inc., 1985).

4 Valium, manufactured by Hoffman-LaRoche, is the most famous of the minor tranquillizers. It came onto the market in 1963; by the mid-1970s it was the second most commonly prescribed drug in Canada; by 1977, the top-selling drug in the world. Increasing evidence shows that minor tranquillizers produce dependency (see Lexchin, *The Real Pushers*, pp. 19-24).

5 Olle Hansson, *Inside Ciba-Geigy* (Penang, Malaysia: International Organization of Consumers, 1989). Written by a doctor deeply involved in the issue, it is the story of clioquinol, an anti-diarrheal, which caused a debilitating central-nervous-system disease, SMON, and the struggle by victims to have Ciba-Geigy, the giant pharmaceutical manufacturer, admit liability and withdraw the drugs.

6 A sample of references, in addition to those cited above, include: United Nations Centre on Transnational Corporations, *Transnational Corporations and the Pharmaceutical Industry* (New York: United Nations, 1979); World Health Organization, *The World Drug Situation: Report Prepared by the WHO Action Programme on Essential Drugs* (Geneva: World Health Organization, 1988); H.C. Eastman, *The Report of the Commission of Inquiry on the Pharmaceutical Industry* (Ottawa: Supply and Services Canada, 1985); John Braithwaite, *Corporate Crime in the Pharmaceutical Industry* (London: Routledge, Kegan and Paul, 1984); Michael L. Tan, *Dying For Drugs: Pill Power and Politics in the Philippines* (Quezon City, Philippines: Health Action Information Network, 1988); and, G. Carruthers et al., *Drug Utilization: A Comprehensive Literature Review* (Toronto: Ministry of Health, Province of Ontario, 1987). These include very useful bibliographies.

7 The landmark study on pharmaceuticals in the third world is Dianna Melrose, *Bitter Pills* (Oxford: Public Affairs Unit, Oxfam-UK, 1982). Other well-documented references include: Andrew Chetley and David Gilbert, *Problem Drugs* (The Hague: Health Action International, 1986); Virginia Beardshaw, *Prescription for Change* (The Hague: International Organization of Consumers Unions, 1984). *Another Development in Pharmaceuticals*, special isssue of *Development Dialogue*, no. 2 (Uppsala, Sweden: Dag Hammarskjold Foundation, 1985) covers a wide range of policy issues on the international regulation of pharmaceuticals.

8 Many anti-diarrheals, cough-and-cold preparations, pain-killers, non-steroidal anti-inflammatory drugs and vitamin preparations are irrational and ineffective. (See Chetley and Gilbert, *Problem Drugs*). For a careful analysis of drug advertising in Canada, see Lexchin, *The Real Pushers*, pp. 112-143.

9 As many sources demonstrate, the majority of improvements in the health of the public are due to improved public health measures – clean water and sanitation, improved nutrition and primary health care, including the availability of essential drugs.

10 *Adverse Effects*, ed. McDonnell; and, Ivan Wolfers, Anita Hardon and Janita Janssen, *Marketing Fertility: Women, Menstruation and the Pharmaceutical Industry* (Amsterdam: WEMOS, 1989). *For Health or for Profit: The Pharmaceutical Industry in the Third World and Canada* (Ottawa: Womens' Health Interaction, 1984), is a useful information kit on women and pharmaceuticals. See also Cary LaCheen, "Population Control and the Pharmaceutical Industry," in *Adverse Effects*, ed. McDonnell, pp. 89-136, where the author analyzes how women are targets for research and marketing of contraceptives.

11 Approximately two-thirds of all mood-altering drugs in Canada and the United States are prescribed to women. See: Ruth Cooperstock and Jessica Hill, *The Effects of Tranquillization: Benzodiazepine Use in Canada* (Ottawa: Health Promotion Directorate, Health and Welfare Canada, 1982); Jim Harding, "Elderly Women in Canada: The Medicalization of Poverty," in *Adverse Effects*, ed. McDonnell, pp. 51-86.

12 *Side Effects*, a play about women and pharmaceuticals, was developed and produced by Women's Health Interaction and the Great Canadian Theatre Company, Ottawa. It toured across Canada in 1985. For a discussion of the achievements and struggles faced by women's groups in Canada and internationally, see Sari Tudiver, "The Strength of Links:

International Women's Health Networks in the Eighties," in *Adverse Effects*, ed. Mc-Donnell, pp. 187-214.

13 An evolving feminist critique of science provides the broad framework for these views. See, for example, Sandra Harding, *The Science Question in Feminism* (Ithaca, N.Y.: Cornell University Press, 1986); and, Ruth Bleier, *Science and Gender* (Toronto: Pergamon Press Canada Ltd., 1984).

14 Hormonal methods include oral contraceptives, two- and three-month injectables depo medroxyprogesterone acetate (Depo-Provera); norethisterone oenanthate (NET-OEN); implants such as Norplant, effective for up to five years; hormone-releasing IUDs. Close scrutiny of research data on these methods has often revealed poor methodology or generalizations about safety made on the basis of small numbers or research over short periods of time. A good summary of the methods and ideology behind their development can be found in Betsy Hartmann, *Reproductive Rights and Wrongs: The Global Politics of Population Control and Reproductive Choice* (New York: Harper and Row Publishers Inc., 1987), pp. 161-207. For a detailed discussion of the research problems pertaining to Depo-Provera, see Judith Weisz et al., *Report of the Public Board of Inquiry on Depo-Provera*, submitted to the U.S. Food and Drug Administration, October 17, 1984. The U.S. Food and Drug Administration rejected the manufacturer's application to have the drug approved for contraceptive use in the United States.

15 An early discussion of these issues can be found in Bonnie Mass, *Population Target: The Political Economy of Population Control in Latin America* (Brampton, Ontario: Charters Publishing, 1976); see also Hartmann, *Reproductive Rights and Wrongs*.

16 W.E. Dieckmann et al., "Does the Administration of Diethylstilbestrol during Pregnancy Have Therapeutic Value?" *American Journal of Obstetrics and Gynaecology* 66 (1953). The study was double-blind; miscarriages were more frequent among DES users than in the control group.

17 For an analysis of sexist images in pharmaceutical advertising, see Anne Rochon Ford, "In Poor Health: Women in Pharmaceutical Advertising," *Healthsharing*, vol. 7, no. 2 (Spring 1986).

18 Estimates indicate that some companies spend more on advertising than on research. See *Multinational Monitor*, special issue on the pharmaceutical industry (August 1980): 17; and, Lexchin, *The Real Pushers*, pp. 112-142.

19 A literature review on psychotropic drugs found that their effectiveness in treating anxiety, physical and psychosomatic conditions was poorly researched and the value of these drugs was overstated (see Joel Lexchin, "Psychotropics," unpublished literature review, 1989); manufacturers' data on minor tranquillizers, provided in the *Compendium of Pharmaceutical Specialties (CPS)* (Ottawa: Canadian Pharmaceutical Associations, 1988) suggest the drugs be administered for three to six weeks.

20 Lexchin, *The Real Pushers*, pp. 191-193.

21 For an analysis of some of these claims, see Patricia Kaufert and Sonia McKinley, "Estrogen Replacement Therapy: The Production of Medical Knowledge and the Emergence of Policy," in *Women, Health and Healing*, ed. E. Lewin and V. Olesen (London: Tavistock, 1985), pp. 113-138; and, Patricia Kaufert, "Menopause, Medicalization and Ideology: A Sociological Critique," paper presented at the 9th International Congress of Psychosomatic Obstetrics and Gynecology, Amsterdam, May 28-31, 1989.

22 See, for example, the advertisement appearing in the *American Journal of Obstetrics and Gynecology* (April 1955), which reads: "Headache is typical of the many distressing but ill-defined symptoms of estrogen deficiency which may occur long before or after cessation of menstruation. Premarin (conjugated estrogens, equine) is an excellent preparation for effective replacement therapy." Adverse effects from the use of Premarin, including headaches, are listed in the *Compendium of Pharmaceutical Specialties (CPS)* (Ottawa: Canadian Pharmaceutical Association, annual editions, 1970s, 1980s).

23 A useful summary of some of these issues is in: Lesley Doyal, *The Political Economy of Health* (London: Pluto Press, 1981); Veronica Strong-Boag, "Canada's Women Doctors:

Feminism Constrained," in *A Not Unreasonable Claim: Women and Reform in Canada, 1880–1920*, ed. Linda Kealey (Toronto: Women's Educational Press, 1979); Wendy Mitchenson, "The Medical Treatment of Women," in *Changing Patterns: Women in Canada*, ed. Sandra Burt, Lorraine Code and Lindsay Dorney (Toronto: McClelland and Stewart Ltd., 1988). Emily Martin's book, *The Woman in the Body: A Cultural Analysis of Reproduction* (Boston: Beacon Press, 1987), offers deeper insights into how women's reproductive processes are viewed by medical science.

24 The injection was probably DES, widely used at that time to suppress lactation.

25 Migraines do run in families, but why some family members suffer and others do not, and the principles of transmission, are not well understood. Some substances (either the taste or smell of them) may trigger a migraine. There appears to be a biochemical basis to migraines. I do not challenge this view but suggest additional conditions that may contribute to increased tensions and stresses that could in turn contribute to migraines, and to the severity and frequency of the headaches. The links to various forms of abuse must be explored.

26 On the new reproductive technologies see, for example: Michelle Stanworth, ed., *Reproductive Technologies: Gender, Motherhood and Medicine* (Minneapolis: University of Minnesota Press, 1987); Elaine Hoffman Baruch et al., eds., *Embryos, Ethics and Women's Rights: Exploring the New Reproductive Technologies* (New York: The Harrington Park Press Inc., 1988); and, Patricia Spallone, *Beyond Conception* (Granby, Mass.: Bergin and Garvey Publishers Inc., 1989).

REFLECTIONS

1 May Sarton, *As We Are Now* (New York: W.W. Norton and Co. Inc., 1973); Margaret Laurence, *The Stone Angel* (Toronto: McClelland and Stewart Ltd., 1964); Barbara Macdonald and Cynthia Rich, *Look Me in the Eye* (San Francisco: Spinsters/Aunt Lute, 1983).

2 An extended family without blood-ties.

3 The first part of this article was originally published as "On Aging" in *Canadian Woman Studies/les cahiers de la femme*, vol. 5, no. 3 (Spring 1984): 67-69. Reprinted here with permission.

4 Kathleen Woodward, "Simone de Beauvoir: Aging and its Discontents," in *The Private Self: Theory and Practice of Women's Autobiographical Writings*, ed. Shari Benstock (Chapel Hill: The University of North Carolina Press, 1988), pp. 92, 95.

5 Ibid., pp. 99, 98.

6 Mary Meigs, *Lily Briscoe: A Self-Portrait* (Vancouver: Talon Books, 1981).

7 Aba Wells, in *The Woman's Eye*, ed. Anne Tucker (New York: Alfred A. Knopf Inc., 1976), p. 129.

8 Diane Arbus, in *The Woman's Eye*, ed. Anne Tucker (New York: Alfred A. Knopf Inc., 1976), p. 109.

9 Woodward, "Aging and its Discontents," pp. 110, 111.

FARM WOMEN FIGHT FOR SURVIVAL

1 N. McClung, *In Times like These* (Toronto: University of Toronto Press, 1972 [originally published by D. Appleton, 1915]), p. 34.

2 P. Smith, "Not Enough Hours, our Accountant Tells Me: Trends in Children's, Women's and Men's Involvement in Canadian Agriculture," a paper presented at the Annual Meeting of the Canadian Agricultural Economics and Farm Management Society, University of Prince Edward Island, Charlottetown, 1985, p. 6.

3 S. Koski, *The Employment Practices of Farm Women* (Saskatoon: National Farmer's Union, 1982), p. 6.

4 Manitoba Advisory Council on the Status of Women, *Some Concerns of Rural and Farm Women* (Winnipeg: 1984), p. 3; and, M. McGhee, *Women in Rural Life: The Changing Scene* (Toronto: Ministry of Agriculture and Food), p. 17.

5 K. Engman, "Rural Areas Issue Emergency Call for Doctors," *Winnipeg Free Press*, January 3, 1988, p. A2.

6 J.L. Walker and L.J. Walker, *The Human Harvest: Changing Farm Stress to Family Success* (Winnipeg: Manitoba Agriculture), pp. 17-21.

7 *Ontario Task Force on Health and Safety in Agriculture: Report* (Ontario: Ministry of Agriculture and Food, Ministry of Labour, 1985), appendix 3, p. 10.

8 J.D. Hatcher and F.M.C. White, *Task Force on Chemicals in the Environment and Human Reproductive Problems in New Brunswick* (Halifax: Faculty of Medicine, Dalhousie University, 1985), pp. 107-108.

9 N.M. Chenier, "Reproductive Hazards at Work: Men, Women and the Fertility Gamble" (Ottawa: Canadian Advisory Council on the Status of Women, 1982), p. 30.

10 *Ontario Task Force on Health and Safety in Agriculture: Report* (Ontario: Ministry of Agriculture and Food, Ministry of Labour, 1985), appendix 3, p. 12.

11 N.I. Colwill, M. Pollock and T.J. Sztaba, "Power in Home Economics," *Canadian Home Economics Journal*, vol. 36, no. 2. (1986): 59-61.

12 L.J. Walker and J.L. Walker, "Lack of Power: A Source of Farm Stress," *Canadian Home Economics Journal*, vol. 37, no. 4 (1987b): 163-167.

13 L.J. Walker and J.L. Walker, "Stressors and Symptoms Predictive of Distress in Farmers," *Family Relations* 36 (1987c): 374-378.

14 *Murdoch v. Murdoch* (1975), 1 S.C.R. 423.

15 B. Sawer, "Predictors of Farm Wives' Involvement in General Management and Adoption Decisions," *Rural Sociology*, vol. 38, no. 4 (1973): 422.

16 J.B. Bullock, "The Farm Credit Situation: Implications for Agricultural policy," *Human Services in the Rural Environment* 10 (1986): 12-20.

17 N. Harl, "Farming for Profit with Financial Resources: A United States Perspective," a paper presented at the Second Century Conference," Opportunities for Agriculture, Edmonton, Alberta, December, 1985.

18 N. Taylor, "All This for Three and a Half a Day" in *Women in the Canadian Mosiac*, ed. Gwen Matheson (Toronto: Peter Matheson Associates), p. 162.

19 A. Ashley, "From the Frontline: Perspectives on Rural Stress," a paper presented at the Policy Forum on Rural Stress, Chicago, Illinois, April, 1986.

WOMAN BY LOG CABIN

This poem, originally entitled "Lady by Log Cabin," was previously published in *Dufferin*, ed. June M. Watson (Carman: Rural Municipality of Dufferin, 1982). Reprinted with permission.

KNITTING EMPOWERING CONFIGURATIONS

I wish to acknowledge the generous support of the Provincial Association of Transition Houses Saskatchewan and the Pennsylvania Coalition Against Domestic Violence. A modified version of this paper was presented at the National Women's Studies Association Tenth Annual Conference, University of Minneapolis, Minnesota, 25 June 1988.

1 On Pennsylvania's communal religious sects, see: John A. Hostetler, *Mennonite Life* (Scottsdale, Pennsylvannia: Harold Press, 1974); and, Elbert Russell, *The History of Quakerism* (New York: Macmillan, 1943.) On Saskatchewan's co-operative movement, see John F. Conway, *The West: The History of a Region in Confederation* (Toronto: James Lorimer and Co. Publishers, 1983).

2 This paper is based upon field studies of the two associations as well as in-depth case studies of three member programs: in Saskatchewan, one house in an urban area with native and non-native populations, and in Pennsylvania, two domestic-violence projects, one in a rural region with a predominately white population and the other in a more settled county with concentrations of minority groups.

3 Jane Mansbridge, "Feminism and the Forms of Freedom," in *Critical Studies in Organization and Bureaucracy*, ed. Frank Fischer and Carmen Sirianni (Philadelphia: Temple University Press, 1984), pp. 472-481; and, Robin Morgan, ed., *Sisterhood Is Powerful: An Anthology of Writings from the Women's Liberation Movement* (New York: Random House Inc., 1970), pp. xxiii-xxviii.

4 For the classical statement on the incompatibility of organization and democracy, see Robert Michels, *Political Parties: A Sociological Study of the Oligarchical Tendencies of Modern Democracy* (New York: Dover Publications Inc., 1959).

5 Myra Marx Ferree and Beth B. Hess, *Controversy and Coalition: The New Feminist Movement* (Boston: Twayne Publishers, 1985), p. 57.

6 Susan Schechter, *Women and Male Violence: The Visions and Struggles of the Battered Women's Movement* (Boston: South End Press, 1982), pp. 29-34.

7 Linda MacLeod, *Battered but Not Beaten: Preventing Wife Battering in Canada* (Ottawa: Canadian Advisory Council on the Status of Women, 1987), pp. 54-55.

8 Joan T. Pennell, "Consensual Bargaining: Labor Negotiations in Battered-Women's Programs," *Journal of Progressive Human Services,* vol. 1, no. 1 (1990): 59-74.

9 These life exigencies need not present insurmountable obstacles since the British women's-aid movement has successfully involved battered women and their children in National Coordinating Group conferences as participating, although not voting, members. See Liz Kelly, "The English Federation: Where Do We Go from Here?" a paper presented at the National Coalition against Domestic Violence Third National Conference on Domestic Violence, St. Louis, July 17, 1986.

10 Voting members of PCADV caucuses include the programs' staff, board, volunteer and service-recipient participants. Others may join as support (but non-voting) members.

11 Although the term *minority* is being employed because of its international interpretability, it is recognized that, as is generally true of scientific words, it obscures reality. By claiming to be a member of the majority, white heterosexual women ignore their own differences and form a bloc excluding other women.

12 Regarding the effect of numbers on organizational subdivison, see Georg Simmel, *The Sociology of Georg Simmel*, ed. and trans. Kurt H. Wolff (New York: Free Press, 1950), pp. 87-89, passim 90-177.

13 Moreover, according to recent census data, although the majority of people in both Saskatchewan and Pennsylvania reside in urban areas, a significantly larger proportion of the Saskatchewan population are in rural areas.

14 Contrary to most organizational theorists, they are not assuming that institutionalization deflects social movement organizations from their radical goals. See Alvin Gouldner, "Metaphysical Pathos and the Theory of Bureaucracy," *American Political Science Review* 49 (June 1955): 496-507.

15 Daniel Guerin, *Anarchism: From Theory to Practice,* trans. Mary Klopper (New York: Monthly Review Press, 1970); Carol Pateman, *Participation and Democratic Theory* (Cambridge: Harvard University Press, 1970).

16 Jean-Jacques Rousseau, *The Social Contract and Discourses,* trans. G.D.H. Cole, rev. J.H. Brumfitt and John C. Hall (London: J.M. Dent, [1762] 1973)1:177.

17 Doug Taylor, *For Dignity, Equality, and Justice: A History of the Saskatchewan Govern-ment Employees' Union* (Regina: Saskatchewan Government Employees' Union, 1984).
18 Schechter, *Women and Male Violence*, p. 109.

REMOVING OUR BLINDERS: THE ECONOMIC PARTICIPATION OF WOMEN

The author wishes to acknowledge the research assistance of Maureen Magee and Simonne Collette in the preparation of this paper. A modified version was published in *New Brunswick in the Year 2000*, published by the Canadian Institute for Research on Regional Development, Moncton, 1989.

 1 New Brunswick Advisory Council on the Status of Women, *We, The Undersigned: A His-torical Overview of New Brunswick Women's Political and Legal History 1784–1984* (Moncton: 1985).
 2 Alberta Women's Bureau et al., "Women are Persons" (n.d.).
 3 Canadian Advisory Council on the Status of Women, *Women and Legal Action* (Ottawa: 1984), pp. 14-15.
 4 Ibid., pp. 20-21.
 5 Gayle M. MacDonald, "Equality: Rationale or Reality?" unpublished article (Fredericton: 1987).
 6 Margrit Eichler, *Families in Canada Today: Recent Changes and their Policy Consequen-ces* (Toronto: Gage Publishing Ltd., 1983), pp. 140-164.
 7 Statistics Canada, *Historical Statistics of New Brunswick* (Ottawa: 1984), p. 33; and, Department of Labour, *New Brunswick Labour Market Report* (Ottawa: 1988).
 8 Task Force on Labour Market Development, *Labour Market Development in the '80s* (Ot-tawa: Employment and Immigration Canada, 1981), p. 102.
 9 Carol Swan, "Women in the Canadian Labour Market" (Ottawa: Task Force on Labour Market Development, Employment and Immigration Canada, 1981); and, Statistics Canada.
10 Department of Labour, Government of New Brunswick, *New Brunswick Labour Market Report* (Fredericton: 1988).
11 Labour Canada, *Part-time Work in Canada* (Ottawa: 1983), pp. 48-59.
12 Ontario Women's Directorate, *Gender Equality Indicator* (Toronto: 1987).
13 National Council on Welfare, *Poverty on the Increase* (1985); and, National Council on Welfare, *Progress Against Poverty*.
14 Statistics Canada, *The Labour Force Annual Average 1975–1983;* and, Statistics Canada, *The Labour Force* (December 1986).
15 Ibid.
16 Statistics Canada, *Survey of Consumer Finances* (1985).
17 Statistics Canada, *Women in the Workplace: Selected Data* (1987); and, telephone inter-view, Statistics Canada, 1988.
18 Statistics Canada, *Survey of Consumer Finances* (1986).
19 Statistics Canada, *Canada, the Provinces and the Territories: A Statistical Profile* (1985), p. 28.
20 Victor R. Fuchs, "Sex Differences in Economic Well-Being," *Science* 232 (April 25, 1986): 459-463.
21 Statistics Canada, *Profiles, New Brunswick, Part 1* (1987), pp. 3-4; Canadian Advisory Council on the Status of Women, *Progress Toward Equality for Women in Canada* (Ot-tawa: 1987); and, Statistics Canada, *Women in the Workplace* (1987).
22 United Nations, *The State of the World's Women 1985* (New York: 1986).

23 Monica Townson, "Women and the Canadian Economy," in *Ottawa's National Symposium on Women and the Economy* (Ottawa: Canadian Advisory Council on the Status of Women, 1986).

24 Ann Porter and Barbara Cameron, *Impact of Free Trade on Women in Manufacturing* (Ottawa: Canadian Advisory Council on the Status of Women, 1987), p. 11; and, Marjorie Griffin Cohen, *Free Trade in Services: An Issue of Concern to Women* (Ottawa: Canadian Advisory Council on the Status of Women, 1987), p. 5.

25 Porter and Cameron, *Impact of Free Trade on Women in Manufacturing*.

26 Marjorie Cohen, "The Razor's Edge Invisible: Feminism's Effect on Economics," *International Journal of Women's Studies*, vol. 8, no. 3 (May-June 1985): 286-298.

27 Margaret A. White, *Breaking the Circular Hold: Taking on the Patriarchal and Ideological Biases in Traditional Economic Theory* (Toronto: Ontario Institute for Studies in Education, 1984).

28 Ibid.

29 Statistics Canada, *Women in the Workplace: Selected Data* (1985), p. 74.

AN INTERNATIONAL FEMINIST BOOK FAIR

An earlier version of this paper was published as an editorial in *Trivia: A Journal of Ideas* (Fall 1988): 3, 4. This paper was edited and reprinted with the permission of the authors. The original paper introduced a special two-part series on The Third International Feminist Book Fair. (*Trivia* 13: *Memory/Transgression, Women Writing in Quebec*; *Trivia* 14: *Language/Difference – Writing in Tongues*). *Trivia* is published three times a year by: *Trivia,* P.O. Box 606, N. Amherst, Maryland, U.S.A., 01059. Write directly or order through your local women's bookstore.

1 The Fourth International Feminist Book Fair was held in Barcelona, Spain, June 19 to 23, 1990.

L'IMMIGRANT/E

This poem was first published in *Prairie Fire*, vol. 2, no. 1 (Spring 1990). Reprinted with permission.

SWIMMING UPSTREAM: REFLECTIONS OF A FEMINIST AT 66

For those who wish to read the works mentioned in the text, bibliographic information is given below, in alphabetical order:

Landsberg, Michelle. *Women and Children First*. New York: Penguin, 1985.

Morgan, Robin. *Sisterhood is Powerful: An Anthology of Writings from Women's Liberation*. New York: Random House Inc., 1970.

Rich, Adrienne. "Adrienne Rich: The Taste and Smell of Life." *Broadside,* vol. 2, no. 8 (June 1981).

Spender, Dale. *Women's Ideas and What Men Have Done with Them*. London: Ark Paper backs, 1983.

van Herk, Aritha. "Planning a Future: Short Story" *Canadian Forum*, vol. 68, no. 787 (March 1990).

OF DESPERATION BORN

1 Rona Grace Achilles, "The Social Meanings of Biological Ties: A Study of Participants in Artificial Insemination by Donor," unpublished Ph.D. dissertation, University of Toronto (Ontario Institute for Studies in Education), 1986.
2 Ibid.
3 The estimates of success rates vary greatly, depending on how they are defined. The 10-percent figure is considered high by some authorities. For a discussion, see Francoise Laborie, "New Reproductive Technologies: News from France and Elsewhere," *Reproductive and Genetic Engineering*, vol. 1, no. 1 (1988): 77-85.
4 Linda S. Williams, "Wanting Children Badly: An Exploratory Study of Parenthood Motivation of Couples Seeking In Vitro Fertilization," unpublished Ph.D. dissertation, University of Toronto (Ontario Institute for Studies in Education), 1988.
5 Margrit Eichler and Phebe Poole, *The Incidence of Preconception Contracts for the Production of Children among Canadians,* report prepared for the Law Reform Commission of Canada, 1988.
6 Based on Margrit Eichler, *Families in Canada Today: Recent Changes and their Policy Consequences* (Toronto: Gage Publishing Ltd., 1988), pp. 258-260.
7 With the aid of the new technology a woman might have a genetic child without ever being aware of it. Let us assume she had a hysterectomy, a doctor removed an egg, successfully fertilized it and implanted it in another woman who eventually gave birth to a child. In this case, the "donor" woman would be an unaware genetic mother.

THE INFERTILITY JOURNEY: DESTINATION UNKNOWN

This paper was earlier published in *Health Information Update* 2 (January 1989): 8. It has been edited and reprinted here with the author's permission.

CLOSING THE CURTAIN

1 T.T. Liang, *T'ai Chi Ch'uan: For Health and Self-Defense* (New York: Vintage Books, 1977), p. 4.
2 Danielle Crittenden, "Let's Junk the Feminist Slogans: The War's Over," *Chatelaine* (August 1990): 37.
3 Carole Etzler, "Standing Before Us," recorded on *Thirteen Ships* (Springfield: Sisters Unlimited, 1983).
4 Donna Reed (director), Margaret Pettigrew (producer), Kathleen Shannon (executive producer), *Goddess Remembered*, 16 mm, video, colour, 54 mins. 29 secs. (Studio D, National Film Board of Canada, 1989).
5 "Editorial," *Canadian Woman Studies/les cahiers de la femme*, vol. 11, no. 1 (Spring 1990): 3, 4. See also *feminist ACTION: News from the National Action Committee on the Status of Women*, vol. 4, no. 4 (May 1990): 1, 2.

6 Laurie Bell, "Good Girls and Bad Girls," quoted in *Everywoman's Almanac* (Toronto: Women's Press, 1988), n.p.

7 Douglas Rodger's *Donut City*, a play performed by the Canadian Stage Company, Toronto, 1988, was a powerful catalyst, propelling me to try to understand what is happening to young women on Canadian streets. See also, for example: Evelyn Lau, *Runaway: Diary of a Street Kid* (Toronto: Harper and Collins, 1989); Tom MacDonnell, *Never Let Go: The Story of Kristy McFarlane* (Toronto: Seal Books, 1988); Margaret A. Michaud, *Dead End: Homeless Teenagers* (Calgary: Detselig Enterprises Ltd., 1988); Social Planning Council of Winnipeg, "Needs Assessment of Homeless Children and Youth," Winnipeg, May 1990.

8 Pat St. Germain, "Home is Worse than Turning Tricks," *The Winnipeg Sun,* Monday, March 19, 1990, p. 3.

Contributors

JACQUELINE BARRAL is a French-born teacher and writer specializing in children's books. Her works include *Solévent* (children's poetry) and *Les Ecuries de la Grenouillère* (a novel), and her poetry is in *Anthologie de la poésie franco-manitobaine*.

MARIK BOUDREAU was a founding member of the Montreal production group called Plessisgraphe. Her photographs have been part of projects such as Optica's art-on-the-buses, Martha Fleming and Lyne Lapointe's *La Donna Delinquenta*, Remue-Ménage's publication, *Women of Quebec in the 80s*, and those of *Possibles, Nouvelle Barre du Jour* and *Ovo*. Her book maquettes have won her several prizes, and her journalistic photography has appeared in newspapers and magazines around the world. She has produced a videotape, *Série Fleuve*, which has been shown in festivals in New York, Seoul and Montreal. Her work has been included in group shows in Montreal, Paris, Liège, Barcelona, Seoul, Sao Paolo, and across Canada. She is currently working on an art project in New York.

DI BRANDT is a writer, teacher and critic. She grew up in a Mennonite farming village in southern Manitoba and now lives in Winnipeg with her two daughters. Her first book of poems, *questions i asked my mother*, was nominated for the Governor General's Award for poetry for 1987 and the Commonwealth Poetry Prize in 1988, and received the Lampert Memorial Award. *Agnes in the sky*, a second poetry collection, was published in 1990. She is currently working on a prison biography with Douglas Marshall entitled *No Tears Allowed*.

JANE BRIERLEY is a Montreal literary translator and president of the Literary Translators Association. Her most recent work includes Elisabeth Vonarburg's science-fiction novel, *The Silent City*, and *A Man of Sentiment: The Memoirs of Philippe-Joseph Aubert de Gaspé (1786–1871)*, which was short-listed for the 1988 Governor General's Literary Award in the English translation category.

ROSEMARY BROWN is executive director of MATCH International Centre in Ottawa. Until 1986, she served for 14 years as a member of the British Columbia Legislature. Coming to Canada from Jamaica in 1950,

Rosemary Brown has also worked as counsellor, social worker, public speaker, motherworker, university teacher and chair of Women's Studies at Simon Fraser University. She has been awarded honorary doctorates by Dalhousie, Mount St. Vincent and York universities. She is featured in *No Way, Not Me* (an NFB film), and is author of *Being Brown: A Very Public Life.*

"CANDY" is the pseudonym of a young woman who knows about life on city streets. She lives in Manitoba.

APRIL D'AUBIN is research analyst for the Coalition of Provincial Organizations of the Handicapped (COPOH), a national advocacy organization located in Winnipeg. She has been active in the development of self-help services for disabled people, serving on the boards of Winnipeg's Independent Living Resource Centre (ILRC) and the Canadian Association of Independent Living Centres (CAILC).

MARGRIT EICHLER is a professor of sociology at the Ontario Institute for Studies in Education. She has written and spoken extensively on many areas of feminist research. Her books include: *The Double Standard: A Feminist Critique of Feminist Social Science; Women in Futures Research; Families in Canada Today: Recent Changes and Their Policy Consequences;* and *Nonsexist Research Methods: A Practical Guide.* She is co-founder of Resources for Feminist Research, past-president of the Canadian Research Institute for the Advancement of Women and president of the Canadian Sociology and Anthropology Association.

HEIDI EIGENKIND lives in Winnipeg, where she co-manages Bold Print, a women's bookstore. At 38, she is engaged in recovering those parts of her self that ran away and hid in response to her father's sexual abuse of her. This quest exhausts, exhilarates and inspires her. It remains the focus of her words and images. Her work has appeared in *CV2* and *Fireweed*, and is included under the name Heidi Muench in *Celebrating Canadian Women*, edited by Greta Nemiroff.

FERRON is best known for her song writing and for her unique singing voice – a powerful blending of alienation and compassion, suffering and spirit. "Testimony," and "Shadows on a Dime," are widely known and loved. Her latest recording, *Phantom Center*, on Chameleon Records of Los Angeles was released in 1990. A Canadian who grew up in a large, working-class family in a suburb of Vancouver, she now lives in Cape Cod, Massachusetts.

ELLEN GOODMAN is a communications officer for the Manitoba Public Insurance Corporation. She has worked as a journalist, editor and photographer for several Manitoba newspapers and magazines.

HEIDI HARMS lives in Winnipeg with her husband and their two children. She works for *Prairie Fire* magazine. This is her first published story.

IRENE HEAMAN is a teacher, motherworker of daughters, and writer, who for years lived on a farm near Carman, Manitoba. She recently moved to Winnipeg. She has published short stories, poems and articles. A Manitoba Arts Council grant is enabling her to prepare a manuscript of poetry.

BARBARA M. HERRINGER is visiting assistant professor at the University of Victoria School of Social Work. She is currently on the Steering Committee of Women for Economic Survival, as well as on the Advisory Board of *F(Lip)*, a journal of innovative feminist writing. She is a writer, editor and researcher, whose interests include issues within the broad area of women and aging and the effect of AIDS on the families of gay men. She is co-editing a book on feminist social-work praxis with Kathryn McCannell.

SHIRLEY KITCHEN, of Winnipeg, has long been interested in the application of feminist principles to relationships in families, community groups and work situations. She is a nurse, has worked as a television researcher, writer and host, and was the co-producer of the video documentary *Perspectives on Women in the 1980s*. She is currently the chair of Women and Religion, Western Canada District, Unitarian Universalist Association.

DEBRA LYNN KRAHN is a self-taught artist, originally from rural Manitoba, now living in Winnipeg. Her drawings celebrate women's spirituality and our unity with the earth. She is a single parent, mother of two sons.

CONNIE KUHNS has written for the *Radical Reviewer, Fuse Magazine, Fireweed, Kinesis, Herizons, Radio Waves, The Georgia Straight* and *Hot Wire: A Journal of Women's Music and Culture*. Since 1981 she has been the producer and host of "Rubymusic" on CFRO Radio in Vancouver. She is writing a book entitled *Rise Up! A History of Women's Music in Canada*. She is the mother of a young daughter and an infant son.

EMMA LAROCQUE is a professor in the Department of Native Studies, University of Manitoba. She is also pursuing Ph.D. studies in Aboriginal history. She is a frequent guest lecturer throughout Canada and the United States. She is author of *Defeathering the Indian,* co-author of *Native Studies: A Selected Bibliography,* and author of numerous articles, including "On the Ethics of Publishing Historical Documents," in *"The Orders of the Dreamed": George Nelson on Cree and Northern Ojibwa Religion and Myth, 1823,* edited by Jennifer S.H. Brown and Robert Brightman. Her poetry was published in 1990 in *Canadian Quarterly.* She contributed to the preface and poetry for *Native Women of Western Canada: Writing the Circle – An Anthology,* edited by Jeanne Perreault and Sylvia Vance.

EVELYN LAU is a Vancouver writer whose poetry has been published in various literary magazines, including *Queen's Quarterly, Prism International* and *Exile.* She is the author of an autobiography, *Runaway: Diary of a Street Kid,* and a collection of poetry, *You Are Not Who You Claim.*

HELEN LEVINE has been actively involved in the women's movement since the late 1960s. She was a member of the faculty of the School of Social Work at Carleton University from the mid-1970s until 1988. Since "retirement," she has been practising feminist counselling as well as speaking and doing workshops on topics related to women's personal and political struggles. She is a member of the Crones, a group of older feminists; of a singing group called Sistersong; and of Woman-to-Woman, a feminist counselling project, all in Ottawa. She has published many articles, most of which have been critiques of the conventional helping professions and of the issues related to a feminist counselling approach. See, for example: "The Power Politics of Motherhood"; and "Feminist Counselling: Approach or Technique?" both in *Perspectives on Women,* edited by Joan Turner and Lois Emery. In October 1989, Helen Levine was one of six women across Canada to receive the Person's Award, in recognition of her contribution to improving the status of Canadian women.

LU-ANN LYNDE has loved drawing since childhood. She received her art training from the Sheridan School of Visual Art in Oakville, Ontario, and the University of Manitoba. She has taught classes in puppetry drawing and painting, and has illustrated three colouring books, including *Free Hand,* a creative colouring book for children with Carol Rose. Also with Carol Rose she illustrated the Walking the Motherpath Cards. She resides in Milton, Ontario, where she is continuing her work as an artist.

MARILYN MACKENZIE is the investigation officer for sexual harassment policy at the University of Manitoba. She is a social worker and a motherworker.

JOSS MACLENNAN is a Toronto freelance illustrator. She has worked for *Fireweed* and other magazines. She is well-known for her posters and designs for the women's movement and the labour movement. A show of 10 years of her political posters was held at Partisan Gallery in Toronto during the summer of 1990.

KATHERINE MARTENS has lived in Winnipeg most of her life, with interludes in Toronto, Urbana, and in Bochum and Erlangen in Germany. She has a B.A. from the University of Manitoba, and taught in an elementary school for seven years. Holistic health, meditation, massage, self-help and spirituality are all interests that have arisen from the need to solve problems in her own life. Her most ambitious project was collecting oral family history in preparation for the publication of a book entitled *All in a Row: The Klassens of Homewood*. Recently she completed an oral-history project for the Mennonite Heritage Centre and the Manitoba Provincial Archives, "Childbirth in the Mennonite Community," which consists of 58 tapes with women of all ages describing their birth experiences. She is married, and has two daughters and a son.

KATHRYN F. MCCANNELL is associate professor at the School of Social Work, University of British Columbia. Prior to this, she taught at the University of Manitoba. In 1986 she edited a special issue of the *Canadian Journal of Community Mental Health* entitled *Women and Mental Health,* and is currently working on a book on feminist social work praxis with Barbara Herringer. Her research interests are in the areas of social networks, diversity in families, and violence. Kathryn Mc-Cannell maintains a feminist counselling practice in Vancouver. She is the mother of two daughters.

MARY MEIGS was born in Philadelphia in 1917, grew up in Washington, D.C., and now lives in Montreal. She was instructor in English at Bryn Mawr College between 1940 and 1942. She served in the WAVES during the War, then studied art, and subsequently had one-woman shows in Boston, New York, Paris and Montreal. Her first book, *Lily Briscoe: A Self Portrait* was published in 1981, followed by *The Medusa Head* in 1983 and *The Box Closet* in 1987. The first two books have been translated into French. Other published work includes illustrations for the deluxe edition of *Une Saison dans la Vie d'Emmanuel*, by Marie-Claire Blais; and *Illustrations for two Novels by Marie-Claire Blais*.

LUCILLE MEISNER is a social worker and a feminist therapist specializing in body-image work and in eating disorders. She is the prevention education consultant for the Women's Centre for Substance Abuse and is vice-chairperson of the Board of the Women's Health Clinic in Winnipeg.

ROSELLA MELANSON is a New Brunswick feminist who has studied in social work and communication. She is director of communications and planning with the New Brunswick Advisory Council on the Status of Women.

LINDA NELSON is associate editor of *Trivia: A Journal of Ideas,* and production manager for the *Village Voice.* She is currently working on a lesbian road novel.

FAITH NOLAN is a singer and song writer. Her music is her political work. Growing up in Halifax and later in Toronto's Cabbagetown deepened her commitment to representing the lives of Black and working-class people in her songs. Whether it is about Black rights or gay rights she is uncompromising in her call for liberation, equality and justice. Her recordings include *Africville, Sistership* and *Freedom to Love.*

DOROTHY O'CONNELL is a long-time activist in welfare rights and public tenants' rights organizations. She has worked as a film editor, teacher, organizer, journalist and mother of five children. She wrote *Chiclet Gomez, Cockeyed Optimists,* and *Sister Goose.* Dorothy O'Connell is the author of "Poverty: The Feminine Complaint," in *Perspectives on Women,* edited by Joan Turner and Lois Emery. She is an appointed member of the Social Assistance Review Board of Ontario.

UMA PARAMESWARAN was born in Madras, India; she was educated at Jabalpur and Nagpur universities in India, and at Indiana and Michigan State universities in the United States. She is professor of English, University of Winnipeg. She is the author of *Cyclic Hope, Cyclic Pain,* published in Calcutta, and *Trishanku* and *Rootless but Green are the Boulevard Trees,* published in Toronto. She has written many scripts for local stage and television productions, and in 1988 wrote a play entitled *Deer Deedi, My Sister.* She is the mother of a teen-aged daughter.

JOAN PENNELL is assistant professor, Faculty of Social Work, University of Manitoba, and has also taught at Memorial University, Newfoundland. She was a founding member of the shelter for battered women in St. John's. She has been active in the feminist movements in Canada and the United States. Joan Pennell completed her Ph.D. at Bryn Mawr College, where the focus of her dissertation was "Democratic Hierarchy in Feminist Organizations."

CAROL ROSE is a Winnipeg child-care teacher, workshop leader and spiritual counsellor. Together with Lu-Ann Lynde, Carol created Walking the Motherpath Cards, depicting images of Biblical women, which she uses in workshops throughout North America. Also with Lu-Ann Lynde, she has illustrated *Free Hand*, a creative colouring book for children. Carol is the mother of four sons and a daughter. In 1990 her writing also appeared in *Healing Voices: Therapy with Women*, edited by Toni Laidlaw and Cheryl Malmo.

KATHLEEN SHANNON has worked at the National Film Board of Canada for many years, where she founded the well-known Studio D, which she headed until recently. Her work as a writer, speaker and facilitator has the same focus as her work in documentary film – the empowerment of all persons through overcoming both social and internalized oppressions. Her work has been recognized by a number of awards including an honorary Doctor of Laws degree from Queen's University. In 1986 she was made a member of the Order of Canada.

LINDA TRIGG was born in Switzerland and has lived in Europe, Great Britain, Canada and the United States. Currently living in Winnipeg with her husband, Linda is a registered psychologist employed as director of clinical services at Children's Home of Winnipeg. Linda served as a member of the Board of Directors of the Women's Health Clinic for six years, for two years as chair. She is involved with the Canadian Mental Health Association, formerly as a member of the Professional Advisory Committee and now chairing a national committee addressing the mental health needs of women.

SARI LUBITSCH TUDIVER is a policy and program officer for the Manitoba Council for International Cooperation, an umbrella organization of the 36 Manitoba agencies involved in development initiatives overseas and in Canada. Her particular interests are in the areas of gender and development, women's health and pharmaceuticals, and the role of grass-roots organizations in social change. She has been active in women's health networks locally, nationally and internationally. She holds a Ph.D. in anthropology from the University of Michigan and is an occasional lecturer in the Women's Studies Program at the University of Manitoba.

JOAN TURNER, of Winnipeg, is editor of *Living the Changes* and co-editor with Lois Emery of *Perspectives on Women*. With Shirley Kitchen, she produced the video documentary, *Perspectives on Women in the 1980s*. Under her former name, Joan Zeglinski, she wrote for social-work journals and edited *Social Work Education for Rural and Northern Practice*. Joan Turner was associate professor at the School of Social Work, University of Manitoba, for almost 20 years. She is the owner of Bold Print Inc., the Winnipeg women's bookstore, which is financed and staffed by women, and where women's books, music and art are actively promoted. For more than six years, she has been in private practice, providing body-work, therapeutic massage, counselling and teaching services for women. Her therapeutic work is described in her chapter, "Let My Soul Soar: Touch Therapy," in *Healing Voices: Therapy with Women*, edited by Toni Laidlaw and Cheryl Malmo. She is the mother of two daughters, both medical doctors.

LILLY JULIA SCHUBERT WALKER, professor and director of Counselling Services at the University of Manitoba, received the Western Manitoba Outstanding Professional Woman of the Year Award in 1985, and the Lawson Award to an Outstanding University Counselling Professional in Canada in 1990. Her current involvement with farm families in transition evolved out of her clinical, counselling and consulting activities in rural Manitoba. She is a consultant to the federal and Manitoba governments on the human issues in agriculture. Lilly Walker's most recent publications include: "The Human Harvest: Changing Farm Stress to Family Success" and "Stressors and Symptoms Predictive of Distress in Farmers" in *The Journal of Clinical Psychology*; and "Fitting Farm Management Strategies to Family Styles" in *The Canadian Journal of Agriculture Economics*.

EMILY ELIZABETH WARNE is a student who lives in Winnipeg and is concerned about peace.

LISE WEIL is editor of *Trivia: A Journal of Ideas*. She is translator of Christina Thurmer-Rohr's *Vagabundinnen* (*Vagabond Women*). She is currently collecting creative responses to the question "What is a Lesbian?" for an upcoming anthology.